The Punitive Imagination

The Punitive Imagination

Law, Justice, and Responsibility

Edited by
Austin Sarat

THE UNIVERSITY OF ALABAMA PRESS
Tuscaloosa

The University of Alabama Press
Tuscaloosa, Alabama 35487-0380
uapress.ua.edu

Copyright © 2014 by the University of Alabama
Press All rights reserved.

Inquiries about reproducing material from this work should be addressed to the University of Alabama Press.

Typeface: Caslon

Manufactured in the United States of America
Cover illustration: *The Punishment of Flatterers, By Gustave Doré*. Gustave Doré, 1832–83, French. Engraving for *The Divine Comedy, Divina Commedia*, by Dante.
Cover design: Michele Myatt Quinn

∞

The paper on which this book is printed meets the minimum requirements of American National Standard for Information Sciences—Permanence of Paper for Printed Library Materials, ANSI Z39.48-1984.

Library of Congress Cataloging-in-Publication Data

The punitive imagination : law, justice, and responsibility / edited by Austin Sarat.
    pages cm.
  "This volume is the product of a symposium held at the University of Alabama School of Law on September 28, 2012."—Acknowledgments.
  Includes bibliographical references and index.
  ISBN 978-0-8173-5799-3 (pbk. : alk. paper) — ISBN 978-0-8173-8796-9 (e book)
1. Punishment—United States—Congresses. I. Sarat, Austin, editor of compilation.
  KF9225.A75P86 2014
  364.601—dc23

                                      2014011270

To Stephanie, Lauren, Emily, and Ben

Contents

Acknowledgments ix

Examining Assumptions: An Introduction to Punishment, Imagination, and Possibility 1
Austin Sarat

1. "To See a World in a Grain of Sand": Dignity and Indignity in American Criminal Justice 19
   Carol S. Steiker

2. Injustice, Authority, and the Criminal Law 42
   Stephen P. Garvey

3. Imprisonment without Justice 82
   Caleb Smith

4. Punishment as an Act of the Imagination 103
   Leo Katz

5. "Which Question? Which Lie?": Reflections on *Payne v. Tennessee* and the "Quick Glimpse" of Life 127
   Michelle Brown

6. Afterword: Time, Imagination, and Punishment 158
   Patricia Ewick

Contributors 173

Index 175

Acknowledgments

This volume is the product of a symposium held at the University of Alabama School of Law on September 28, 2012. I want to thank the colleagues, students, and skilled research assistance of Heather Richard and the staff who helped make that such a successful event. I am grateful for the financial support of the University of Alabama Law School Foundation. A special word of thanks to former Dean Ken Randall for his unstinting support, for sharing the vision of legal scholarship reflected in these pages, and for making me feel so at home at the law school.

The Punitive Imagination

Examining Assumptions
An Introduction to Punishment, Imagination, and Possibility
Austin Sarat

From the Gospel of Matthew[1] to George Bernard Shaw[2] and former Supreme Court Justice William Brennan,[3] many have remarked that how a society punishes reveals its true character. Punishment then tells us who we are.[4] The way a society punishes demonstrates its commitment to standards of judgment and justice, its distinctive views of blame and responsibility, its understandings of mercy and forgiveness, and its particular ways of responding to evil. *The Punitive Imagination* seeks to understand what America's practices of punishment tell us about who we are. Offering an exegesis of some of the basic assumptions and purposes of our systems of punishment, this book brings together cultural, philosophical, and legal perspectives to offer a distinctive take on the meaning of punishment in America.

Punishment is, of course, only one of the ways that the state responds to violations of norms and rules and for the state to express its displeasure and disapproval of the behavior of its citizens.[5] While many scholars have tried to identify the essential elements of punishment,[6] perhaps the most famous and influential of those efforts is found in H. L. A. Hart's *Prolegomenon to the Principles of Punishment*.[7] There, Hart establishes the following criteria for an act to be considered punishment: (1) It must involve pain or other consequences normally considered unpleasant; (2) It must be for an offense against legal rules; (3) It must be of an actual or supposed offender for his offense; (4) It must be intentionally administered by human beings other than the offender; and (5) It must be imposed and administered by an authority constituted by a legal system against which the offense is committed.[8]

In the jurisprudence of double jeopardy and the Eighth Amendment, courts regularly engage in similar definitional efforts. Judges insist that the mere fact that pain is imposed by, or that unpleasant consequences are associated with, a legal enactment is not sufficient to establish that such a law is punitive.[9] One of the most instructive of these judicial efforts is found in a decision of the Third Circuit Court of Appeals concerning a challenge to the constitutionality of Megan's Law. This New Jersey law increased penalties for sex offenders and required them to register with local law enforcement whenever offenders established a new residence. It also required law enforcement to provide notification of the whereabouts of sex offenders to the communities in which they reside. The petitioner in *Artway v. The Attorney General of the State of New Jersey*, the legal challenge to Megan's Law, insisted that its registration and notification requirements were a form of punishment. He claimed, among other things, that they constituted a second punishment for sex offenders, who had already been imprisoned, and therefore violated the prohibition of double jeopardy.[10]

The court began its decision by noting that if registration and community notification did not count as "punishment," then they could not violate double jeopardy no matter how painful and burdensome registration and notification might be to those subject to them. In its effort to categorize those requirements, the court developed a three-part test. The court argued that whether registration and community notification was punishment depended on the legislation's "(1) actual purpose, (2) objective purpose, and (3) effect."[11]

Starting with the law's actual purpose, the court noted that "[i]f the legislature intended Megan's Law to be 'punishment,' that is retribution was one of its actual purposes, then it must fail constitutional scrutiny. If, on the other hand, 'the restriction of the individual comes about as a relevant incident to a regulation,' the measure will pass this first prong."[12]

If the legislature's actual purpose does not appear to be to punish, "we look next to its 'objective' purpose. This prong," the court said, "in turn, has three sub-parts.

> First, can the law be explained solely by a remedial purpose? . . . If not, it is "punishment." Second, even if some remedial purpose can fully explain the measure, does a historical analysis show that the measure has traditionally been regarded as punishment? . . . If so, and if the text or legislative history does not demonstrate that this measure is not punitive, it must be considered "punishment."

Third, if the legislature did not intend a law to be retributive but did intend it to serve some mixture of deterrent and salutary purposes, we must determine (1) whether historically the deterrent purpose of such a law is a necessary complement to its salutary operation and (2) whether the measure under consideration operates in its "usual" manner, consistent with its historically mixed purposes.... Unless the partially deterrent measure meets both of these criteria, it is "punishment."[13]

The court continued, "[I]f the purpose tests are satisfied, we must then turn to the effects of the measure. If the negative repercussions—regardless of how they are justified—are great enough, the measure must be considered punishment."

Focusing on Megan's Law itself and reconstructing its legislative history, the court found "that the legislature's actual purpose was not punishment. It speaks of 'identify[ing] and alert[ing] the public' to enhance safety and 'preventing and promptly resolving incidents.' Protecting the public and preventing crimes are . . . 'regulatory' and not punitive."[14] With respect to "objective purpose," the court again invoked the regulation/punishment distinction. Comparing the registration of sex offenders to required registration of membership corporations, lobbyists, professional gamblers, and of citizens under a military draft, the court held that "[r]egistration is a common and long-standing regulatory technique with a remedial purpose."[15] Here the court explained,

> [T]he solely remedial purpose of helping law enforcement agencies keep tabs on these offenders fully explains requiring certain sex offenders to register. Registration may allow officers to prevent future crimes by intervening in dangerous situations. Like the agent who must endure the snow to fetch the soupmeat, the registrant may face some unpleasantness from having to register and update his registration. But the remedial purpose of knowing the whereabouts of sex offenders fully explains the registration provision just as the need for dinner fully explains the trip out into the night. And the means chosen—registration and law enforcement notification only—is not excessive in any way. Registration, therefore, is certainly "reasonably related" to a legitimate goal: allowing law enforcement to stay vigilant against possible re-abuse.[16]

Finally, turning to the actual effect prong of its three-part test, the court acknowledged that "there doubtless are some unpleasant consequences of registration." It found, however, that this "impact, even coupled with the registrant's inevitable kowtow to law enforcement officials, cannot be said to have an effect so draconian that it constitutes 'punishment' in any way approaching incarceration."[17]

Several things may be said about the court's effort to define punishment and differentiate it from regulation. First, its test is complicated and difficult to administer.[18] Second, it reflects an anxious effort to police and stabilize an uncertain and blurred boundary, trying to name different forms of state power and different experiences of that power. Third, it insists on an absolute distinction between punishment and regulation instead of attempting to understand regulation and punishment in relational terms, with regulation the more inclusive concept. In this effort what is crucial is the perspective of those who authorize or administer the state's regulatory and punitive power.[19] Punishment, in this account, might be seen as a particular type or manifestation of the state's effort to regulate human conduct and subject it to the "governance of rules."[20]

Such efforts and the practices of punishment that they embody are all around us, mainly proceeding unnoticed in the daily world of crime and justice or in the work of our social institutions.[21] But occasionally they galvanize attention and remind us of punishment's importance as a mirror of our political, legal, and cultural values. Thus, the 1998 execution of Karla Faye Tucker in Texas led many to think about the significance of repentance and whether someone whose character seems to change dramatically nonetheless should be executed.[22] In the fall of 1999, after a fight at a football game, seven African American students from Eisenhower High in Decatur, Illinois, were expelled, which was required by the school district's "zero-tolerance" policy.[23] Because of the intervention of the Rev. Jesse Jackson, what otherwise might have been a little-noticed incident of school discipline became the focus of a well-publicized conversation about who we punish, how we punish, and why we punish as we do.[24] The controversy surrounding the impeachment of former president Clinton was a kind of national seminar on morality, truthfulness, and proportionality.[25] High-profile trials of persons accused of crimes against humanity, from World War II to the present, ask us to think about how we respond to the most serious forms of human evil.[26]

In addition to such events, there is the stark reality of the population of our jails and prisons. Despite the fact that the total prison population has been declining slightly in the last few years, approximately 2.2 million people are held in federal or state prisons or in local jails.[27] The United States still has the highest documented incarceration rate in the world at 738 persons in prison or jail per 100,000. It is estimated that the United States has 5 percent of the world's population and approximately 23.6 percent of the world's prison population.[28] About 10.4 percent of all black males in the United States between the ages of 25 and 29 were sentenced and in prison, compared to 2.4 percent of Hispanic males and 1.3 percent of white males.

The Punitive Imagination examines some of the critical presuppositions that undergird America's approach to punishment. Among the questions addressed in this book are: What is the place of concern for human dignity in our prevailing ideologies of punishment? Can we justly punish the socially disadvantaged? What assumptions about persons, social institutions, and the ordering of social space provide the basis for American punitiveness? Who, if anyone, can be held responsible for excessively punitive criminal sentences? How does punishment depend on prevailing views of free will, responsibility, desert, blameworthiness? Where/how are those views subject to challenge in our punitive practices?

In taking up these questions this book continues a line of commentary dating back to the early nineteenth century. Such commentary portrays punishment as a key part of the American story, revealing hopes and fears, fissures and conflicts at different moments in our history. Beaumont and Tocqueville illustrated these connections by noting that "there is a spirit of obedience to the law, so generally diffused in the United States, that we meet this characteristic trait even within the prisons."[29] In *Democracy in America*, Tocqueville returned to the subject of punishment as part of his effort to understand what he called the "tyranny" of democratic republics, noting "prisons made violence a physical thing, but our contemporary democratic republics have turned it into something as intellectual as the human will it is intended to constrain."[30]

From Richard Nixon's "law and order" rhetoric to Bill Clinton's pledge to represent people who "work hard and play by the rules" to George W. Bush's promise to bring terrorists to justice and "punish the evil doers," issues of punishment have been crucially important in our recent political life.[31] Some believe that the rhetoric of law and order adds clarity to our moral thinking, rightly separating good from evil, victim from villain.[32] Others contend that the problems to which punishment responds are too complicated to be comprehended using those stark categories.[33]

From the nineteenth century to the present, punishment in the United States has modeled socially appropriate ways of responding to injuries done to us. It "teaches, clarifies, dramatizes and authoritatively enacts some of the most basic moral-political categories and distinctions which help shape our symbolic universe."[34] A number of social theorists have explored the connections of the punitive imagination and particular styles of punishment. To take but one example, Emile Durkheim saw penal institutions as providing concrete instances of the "collective conscience" at work in a process "that both expressed and regenerated society's values."[35] For Durkheim, when a society decides whom and how to punish, it establishes boundaries, creates social solidarities, and vividly marks "we-they" distinctions.[36]

Today we are entering a period of transition and reconsideration of the prevailing assumptions and practices of our system of crime and justice. Citing declining use of capital punishment, slight declines in our prison and jail populations, and the "financial pressures of sustaining a never ending war on crime," Patricia Ewick argues that "the unabated and largely uncontested intensification and expansion of the carceral system has moderated and there is some compelling evidence that there is a cultural and political turning away from the politics of revenge and all that it entails."[37] Yet today arguments about punishment and the assumptions that provide its basis continue unabated. Some defend punishment, even severe punishment, as essential in protecting society and defending society's values. Some also believe that it expresses respect for human dignity and allows for atonement and expiation of guilt.[38] Critics respond that we should punish less and forgive more, that punishment is often an inadequate response to evil.[39]

If Ewick is right, we need to carefully consider the assumptions that underlie our punishment policies and of the meanings and purposes of punishment in the United States. In this period of transition and reconsideration, *The Punitive Imagination* seeks to provide such a consideration. The contributors to this volume examine the ways our practices of punishment are discursively constructed in and by law and explore various contexts within which we can explore the punitive imagination. They do not offer a comprehensive survey of those assumptions so much as a set of critical interventions pointing the way for further inquiry.

This book begins with three chapters that examine large-scale background assumptions that underlie the punitive imagination and that provide vantage points from which punishment in the United States can be subject to critique. The next two chapters focus more particularly on examples of how those assumptions play out in particular cases.

We start with the concept of human dignity and the question of how American punishment should be thought of in light of our commitment to that value. Carol Steiker's chapter offers an overview of the punitive turn of the last part of the twentieth century, with its dramatic increase in incarceration rates, the rise of supermax prisons, the proliferation of mandatory and life without parole sentences, the adult treatment of juvenile offenders, and the resurgence of capital punishment. Her chapter contextualizes and evaluates those developments through the lens of "human dignity." However, unlike others for whom the idea of human dignity is itself seen as an "antidote to the unchecked punitive turn," Steiker, quoting Pinker, worries that this idea is "'hardly up to the heavyweight moral demands assigned to it.'"

For Steiker, a more useful conception of dignity focuses on the collective dignity of those who punish rather than the individual dignity of those subject to punishment. For her, collective dignity is a "societal value," which is "distinct from the harms that indignity may impose on an individual." Current punishment practices, she argues, pose an especially severe threat to collective dignity as a shared value in our community. The act of punishment is itself a collective act and thus has the force to "affect more powerfully our collective life."

Asserting our stake in collective dignity provides a framework for evaluating our particular criminal punishments. She offers three examples of how this might work: punishments that induce shame in offenders, those that impose extreme physical or psychological pain, and those that do not take account of offenders as individuals.

Shame. "Shaming punishments" involve the deliberate public humiliation of the offender. Moreover, these punishments require that members of the public experience the offender's shame. In Steiker's view shaming exposes the public to modes of feeling and thinking that can pose a threat to our communal life. As she argues, "Permitting prison officials—public officials of the state—to violate the dignity of prisoners under their control threatens to promote and condone official attitudes that are inconsistent with a democratic commitment to the fundamental equality of persons before the government and by extension in the eyes of the community that both creates and is created by government." Shaming punishment is, in her view, incompatible with our "collective ways of seeing and thinking about status."

Extreme Pain. Challenges to punishment practices that produce extreme physical or psychological pain have had more success in American courts than challenges to "merely" humiliating practices. Steiker cites two examples. The Supreme Court rejected both Alabama's "hitching post" punishment of an inmate and California's severely overcrowded prisons as inconsistent with "'the basic concept underlying the Eighth Amendment,'" namely, "'nothing less than the dignity of man.'" Nonetheless, only Justices Brennan and Marshall—in *Furman v. Georgia*—have argued that capital punishment is a violation of the Eighth Amendment on the grounds of human dignity. Solitary confinement has likewise been left unscathed by dignity-based arguments.

Steiker argues that we will be better served if we connect situations of extreme pain to concerns about collective dignity. In her view, the imposition of punishment involving severe pain entails the same kind of "dehumanization" as the imposition of shaming punishments. Furthermore, Steiker argues, such punishment promotes the "suppression of emotions (sympathy) and capacities (empathy, or the ability to feel sympathy for the pain of others) that are central to the experience of the fellowship of humanity." In so doing they offend our collective dignity.

Individualization. The "explosion" of mandatory minimum sentences during the last part of the twentieth century has forced us to rethink the logic of sentences governed only by consideration of the offense being punished. In her view, such sentences offend against a collective interest in punishing individuals as individuals. As she puts it, taking both the offender and the offense into account at the time of sentencing is a "'progressive and humanizing development'" for those who punish and the community they represent. "Individualization," Steiker explains, "shapes what the sentencer must actively consider and thus the public story that is told and received more widely about the punishment that is eventually imposed on an offender."

Steiker concludes by evoking the poetics of William Blake. Dignity's absence from our constitutional and criminal justice discourse, she says, reflects the "absence of an imagined identity of each individual with one another and with the collective." The next chapter offers a very different framework for imagining punishment. Instead of Steiker's effort to think about punishment through the lens of a particular moral commitment, Stephen Garvey argues that we should focus instead on political authority. In his view, states can and do have authority to punish that is separate from morality. This authority is founded in the fact that the state satisfies the conditions that make it a legitimate state. He offers a framework for helping to see the bases and limitations of the state's authority to punish.

Garvey develops that framework as a response to the following question: "Should it matter that a criminal defendant has been burdened, not only with a rotten social background, but with a rotten social background he was entitled *not* to suffer, or to put it another way, with a rotten social background for which the state is to blame? If it should matter, why and in what way?" That is, can a state punish a defendant whom it has essentially forced into the position of a second-class citizen? Shouldn't his crime, then, be considered in some way also inherently "second-class"?

Taking up the 1968 murder case of a black man accused of killing two white marines as his exemplary systemically excluded second-class citizen, Garvey argues that a "state that treats a citizen as second-class loses the authority to punish him for having committed a crime." The second-class citizen cannot be said to be guilty of a crime. Recalling my earlier discussion of the meaning of punishment, Garvey claims that the state may "impose a hardship upon him" but not punish his crime.

Generally criminal responsibility is said to depend on a type of freedom; that is, "an actor chooses to do unless he could have chosen [unless he were 'free'] to do otherwise." This account, Garvey contends, demands too much. Instead, he says, responsibility should rest on "the capacity to respond to reasons." This capacity might also be described as the "capacity for self-control." Responsibility for crime is, in turn, reduced to the extent that an actor's capacity to respond to reasons is diminished. Diminished capacity to respond to reasons applies equally to second-class and first-class citizens—it does not depend on how "poorly one had been treated at the hands of the powers that be."

Garvey argues that freedom might only be *necessary* for responsibility but not sufficient. "Ownership" might be required too. What this means is that we can only be responsible for choices we fully own. As he suggests, "[T]he debate over the relationship between social deprivation and excuse is part of a larger and ongoing debate about the morality of responsibility. Even if we all agree that the freedom responsibility requires is nothing more than the freedom associated with the capacity to respond to reasons, and not the capacity to do otherwise, the question of ownership remains." This question, he suggests, leaves the state's authority to punish the crimes of second-class citizens in doubt.

In addition, in Garvey's view, the state's right to hold responsible depends on the nature of the wrong—it must be a "public wrong." The commission of a public wrong violates the "core values" by which a community "defines itself as a polity." The state can lose the standing to condemn by *hypocrisy* and also by *complicity*. If this is right, then the effort to punish criminal wrongdoers, who the state itself has wronged (by relegating them to second-class citizenship), might make the state guilty of hypocrisy or complicity.

These difficulties are avoided, Garvey contends, if we assume that the state's authority to punish does not depend on how well its criminal law conforms to the morality. Yet even if we focus exclusively on authority, Garvey suggests that when a state treats a citizen as second-class, "it violates his right not to be so treated and thus can no longer claim to have the authority to punish him for disobedience." It may "coerce him in order to elicit his obedience," but it does not have the authority to punish him.

We grant the state the authority to punish insofar as it "gives us peace and repose." A state can lose its authority in two ways. First, a state loses its authority if it fails to deliver the goods that justify its existence. A failure, therefore, to stave off the state of nature would cause a state to lose its authority. Second, a state loses its authority if it fails to respect the rights without which its citizens have no obligation to obey. In Garvey's view both of these two ways in which a state can lose its authority are implicated in any case involving a crime of a member of the second-class.

That said, Garvey argues, "The state nonetheless *did* wrong Murdock when it failed to give him his fair share of the fruits of social cooperation." By treating Murdock as a second-class citizen, the "nature" of the state's authority has changed. It no longer possesses the right to impose obligations. In this sense, crimes of second-class citizens are second-class "crimes," which is to say, they are not really crimes at all. When a state treats you like a second-class citizen, Garvey suggests, its relationship with you is no longer a moral one. Instead, the relationship is more like that "between an occupying power and those within the territory it occupies." In such a situation the state may coerce, but it has lost its authority to punish. Unlike Steiker for whom the punitive imagination should be focused on preserving collective dignity, for Garvey distributional and status questions should be at the center of our concerns.

From assumptions about dignity and authority, Caleb Smith's chapter considers what we do when we punish in terms of the dynamics of social space. He notes that any consideration of the underlying assumptions of the punitive imagination must begin with the fact that our system of mass incarceration has "detached itself, more or less explicitly, from any claim to justice at all." Since the 1980s, Smith suggests, prisons have become less sites of justice done and more sites of containment—pure, simple, and unjust.

During the 1960s and 1970s, as the United States constructed its "'penal state,'" both the "material form" and the "ideological function" of imprisonment were transformed. The rise of mass incarceration "was legitimated by an "increasingly harsh rhetoric" that announced the decline of the liberal "'rehabilitative ideal.'" Like Steiker, Smith notes that our conception of offenders changed dramatically. Offenders were no longer "lost souls to be reclaimed" but, instead, came to be thought of as "enemies of society to be captured, humiliated, and broken down."

Drawing on the work of cultural geographer Ruth Wilson Gilmore, Smith focuses on California's contemporary prison system, the largest state system in the country. He notes that our "metastasizing prisons" are "'partial geographic solutions to political economic crises, organized by the state, which is itself in crisis.'" Our prison system has discarded most of the conventional justifications for punishment—rehabilitation, retribution, and deterrence—in favor of incapacitation. Among the traditional justifications for punishment, incapacitation is unique in that it does not justify itself in relation to the offender's crime. Instead, it is purportedly designed to prevent the commission of some unspecified *future* crime. In this sense, Smith claims, incapacitation is not really a theory of punishment at all, but "a policy for the management of social instability and social space."

In addition, Smith sees a direct correlation between the demise of the welfare state and the emergence of the penal state. Quoting from Loïc Wacquant's *Prisons of Poverty*, Smith notes: "'Incarceration has de facto become America's largest government program for the poor.'" Like Garvey, Smith wants us to imagine punishment in relation to social deprivation. As Smith argues, again quoting Wacquant, the prison system has been accompanied by a "'new cultural industry of the fear and loathing of (lower-class and dark-skinned) offenders.'" In Smith's view the work of our penal system is today largely "spatial." As Wacquant notes, it functions to clean up urban spaces by ridding them of the "'subproletariat that mars the scenery.'"

Smith argues that the fantasy that drove the expansion of imprisonment is that of "urban space as a smooth, clean zone of circulation and consumption." The system of mass incarceration is really "a machine for the transformation of public space." Perhaps, Smith observes, "[T]he system of mass incarceration legitimates itself today by appealing not only to a punitive imagination but also, more subtly, to an *insecure* one."

To study the punitive imagination in the era of mass incarceration, according to Smith, would "require a critical research program into cultural representations of the geographies of contemporary life." More careful thought needs to be given to understanding how governments and their people have come to imagine crime more "as a disturbance in the landscape, especially the cityscape." "Ultimately," such research, "would seek to explain how the vagrant in the park or the dealer on the corner came to be imagined as a disturbance that could best be eliminated though the construction of warehouses of incapacitation on a vast scale."

The next chapter combines a thought-experiment and a historical example. If it is true that our punishment practices have violated our collective dignity, forfeited our authority to do more than coerce a large portion of our population, and indulged a fantasy of ridding our cities of a subproletariat, can anyone be held responsible? This question animates Leo Katz's contribution to this volume. Katz begins his "Punishment as an Act of the Imagination" by asking whether American judges should feel at all concerned about handing down inordinately long sentences. "How confident should they feel that they are doing the right thing by suppressing their unease and doing what the law demands of them?"

To frame that question Katz examines a case taken not from the United States but from Germany. After World War II, a case arose that involved the prosecution of a former judge (A) from Communist East Germany who had fled to West Germany. While serving as a judge in East Germany, A sentenced several members of the Jehovah's Witnesses for refusing to do their obligatory military service. They were charged with various treason-related offenses—the accusation was basically that they were dissenters.

As was customary, A received very firm and specific instructions from the Communist Party as to their sentences. He complied. Not long after presiding over the case, A moved to West Germany, where he subsequently was prosecuted by West German authorities for his actions as an East German judge in the case against the Jehovah's Witnesses.

According to Katz, there are three grounds why one might balk at the idea of prosecuting A—and three reasons why an American judge might similarly balk at the notion that he could be held accountable for imposing excessively harsh sentences. The first ground is simply the contention that there seems to be no legitimate legal basis for the judge's prosecution. A was charged with two offenses. The first was "false imprisonment," and the second was *Rechtsbeugung*, literally "bending the law." *Rechtsbeugung*, misapplication of the law, was interpreted to include cases in which the law was faithfully applied but in which that law was an extremely immoral one and therefore never valid in the first place. Yet Katz asks, why should we be reluctant to create a new track for wrongdoers who utilized the machinery of the state for their criminal actions?

Katz next moves on to consider the second reason why an American judge would balk at the prosecution of the East German judge. It has to do with the concept of disproportionate punishment—how do we determine whether the sentences imposed on the Jehovah's Witnesses were in fact "draconian"? Where do disproportionality judgments come from, anyway? In response Katz argues that desert judgments are not vacuous or conclusory. Instead, he says, they "build on widely shared and surprisingly robust intuitions."

The third reason why a judge might object to being held responsible for applying the law in such a way as to mete out excessively long sentences has to do with mental state, or mens rea. The West German court acknowledged this concern more seriously than any other. Arguably, A did in fact lack the requisite consciousness of wrongdoing. The court eventually concluded that A did have mens rea, ironically, on the ground that he decided to flee from East Germany.

Katz argues that the court made the mental state problem much too easy for itself. Katz notes that the usual understanding of mens rea fails to take into account how a defendant "sees" or "understands" his actions. He identifies several contexts in which what someone is doing changes its moral character depending on how he conceives of it and says that "[i]n the end, then, a judge who subjects a criminal to excessive punishment, might escape sanction—both legal and moral sanction—not for the reasons we might at first think of: not because doing so would involve violating the norm against retroactive laws or because proportionality is too vague a concept. Instead, the judge can escape punishment *because punishment, like the award of rewards and prizes, is to an unappreciated extent an act of the imagination.*" He concludes that figuring out whether American judges can fairly be held responsible for imposing excessive sentences depends "to an unappreciated extent on the way in which the person meting it out conceptualizes what he is doing."

This interest in how we understand the acts of others animates Michelle Brown's examination of the well-known case *Payne v. Tennessee*, a case in which the Supreme Court allowed the admission of victim impact statements in capital trials. Taking up concerns similar to those of Steiker, Garvey, and Smith, Brown contends that the key question addressed by the court in *Payne* is the worth of individuals acting under, and acted upon by, the law. She worries that "*Payne* gives us an unfortunate roadmap for the broad devaluation of suffering in criminal justice contexts." However, unlike Steiker and Katz, who want to change the focus of our punitive imagination from the conditions of those we punish to the conditions of those who impose the punishment, Brown argues that empathy must occupy a large place in the punitive imagination.

Brown describes victim impact statements of the sort allowed in *Payne* as allowing, in the language of the court, only a "quick glimpse" of life. She highlights how, according to post-*Payne* social science research, this "quick attention" has been demeaning to the lives and deaths of capital victims, defendants, and their families. She says that *Payne* subsumes whole, unique lives into particularized and partial half-depictions. In this way, Brown argues, the "jurisprudence of life and death" that *Payne* promotes is not simply about the worth of lives but "about a marked determination to disregard life and death in all of its complexity." This disregard, Brown notes, governs the practice of law and punishment in the United States "at its visceral base level."

Payne, she writes, is "preoccupied with the living dead" in a way that is highly problematic. It is but one example of the "symbolic use" of suffering, pain, and death in our punitive imagination. "Punishment—and punitive imaginations—are," Brown argues, "no real use in response to loss." But we seem to have no alternative discourse. "Nothing" can be done—so we ritualistically recite tailored and shallow statements of suffering so we can punish and sentence to death. Returning to Garvey's interest in social inequality and its consequences in punishment, Brown argues that in our punitive imagination we maintain the grieving in the position of "living corpses," somewhere between life and death and we do this with a knowledge of the unequal worth of victims. Punishment attempts to "raise the dead" yet in so doing it inevitably distances us from the lives of these real dead, and their race and class positions.

In the end, Brown suggests that the logic of punishment encourages a very particular form of emphatic judgment: one that is inevitably both superficial and suspect. In this logic we remain, she says, "irritated by the scene of suffering always in some way." Ultimately, we come to believe that "this is something about which there is nothing we can do." Thus, Brown argues, in punishment, empathy and compassion "risk taking on the most artificial of constructions and may result in the creation of a pure fiction largely centered upon the needs of self, not others." It is the "dark side" of empathy that is tied to the punitive imaginary where retribution and revenge are privileged over more "complex forms of solace and long-term attention to loss and grief." *Payne* is, in this way, exemplary in that it is not about the suffering of others, but the suffering of us. We have yet to see, Brown says, "what it might be to sustain 'an intimate and heartfelt expression of reverence for dead and living victims' within the law."

This volume concludes with an afterword by Patricia Ewick. In Ewick's view, what unites the previous chapters is an interest in exploring various ways in which "the punishing state has been as much a result of the *suppression* of imagination as it has been a *product* of imagination." In Ewick's account, they also each illustrate how a particular orientation toward "time—or temporality—is implicated in our contemporary practice of mass incarceration." As Ewick puts it, "the carceral state has been constructed on a perversion of the temporality inherent in imagination." How much of the punishing state, Ewick asks, is based on "the annihilation of past and future and, consequently, the foreclosure of any possibility of change, alteration, or becoming."

For Ewick, this book's particular contribution is a reminder to its readers that "a penal system that denies its captives a past or a future denies itself one as well." The punitive imagination should help us, she concludes, see "the present in terms of the past and future and . . . ourselves and what we do in terms of others with whom we navigate this temporality."

Notes

1. See Matthew 25:31–46, found at http://www.unc.edu/~megw/Matthew.html.

2. See George Bernard Shaw, "Capital Punishment," *Atlantic Monthly* (June 1948), found at http://www.theatlantic.com/past/docs/unbound/flashbks/death/dpenshaw.htm.

3. *Furman v. Georgia*, 408 U.S. 238, 305 (1972). Justice Brennan concurring.

4. Joel Feinberg, "The Expressive Function of Punishment," *Monist* 49 (1965): 397.

5. This argument is developed in Austin Sarat, Lawrence Douglas, and Martha Merrill, "On the Blurred Boundary between Punishment and Regulation," in *Law as Punishment/Law as Regulation* (Stanford, CA: Stanford University Press, 2011). What follows is taken from that essay.

6. For example, George Fletcher, "What Is Punishment Imposed For," *Journal of Contemporary Legal Issues* 5 (1994): 101. Also, Thomas McPherson, "Punishment: Definition and Justification," *Analysis* 28 (1967): 21.

7. H. L. A. Hart, *Prolegomenon to the Principles of Punishment*, reprinted in H. L. A. Hart, *Punishment and Responsibility: Essays in the Philosophy of Law* (New York: Oxford University Press, 1968).

8. Id. See also Michele Cotton, "Back with a Vengeance: The Resilience of Retribution as an Articulated Purpose of Criminal Punishment," *American Criminal Law Review* 37 (2000): 1313, and Joel Feinberg, "The Expressive Function of Punishment," in *Doing and Deserving: Essays in the Theory of Responsibility* (Princeton, NJ: Princeton University Press, 1970), 95.

9. See Charles L. Scott and Joan B. Gerbasi, "Sex Offender Registration and Community Notification Challenges: The Supreme Court Continues Its Trend," *Journal of the American Academy of Psychiatry and Law* 31 (2003): 494.

10. *Artway v. The Attorney General of the State of New Jersey*, 81 F.3d 1235 (1996). See also "Megan's Law and Its Progeny: Whom Will the Courts Protect?" *Boston College Law Review* 39 (1997): 201, and Alexander D. Brooks, "Megan's Law: Constitutionality and Policy," *Criminal Justice Ethics* 15 (1996): 24.

11. *Artway v. The Attorney General of the State of New Jersey*, 1264.

12. Id. at 1284.

13. Id.

14. Id. at 1285

15. Id.

16. Id. at 1286.

17. Id. at 1287

18. See Carol S. Steiker, "Punishment and Procedure: Punishment Theory and the Criminal–Civil Procedural Divide," *Georgetown Law Journal* 85 (1997): 775. Referring to the Supreme Court's efforts to distinguish punishment from regulation, Steiker observes, "The Court's work has been conceptually muddled, to say the least. Sometimes the Court seems to be attempting to define punishment either for the purposes of particular types of state activity (such as forfeitures or contempt proceedings) or for the purposes of particular types of constitutional protections (such as the prohibitions of double jeopardy or excessive fines). On the rare occasion when the Court has attempted to define punishment more globally, it has resorted to a list of 'factors,' which it has acknowledged are neither necessary nor sufficient for its purposes, and for which it has been unable to offer an underlying rationale," at 781.

Also John Coffee Jr., "Paradigms Lost: The Blurring of the Criminal and

Civil Law Models—And What Can Be Done About It," *Yale Law Journal* 101 (1992): 1875; Abraham Goldstein, "White-Collar Crime and Civil Sanctions," *Yale Law Journal* 101 (1992): 1895; Kenneth Mann, "Punitive Civil Sanctions: The Middleground between Criminal and Civil Law," *Yale Law Journal* 101 (1992): 1795; Paul H. Robinson, "Foreword: The Criminal-Civil Distinction and Dangerous Blameless Offenders," *Journal of Criminal Law and Criminology* 83 (1993): 693; Franklin Zimring, "The Multiple Middlegrounds between Civil and Criminal Law," *Yale Law Journal* 101 (1992): 1901; Symposium: "The Civil-Criminal Distinction," *Journal of Contemporary Legal Issues* 7 (1996): 269; Symposium: "The Intersection of Tort and Criminal Law," *Boston University Law Review* 76 (1996): 1.

19. For a different perspective see Adam Kolber, "The Subjective Experience of Punishment," *Columbia Law Review* 109 (2009): 182.

20. Lon Fuller defines law as "the enterprise of subjecting human conduct to the governance of rules." See *The Morality of Law* (New Haven, CT: Yale University Press, 1964) 106.

21. See Jean Hampton, "The Moral Education Theory of Punishment," *Philosophy and Public Affairs* 13 (1984): 208.

22. Beverly Lowry, *Crossed Over: A Murder, A Memoir* (New York: Vintage Books, 2002).

23. Dirk Johnson, "7 Students Charged in a Brawl That Divides Decatur, Ill.," *New York Times*, November 10, 1999, found at http://partners.nytimes.com/library/national/race/111099race-ra.html.

24. Flynn McRoberts, "Jackson Fights Expulsion of Black Decatur Youths," *Chicago Tribune*, November 8, 1999, found at http://articles.chicagotribune.com/1999-11-08/news/9911080250_1_zero-tolerance-policies-eisenhower-high-school-decatur-school-board.

25. See Ben G. Bishin, Donald Stevens, and Charles Wilson. "Character Counts?: Honesty and Fairness in Election 2000," *Public Opinion Quarterly* 70 (Summer 2006): 235.

26. Lawrence Douglas, *The Memory of Judgment: Making Law and History in the Trials of the Holocaust* (New Haven, CT: Yale University Press, 2005), and Lawrence Douglas, "Ivan the Recumbent or Demanjanjuk in Munich: Enduring the 'Last Great Nazi War-Crimes Trial,'" *Harpers*, March 2012, found at http://harpers.org/archive/2012/03/ivan-the-recumbent-or-demjanjuk-in-munich/.

27. Paul Guerino, Paige M. Harrison, and William J. Sabol, "Prisoners in 2010," *Bureau of Justice Statistics*, December 2011.

28. See Adam Liptack, "U.S. Prison Population Dwarfs That of Other Nations," *New York Times*, April 23, 2008, found at http://www.nytimes.com/2008/04/23/world/americas/23iht-23prison.12253738.html?pagewanted=all.

29. Gustave de Beaumont and Alexis de Tocqueville, *On the Penitentiary System in the United States and Its Application in France* (Carbondale: Northern Illinois University Press, 1964), 188.

30. Alexis de Tocqueville, *Democracy in America*, vol. 1, trans. Henry Reeves (Boston: John Allyn Publisher, 1876), 337.

31. See Stuart Scheingold, *The Politics of Street Crime: Criminal Process and Cultural Obsession* (Philadelphia, PA: Temple University Press, 1991).

32. James Q. Wilson, *Thinking about Crime* (New York: Basic Books, 1975).

33. Linda Ross Meyer, *The Justice of Mercy* (Ann Arbor: University of Michigan Press, 2010).

34. David Garland, "Punishment and Culture: The Symbolic Dimension of Criminal Justice," *Studies in Law, Politics and Society* 11 (1991): 198.

35. Quoted in David Garland, *Punishment and Modern Society: A Study in Social Theory* (Oxford: Clarendon Press, 1990), 23.

36. Id.

37. Patricia Ewick, "The Return of Restraint: Limits to the Punishing State," unpublished manuscript, 2012, 5.

38. Herbert Morris, "Persons and Punishment," *Monist* 52 (1968): 475.

39. See Meyer, *Justice of Mercy*.

"To See a World in a Grain of Sand"
Dignity and Indignity in American Criminal Justice
Carol S. Steiker

Carol Steiker is the Henry J. Friendly Professor of Law at Harvard Law School. She is a scholar in the broad field of criminal justice, where her work ranges from substantive criminal law to criminal procedure to institutional design, with a special focus on issues related to capital punishment. Recent publications address topics such as the relationship of criminal justice scholarship to law reform, the role of mercy in the institutions of criminal justice, and the likelihood of nationwide abolition of capital punishment. In addition to her scholarly work, Professor Steiker contributes to numerous law reform efforts as a litigator, nonprofit board member, consultant, and expert witness.

The starting point for this symposium is the striking punitive turn that has occurred in the United States over the past forty years—a change in public discourse and public policy that has yielded a staggering increase in the rate of incarceration, along with other dramatic changes such as the rise of the "supermax" prison, the proliferation of mandatory sentences and sentences of life without parole, the increasing treatment of juvenile offenders as adults, the resurgence of the use of capital punishment, and the criminalization of immigration policy.

During roughly the same time period, the concept of "human dignity" has been elaborated in a robust jurisprudence in a number of domestic legal systems outside the United States and in international human rights law.[1] In contrast, although "dignity" makes an occasional appearance in American constitutional law, it has been much less robustly developed here than elsewhere, especially with regard to criminal justice. We have highly developed (albeit hotly contested) accounts of the constitutional norms of "liberty" and "equality," both of which are textually present in the Constitution; we also have highly developed accounts of "privacy" and "proportionality," neither of which are textually present but which are often taken to be the central animating principles of the Fourth and the Eighth Amendments, respectively. But dignity remains largely a rhetorical cipher, lacking a home in any specific amendment of the Bill of Rights or a substantial or well-theorized role in American constitutional jurisprudence more broadly. As one scholar of comparative constitutional law has wryly observed, "One might conclude that Americans have no dignity, only rights."[2]

A number of scholars have argued that these two phenomena are related—that the lack of a constitutional jurisprudence regarding dignity in the United States is connected in some important way to the punitive turn or that incorporating dignity into our constitutional jurisprudence would provide an antidote to the punitive turn. For example, legal historian James Whitman has argued that the greater harshness of penal policy in the United States in comparison to that of Western Europe is the product primarily of a "leveling down" egalitarian tradition in the United States in contrast to a "leveling up" egalitarian tradition in Europe that extended the notion of "dignity" in punishment—formerly the privilege only of high-status offenders—to all.[3] On this view, it should not be surprising that dignity, with its historical overtones of status-based privilege, has been neglected in policy discourse and constitutional law regarding criminal punishment in the United States; we should not expect dignity to be the primary normative resource for fleshing out the content of the constitutional promise of "equal protection of the laws" or the protections against "cruel and unusual punishments" and deprivations of life or liberty without "due process of law."

Other legal scholars have moved beyond descriptive accounts of the reasons for dignity's relative absence from American discourse and penal policy into the prescriptive arena, arguing that the development of dignity as a constitutional value may prove to be a useful—even necessary—antidote to the unchecked punitive turn. For example, Jonathan Simon has argued that a reinvigorated constitutional value of dignity is a key weapon in the battle against the proliferation of sentences of life without parole in the United States.[4] Eva Nilsen has generalized the argument and urged that a more robust constitutional conception of human dignity is crucial to responding to the problems of mass incarceration and the inhumane treatment that incarcerated American prisoners routinely face.[5] At a more theoretical level, Kyron Huigens has argued that a return to an Aristotelian or "aretaic" conception of dignity in the moral philosophical grounding of criminal punishment is necessary to transform our current system of massive "quarantine" back into a system of value-oriented criminal justice.[6]

Not everyone agrees that an increased focus on dignity would improve constitutional law or moral discourse. Some, like Neomi Rao, worry that a focus on human dignity as a moral *value* might lead modern constitutionalism to deprive legal *rights* of their special force.[7] Others, like Reva Siegel, argue that the concept of dignity can be so fundamentally contested that its future normative and political valence is unpredictable, as Siegel demonstrates in the context of public and constitutional discourse about sexuality (abortion and same-sex marriage).[8] Others, perhaps most famously Steven Pinker in an essay in the *New Republic* entitled "The Stupidity of Dignity," claim that the concept of dignity is fundamentally incoherent; Pinker argues that dignity's amorphousness has permitted its use as a front for "theocon" (religious conservative) interventions in bioethics.[9] In Pinker's view, "The problem is that 'dignity' is a squishy, subjective notion, hardly up to the heavyweight moral demands assigned to it."[10]

My contribution to this discussion is not to defend or develop the causal argument linking dignity's relative absence in American legal discourse to our punitive turn, nor to urge greater reliance on the value of dignity in American constitutional law in a wholesale manner. Rather, I hope to illuminate further what a commitment to dignity might entail, by unraveling a single strand of its possible meanings. Thus, I do not try to develop a comprehensive account, either philosophically or legally, of human dignity. Instead, I focus on one feature of what respect for dignity might entail that distinguishes it from other allied norms such as liberty, equality, privacy, and proportionality—the idea of human dignity as a societal value rather than an individual right, as something distinct from the harms that indignity may impose on an individual. My focus is on the role that the concept or value of dignity might play in protecting something in our collective, communal life—*our* dignity, if you will—in addition to and apart from the individual suffering of those who are harmed by our failures to respect *their* dignity. Appeals to this "collective" aspect of dignity arise occasionally in American moral and constitutional discourse and more often abroad, but such appeals tend to be controversial—partly because of their "squishy" nature and partly because of the ways in which collective dignity can clash with individual rights of autonomy in some contexts. My claim is that the collective aspect of dignity may be less controversial and more normatively attractive in the context of the imposition of state punishment, both because the meaning of appeals to collective dignity may be less amorphous in the criminal context and because the stakes of dignitary violations in this context may be especially high.

To develop this collective strand of dignity, I will explore three general circumstances within the context of criminal punishment that have invited dignity arguments along these lines, albeit arguments that are often nascent or gestural in form. Specifically, punishment practices that deliberately or unnecessarily induce shame in offenders, punishment practices that impose extreme physical or psychological pain on offenders, and punishment practices that fail to take account of offenders as individuals all have engendered arguments along dignity lines—arguments that either explicitly or implicitly appeal to notions of collective dignity in addition to (and as distinct from) individual dignity. Of course, the collective strand of dignity arguments that I am trying to tease out is not the whole of what a commitment to dignity might mean; indeed, it is probably not the most familiar or obvious meaning of a moral or constitutional commitment to dignity. But the peripheral nature of the collective strand of dignity is precisely what recommends it here, as it has not been sufficiently developed—especially in the context of criminal justice, where its greater elaboration might help illuminate the causal, policy, and constitutional arguments about the relationship between dignity discourse and punishment practices.

Shame. The punishment context in which appeals to a collective notion of dignity are most apparent is the debate over so-called shaming punishments—punishments that involve the deliberate public humiliation or degradation of the offender.[11] Such punishments were familiar mainstays of criminal justice in earlier times, including the American colonial era (think stocks and pillories), before incarceration became the dominant mode of response to serious criminal offending. More recent proponents, like Dan Kahan, of modern shaming punishments (such as requirements that offenders wear distinctive garb or carry signs advertising their offenses) are drawn to these punishments by concerns about the longer and costlier degradation of offenders that incarceration entails—that is, at least in part by concerns about the harshness of our current penal regime that could itself be deemed a concern about the "dignity" or suffering of offenders.[12] But opponents of shaming punishments tend to frame their concerns in dignitary terms that reach beyond the individual suffering of offenders. The main arguments made against shaming punishments tend to emphasize their broader social impact and meaning.

One distinctive feature of shaming punishments is the way they directly involve the public in the administration of punishment. By their nature, shaming punishments generally require an audience to experience the offender's shame, whether in Hester Prynne's Puritan village or a modern metropolis. Critics of shaming punishments worry about the attitudes and behavior that such punishments might call forth on the part of the public audience. James Whitman brings to bear consideration of historical experience with shaming punishments. He argues that such sanctions "involve an ugly, and politically dangerous, complicity between the state and the crowd."[13] He worries that that by public shaming, the state invites—or even incites—the public to feel and express anger and contempt toward the offender that may produce a degree of abuse that the state cannot moderate or control. Some such vengeful emotions are inevitably produced by the commission of serious crimes, but the state's mode of punishment can exacerbate and celebrate those emotions, producing results that are antithetical to an "ethic of restraint and sobriety"[14] and to a commitment to "*measured* punishment."[15] Moreover, Whitman warns that allowing public officials the authority to "pluck on the bass strings of public psychology" and to thus "stir up demons" reverts to "a style of twentieth-century mass politics" that we should have learned to eschew after the excesses of Nazism and its frightening ilk.[16]

Richard Posner adds to Whitman's critique of shaming penalties by emphasizing the need for criminal punishment to express "official respect for the dignity of even the lowest of the low, namely hateful criminals."[17] This expressive function is necessary, in Posner's view, to prevent the proliferation of public attitudes that threaten the foundations of a free society. For Posner, to treat criminals as less than "errant members of the community"—to treat them like "children or animals"—is to "introduce into government a kind of we-they thinking that can lead . . . to barbarous prison conditions, summary justice, and savage punishments."[18] Thus, for Posner as for Whitman, avoiding public humiliation and preserving dignity in the punishment of individual offenders is primarily a means of protecting the broader public from modes of feeling or thinking that can pose a threat to our communal life.

Such appeals to what I call the "collective" aspect of dignity have special force in the context of shaming punishments because of the way that shaming punishments directly involve the collective in the punishment itself. But a version of this collective dignity argument can extend to humiliating aspects of incarceration that occur inside jail and prison walls and away from public view. Many of the dignity-based arguments against humiliating aspects of incarceration have involved, not surprisingly, practices relating to bodily functions and sexuality—such as prison and jail policies authorizing strip searches and body-cavity searches, policies placing male inmates under female guard surveillance while using toilet and shower facilities, practices of stripping naked some Muslim detainees at Guantanamo Bay or adorning them with women's underwear, and the decision of one infamous sheriff to issue pink-dyed underwear to all male jail inmates. Some of these practices are intended to humiliate (like the treatment of the Muslim detainees), others are generated primarily by security concerns (such as strip searches), and some are contested (the sheriff claimed that he dyed inmates' underwear pink to prevent them from taking it home with them upon release[19]). Whether or not these practices are intended to humiliate, detention practices that involve bodily functions or sexuality are powerful in their capacity to do so. Freud posited that our disgust and shame regarding our excretory functions and sexuality derives from our need to distance ourselves from lower animals,[20] and this disgust around the body tends to engender special fear and loathing of female sexuality and male homosexuality.[21]

These insights lay behind a federal appeals court ruling permitting the introduction of evidence about the pink underwear policy in a wrongful death action brought on behalf of a mentally ill man who died from a heart arrhythmia, which was allegedly caused in part by the stress he suffered after being physically forced to "dress out" in the pink inmate garb. The court explained that the pink garb could be construed as an impermissibly punitive measure intended to humiliate the inmate: "Given the cultural context, it is a fair inference that the color is chosen to symbolize a loss of masculine identity and power, to stigmatize the male prisoners as feminine."[22] As Caleb Smith recognizes in his contribution to this collection, there was an intentionally mocking element to the pink underwear policy: the "celebrity sheriff" who promulgated the policy did so knowing that he was "inviting decent citizens to laugh at the humiliation of [the] inmates."[23]

Psychological insights about body taboos and shame also help to explain the degree of outrage that greeted the Supreme Court's recent decision upholding the automatic strip search and visual body-cavity inspection of any arrestee admitted to the general population of a jail.[24] Mr. Florence, the plaintiff in the case, had been arrested during a traffic stop (when his wife was driving) on a mistaken outstanding warrant for a fine that he had paid years ago. Before the mistake was cleared up, Mr. Florence had been strip searched twice, an experience that left him feeling deeply humiliated—"less than a man" in his own words.[25] The four-justice dissent, authored by Justice Breyer, contended that the majority failed to take seriously enough the intrusion at issue and went so far as to list the words that lower courts had used to describe similar practices: "demeaning, dehumanizing, undignified, humiliating, terrifying, unpleasant, embarrassing, [and] repulsive, signifying degradation and submission."[26] Criticisms of the decision in the media were similarly strongly worded; one op-ed in the *Chicago Tribune* characterized the decision as "perhaps the largest judicial assault on human dignity since *Buck v. Bell* justified eugenics or since *Plessy v. Ferguson* gave us 'separate but equal.'"[27]

But granting that some treatment of inmates can be just as humiliating as public-shaming penalties (or even more so), if the public is not involved as an audience or participant in an inmate's shame, how do such humiliating practices raise the *collective* dignity concerns that are my particular focus? We can see some possible connections in Judge Posner's dissenting opinion from an appeals court decision that dismissed an inmate's claim that his Eighth Amendment right against "cruel and unusual punishment" was violated by his continuous surveillance by female guards, including while he was naked and using the toilet or the shower. Posner—wearing his judge's robe rather than his scholar's hat—associated exposing prisoners' nudity to guards of the opposite sex with seeing them "as members of a different species . . . devoid of human dignity and entitled to no respect."[28] In a particularly provocative passage, Judge Posner noted that from this dehumanizing perspective, "no issue concerning the degrading or brutalizing treatment of prisoners would arise. In particular there would be no inhibitions about using prisoners as the subject of experiments, including social experiments such as the experiment of seeing whether the sexes can be made interchangeable. The parading of naked male inmates in front of female guards, or of naked female inmates in front of male guards, would be no more problematic than 'cross-sex surveillance' in a kennel."[29]

The first and more obvious concern raised by Posner regarding humiliating practices in prisons and jails is the likelihood that such practices will lower the inhibitions of prison officials against further brutal treatment. Conditions and practices that "dehumanize" prisoners encourage those in charge of them to see them as less than human and thus to treat them as such. This tendency was powerfully demonstrated by Philip Zimbardo's famous Stanford Prison Experiment, in which college student "guards" engaged in increasingly brutal treatment of their peer "inmates" when the inmates were dressed in smocks and ankle chains, with their hair hidden by stocking caps and their names replaced by inmate numbers.[30] Zimbardo's experiment suggests, as Posner argues, that protecting the dignity of prisoners protects them—and their keepers—from a slide toward greater brutality. I will say more about how brutal treatment implicates the "collective" aspect of dignity below under the heading of "pain," but it is enough to note here that one concern about shaming is that it can be causally linked to such treatment.

However, distinct from the worry about loosening inhibitions against brutal treatment, there is a less obvious but even larger concern in Posner's dissent. His reference to using prisoners as "the subject of experiments" calls to mind, almost certainly intentionally, Nazi experimentation on prisoners in concentration camps. I hazard a guess that Posner was not really worried that permitting female guards to oversee male prisoners would *actually* lead to Nazi-era prisoner experimentation in Chicago's prisons and jails (nor has the practice—which was upheld—done so to date). Rather, Posner's reference to prisoner experimentation was a way of underscoring a social and political dimension to the way we collectively, through our official institutions and practices, "see" the status of our prisoners. Posner's concern about what he called "a kind of we-they thinking" is explicitly a concern about thought as distinct from action, about how prisoners are viewed as distinct from how they are treated, about the attitudes of the punishers rather than the suffering of offenders. Permitting prison officials—public officials of the state—to violate the dignity of prisoners under their control threatens to promote and condone official attitudes that are inconsistent with a democratic commitment to the fundamental equality of persons before the government and by extension in the eyes of the community that both creates and is created by government.

This kind of dignitary concern is not dependent on how much offenders subjectively suffer from humiliating punishments. Hence, it would not matter whether some offenders might prefer public-shaming punishments to incarceration, as Dan Kahan suggests is the case.[31] Nor would it matter if prisoners got used to female guards and ceased to feel humiliated by their surveillance. The concern about collective dignity is about the larger, more subtle, and concededly more difficult-to-measure effects of humiliating punishment practices on our collective ways of seeing and thinking about status. Humiliating punishment, in this view, is a kind of official pornography that has the capacity to get inside of our public institutions and through them into our collective life and imagination to wreak a kind of perversion of thought—a perversion that threatens both the justice of our criminal punishments and the egalitarian foundations of a liberal democratic state.

Pain. A second and related context in which the collective strand of dignity arguments arises is the imposition of punishments that involve offenders' extreme physical or psychological suffering. Granted, it is widely accepted that punishment by its very nature involves deliberately unpleasant consequences or "hard treatment," just as it is unavoidably true that the practice of incarceration involves some irreducible element of humiliation. Hence, to claim that pain or shame in punishment unacceptably violates human dignity, and thus morally and/or legally invalidates some punishment practices, is to make a claim about matters of degree (unless one is willing to jettison the entire structure of current punishment practices, including the use of incarceration, and to rebuild from the ground up[32]).

Challenges to punishment practices that produce extreme physical or psychological pain have had more (though still modest) success in American courts than challenges to conditions and practices that are "merely" humiliating—probably because the most dramatically humiliating practices end up involving pain as well. For example, the Supreme Court gave a rare civil rights victory to an Alabama inmate who sued a group of prison guards for employing the "hitching post" as a form of prison discipline.[33] Mr. Hope, the inmate, was twice handcuffed above shoulder height to a restraining bar exposed to the sun; the second incident, which took place in June, lasted for seven hours, during which Hope was ordered to remove his shirt, not permitted bathroom breaks, given inadequate water, and taunted by a guard about his thirst. (Hope testified that the guard first gave water to some dogs, then brought the water cooler closer to Hope before kicking it over and spilling the water onto the ground.[34]) The court ruled that the Eighth Amendment proscription of "cruel and unusual punishments" had been clearly violated in light of the "obvious cruelty" inherent in the use of the hitching post and the "degrading and dangerous" nature of the circumstances of Hope's particular treatment.[35] The court concluded that "Hope was treated in a way antithetical to human dignity."[36]

More recently, the Supreme Court also adverted to human dignity in construing the Eighth Amendment to require California to release inmates in order to relieve extreme overcrowding in the state's prison system.[37] The court reviewed the catastrophic consequences for inmates of running the California prisons at approximately 200 percent capacity for more than a decade—from the rampant transmission of disease, to the severe lack of adequate medical care, including mental health care, to the increase in violence, all of which contributed to what the court concluded was an "unconscionable degree of suffering and death."[38] The court reached into its proportionality jurisprudence to retrieve a pronouncement that it has used with some frequency (if not much clarity) in that context: "The basic concept underlying the Eighth Amendment is nothing less than the dignity of man."[39] The court insisted that prisoners "retain the essence of human dignity" and noted that a prison's failure to provide adequate sustenance for inmates "may actually produce physical torture or a lingering death"[40] in violation of that "essence" (whatever it is).

Despite the Supreme Court's rejection of Alabama's hitching post and California's overcrowded prisons as inconsistent with human dignity, the court has not been receptive to dignity-based challenges to the punishment that is most commonly associated with "torture" in its extremity—the punishment of death. Only Justices Brennan and Marshall argued that imposition of the death penalty was a per se violation of the Eighth Amendment on the ground that it violated human dignity. These two justices were part of the five-justice majority that temporarily invalidated capital punishment in America in *Furman v. Georgia* in 1972;[41] they remained dissenters for the rest of their days on the court, even after the Supreme Court reinstated capital punishment four years later.[42] Justice Brennan's solo opinion in *Furman* represents the most elaborate dignity-based challenge to the death penalty yet mounted under the Eighth Amendment, developing four principles or considerations to flesh out the abstraction of dignity: severity, arbitrariness, societal unacceptability, and excessiveness. The first of these four principles encompasses the consideration of pain, both physical and mental. Justice Brennan's conclusion that the death penalty violated human dignity thus rested in part on his conclusion that death is "an unusually severe punishment, unusual in its pain, in its finality, and in its enormity. No other existing punishment is comparable to death in terms of physical and mental suffering."[43] A majority of the Supreme Court had little trouble rejecting Brennan's argument because it concluded that the pain involved in capital punishment was not "gratuitous" in light of its long historical acceptance as necessary for the achievement of the valid penological ends of retribution and deterrence.[44]

Dignity-based arguments regarding pain have likewise been unsuccessful in constitutionally challenging the use of solitary confinement—a relative newcomer in the penological world compared to the death penalty but another punishment that has been likened to torture. Despite evidence of dramatic psychological and even physiological reactions to solitary confinement, so well documented in surgeon Atul Gawande's recent article in the *New Yorker*,[45] prisoners seeking to challenge the practice on Eighth Amendment grounds have generally failed in the absence of proof of some other more tangible deprivation of basic human needs, or proof that they were seriously mentally ill when placed in segregation. A recent scholarly survey concluded, "Virtually every court which has considered the issue has held that the imposition of solitary confinement, without more, does not violate the Eighth Amendment. Arguments that isolation offends evolving standards of decency, that it constitutes psychological torture, and that it is excessive because less severe sanctions would be equally efficacious, have routinely failed."[46] There is some reason, however, to think that the tide may be turning with regard to the humanity and legality of solitary confinement, in light of both renewed litigation in federal courts and the first ever Senate hearings in 2012, where substantial testimony was received about the suffering produced by current use of the practice.[47]

The dignity-based arguments about the pain involved in the various forms of state punishment canvassed above, whether legally successful or not, all relied heavily on the individual suffering that the punishment entailed. In the successful legal claims—against Alabama's hitching post and California's overcrowded prisons—the Supreme Court gave careful attention to the details, the nitty-gritty mechanics, of the suffering endured—how the sun heated the handcuffs attached to the hitching post so as to burn and chafe Mr. Hope's wrists; how one young inmate in California died of undiagnosed and untreated testicular cancer after seventeen months of testicular pain. In both cases, photographs were part of the legal record. These concrete depictions of pain featured in the successful claims may explain something about the lack of persuasiveness of the unsuccessful claims, in that both the death penalty and solitary confinement involve less visible or accessible forms of pain. The introduction of progressively more "humane" methods of execution has reduced the physical pain that execution entails, so that much of the "pain" involved in the death penalty is more abstract—the psychological anguish over impending loss of life, and the so-called "death row syndrome" of enduring a lengthy and uncertain period of incarceration leading up to execution. Similarly, the horrifying psychological effects of solitary confinement are less intuitively accessible to those who have not experienced them. We can *see* visceral human pain; it makes us flinch and turn away (or stare in disgusted fascination). Extreme physical pain that is literally torturous seems to have a more direct link, both historically and intuitively, to the "cruelty" forbidden by the Eighth Amendment in its promised protection of "dignity."

Consideration of the role of concrete, individual suffering in these pain-based dignity arguments seems, at first glance, to place them far afield from the collective strand of dignity arguments that are my focus. The right of an individual offender to be free from extreme and gratuitous pain seems to lie in the heartland of an individual-rights-based formulation of dignity. How, if at all, does the extremity of pain suffered by an offender connect to concerns about collective dignity? One plausible answer would be to claim that the imposition of punishment involving severe physical or mental pain on an offender necessarily entails the same kind of "dehumanization" as the imposition of humiliating, shaming punishments (not least because many extremely painful punishments could also be described as extremely humiliating ones). Those who actually authorize, inflict, or tolerate offenders' extreme pain must rationalize their roles, which likely involves the "kind of we-they thinking" that Posner warned of in the context of shaming punishments. Moreover, official indifference (or worse, satisfaction) in the face of vividly extreme suffering enacts an official rejection of the humanity of the offender in the same way that shaming punishments enact a debased status incompatible with equality. On this account, pain and shame in punishment pose similar, perhaps even identical, threats to collective dignity.

Moreover, official imposition of extreme physical or psychological pain has a further dimension that implicates us collectively. Brutal punishments require those who actually inflict the pain or directly witness the suffering of offenders to steel themselves and repress their natural instincts to flinch and to suffer empathetically with the offender. Those who are unable to distance themselves sufficiently from their brutal work are apt to experience trauma, as Werner Herzog's recent documentary about a capital case in Texas illustrated in its interview with a former "execution team" member.[48] Thus, as Michelle Brown explains in her contribution to this collection, while suffering may invite empathy, it also may simultaneously generate empathy's "dark undertow," in that "scenes of vulnerability produce desires to *withhold* attachment."[49] This withholding in the context of brutal punishment is precisely what implicates us collectively.

As Jeffrey Reiman argues, in the context of capital punishment, "[T]he pain of foreseen, humanly administered death strikes us with the urgency that characterizes intense physical pain, causing grown men to cry, faint, and lose control of their bodily functions. There is something to be gained by refusing to endorse the hardness of heart necessary to impose such a fate."[50] Reiman urges that by rejecting punishments that share this feature modern states will advance their "civilizing" function, an idea that informs the many inchoate invocations of "decency" and "civilized society" in arguments about criminal punishment and human dignity.

Reiman's argument gains support from the fact that, in order to achieve the "hardness of heart" necessary to resist the body in pain, those who directly impose extremely painful punishments must suppress not only their sympathy with the offender's suffering but also the disgust and revulsion that are natural reactions to physical brutality. One way to manage this necessary suppression is to channel these emotions of disgust and revulsion onto the offenders themselves, which both provides an outlet for such uncomfortable feelings and justifies the punishers' participation in the brutal treatment of the offenders. Thus, the infliction of punishments involving extreme pain promotes the suppression of emotions (sympathy) and capacities (empathy, or the ability to feel sympathy for the pain of others) that are central to the experience of the fellowship of humanity, while simultaneously excluding offenders from that circle of fellowship. Kant himself, a foundational proponent of retributivism, warned of just this danger, when he maintained that the just imposition of the death penalty on a murderer "must be kept free from all maltreatment that would make the humanity suffering in his person loathsome or abominable."[51]

Still, it seems fair to ask how the experience of officials involved in the infliction (or toleration) of punishments involving extreme pain carries over into our broader collective life. For example, how does the experience of the executioner (which we try to normalize and diminish through the promulgation of execution "protocols" and the use of execution "teams") make its way out of the execution chamber? How does the brutal use of the Alabama hitching post behind prison walls implicate us collectively? Several distinctive features of punishment as a social practice link the experience of state officials inflicting punishment to the broader polity. At the most concrete level, state punishment is performed in our collective name: criminal cases are entitled "The People" or "The State" or "The United States" against the defendant. But punishment is not our collective doing merely as a formal matter. Rather, a unique feature of the pain involved in formal criminal punishment is that it is intended and expected to be welcomed, even celebrated, by the broader community as justice being done. The rituals and drama of the criminal process are designed to channel powerful human emotions toward a resolution of moral satisfaction with an offender's punishment. As a result, we are not only formally but also emotionally linked to the officials who carry out punishments—even, perhaps especially, the most brutal ones—in our names.

As for the haziness of our knowledge of exactly what happens during an execution, inside a "supermax" segregation wing, in a crowded California prison, or on an Alabama hitching post, that haziness may well intensify rather than diminish our collective engagement with the suffering these practices entail. As Austin Sarat lyrically explains, "Punishment is inscribed in both our unconscious and our consciousness. It lives in images conveyed, in lessons taught, in repressed memories, in horrible imaginings. Some of its horror and controlling power is, in fact, a result of its fearful invisibility."[52] Our taming of the "horrible imaginings" produced by hazy knowledge of brutal punishment practices behind prison walls requires us to collectively join our agents within those walls in suppressing and redirecting our natural revulsion toward brutality and rationalizing our detachment from its objects.

Individualization. A third context in which collective dignity might operate as a constraint is the sentencing process by which criminal punishment is imposed, rather than the nature of the punishment selected. This context is different in kind from the preceding two, and it may seem that it is the least likely to be susceptible to collective concerns, especially since this constraint appears to invoke individual "rights," in particular the right to be considered *as* an individual. But bear with me as I explore the foundation of this right in American constitutional law and its normative connection—albeit one that is more implicit than explicit—to the preservation of collective dignity.

Mandatory sentences are not a novel feature of American law; indeed, the death penalty as mandated punishment for certain crimes came to our shores from England and endured on both sides of the Atlantic well into the nineteenth century. However, the explosion of mandatory minimum sentences over the past several decades has given new urgency to old questions about the wisdom and justice of sentences mandated entirely by consideration of the offense rather than the offender. Generally, such questions have been treated as policy determinations in which prudential considerations such as accuracy and uniformity loom largest. However, the sudden return of the mandatory death penalty in the mid-1970s introduced a moral and constitutional dimension to the debate. Numerous state legislatures responded to the Supreme Court's rejection of standardless capital sentencing in its 1972 decision in *Furman v. Georgia* by enacting the least discretionary mode of sentencing they could conjure—mandatory death sentences for the commission of enumerated capital offenses.

The Supreme Court's consideration of these new mandatory capital statutes in its 1976 decisions in *Woodson v. North Carolina*[53] and *Roberts v. North Carolina*[54] took a peculiar constitutional form. It would have seemed natural for the court to evaluate mandatory capital sentencing under the Fourteenth Amendment's due process clause, which requires that states provide appropriate procedures for deprivations of life, liberty, and property. The hierarchical listing of the three sorts of deprivations invites inquiry into what process is due in each of the three contexts. However, the court decided the question of the constitutionality of mandatory capital sentencing not under the due process clause but rather under the Eighth Amendment's cruel and unusual punishments clause, which, as the *Woodson* plurality opinion explained, serves to assure that "the State's power to punish is exercised within the limits of civilized standards."[55] This choice moved the discussion from what procedures are "due" to what procedures are "civilized"—a more abstract and less individually focused question.

The *Woodson* plurality rested its decision in part on its identification of a historical consensus against the imposition of mandatory death sentences. However, in one of the most openly normative passages of the court's entire Eighth Amendment jurisprudence, the plurality explained that "[c]onsideration of both the offender and the offense in order to arrive at a just and appropriate sentence has been viewed as a progressive and humanizing development."[56] The court went on to note that "[w]hile the prevailing practice of individualizing sentencing determinations generally reflects simply enlightened policy rather than a constitutional imperative, we believe that in capital cases the fundamental respect for humanity underlying the Eighth Amendment requires consideration of the character and record of the individual offender and the circumstances of the particular offense as a constitutionally indispensable part of the process of inflicting the penalty of death."[57] To rule otherwise would permit the sentencing process to "treat[] all persons convicted of a designated offense not as uniquely individual human beings, but as members of a faceless, undifferentiated mass to be subjected to the blind infliction of the penalty of death."[58]

The court's claim that "respect for humanity" requires consideration as a "uniquely individual human being" echoes David Luban's persuasive argument that "subjectivity" lies at the heart of human dignity—that "having human dignity means, roughly, *having a story of one's own*."[59] Luban describes the metaphysical case for placing subjectivity at the heart of dignity as follows: "[H]uman beings have ontological heft because each of us is an 'I', and I have ontological heft. For others to treat me as though I have none fundamentally denigrates my status in the world. It amounts to a form of humiliation that violates my human dignity."[60] Luban also offers a "naturalized" or common-sense account of human dignity as "having a story of one's own" by working backward from "the characteristic features of humiliation," which he identifies as "treating a person's story and viewpoint as insignificant" to an understanding of what respect for dignity necessarily entails.[61]

Luban's subjectivity-based account of human dignity helps to explain why respecting the individuality of offenders in sentencing implicates collective as well as individual dignity interests. Luban's use of the word "humiliation" echoes the concerns raised above about shaming penalties, as does the *Woodson* Court's reference to the "humanizing" function of individualized sentences. Humiliation and dehumanization, whether through shaming or through refusal to consider an offender as an individual, implicate us collectively through the official attitudes such practices enact and promote. Concerns about respecting subjectivity, however, do not merely echo concerns about humiliating punishments. Respect for subjectivity through individualized sentencing adds a new dimension to the concerns about "official pornography" raised in the shame context and the "hardening of heart" raised in the pain context. The agent in any sentencing process is the sentencer, and individualization shapes what the sentencer must actively consider and thus the public story that is told and received more widely about the punishment that is eventually imposed on an offender. If the collective strand of dignity is concerned with shaming because of how it affects what we collectively *see* as a result of our punishment practices and with pain because of how it affects what we collectively *feel*, this strand of dignity is concerned with individualized sentencing because of how it affects what we collectively *consider* as part of the province of punishment—and thus how we understand the narrative or story of our practices of criminal punishment.

Collective Dignity and Criminal Punishment. Elaboration of the concerns that fall within the collective strand of dignity as it relates to criminal punishment raises at least as many questions as it answers. As a moral and constitutional matter, concerns about dignity in punishment are inevitably matters of degree, given that some form of indignity is inherent in any practice of intentionally imposing hard treatment on criminal offenders. Which practices are so humiliating or so painful as to fall on the morally and legally prohibited side of the line? In what kinds of cases and to what extent must offenders be considered as individuals? For example, during the 2012 term, the Supreme Court extended its requirement of individualized sentencing to apply beyond the capital sphere to juveniles facing sentences of life without possibility of parole.[62] But this is obviously a very tenuous stopping place. How should the court determine whether and how to extend this requirement—to all juveniles facing lengthy mandatory sentences (or any mandatory sentences, even relatively short ones)? To all defendants—juvenile or not—facing life without possibility of parole (or facing lengthy mandatory sentences or any mandatory sentences, even relatively short ones)? Understanding what is at stake in collective dignity does not generate anything like a fine-gauged metric to weigh the stakes in particular circumstances.

Moreover, I have left unexplored here a fundamental question prior to the difficult one of application, but one that might help inform it: the question of *why* collective dignity matters. In exploring *what* collective dignity is concerned with, I have left largely unstated the possible foundational reasons for those concerns. Collective dignity might be rooted, as Leslie Meltzer Henry has argued, in Aristotelian virtue ethics—in a vision of "humanity's excellence" that human society is morally bound to promote.[63] Or, collective dignity might be rooted, as I have claimed elsewhere, in the need to preserve the collective moral agency upon which our punishment practices themselves are premised.[64] Or, collective dignity might be rooted, as Austin Sarat has suggested, in a vision of democratic politics, as its "enlivening value."[65] The theoretical roots of a commitment to collective dignity will help save it from the "squishiness" that Steven Pinker deplores and guide its application in particular cases.

Even without such a theoretical foundation, however, an elaboration of the concerns of collective dignity in the punishment context suggests that this strand of dignity, while not unproblematic, is perhaps less problematic in the context of criminal punishment than in some other arenas in which it has been deployed. The first of the two most prominent critiques made of collective dignity is the concern about the potential conflict between collective dignity and individual autonomy. Reva Siegel, for example, has explored this conflict in the abortion context in her critique of the Supreme Court's reliance on the dignity of life to restrict abortion rights in its *Casey* and *Carhart* decisions.[66] The conflict between dignity and autonomy is brought into focus perhaps most sharply by the famous "dwarf tossing" decision of the United Nations Human Rights Committee.[67] After France outlawed the "sport" of dwarf tossing on the grounds of human dignity, a dwarf, who made his living by being paid to be tossed, challenged the ban as a violation of his own individual dignity, autonomy, and right to be free from discrimination. The Human Rights Committee rejected the dwarf's challenge, agreeing with the state that the ban "was necessary in order to protect public order, which brings into play considerations of human dignity that are compatible with the objects of the [International Covenant on Civil and Political Rights]."[68] The decision has generated much commentary, on both sides, much of it genuinely anguished by the difficult conflict raised by the case.[69]

Conflicts of this kind are possible in the criminal context, too—but to a lesser extent. At the rhetorical level, just as dignity can be invoked on behalf of unborn fetal life *and* by pregnant women, so too can dignity be invoked by the victims of crime in addition to criminal offenders. Failing to punish (or to punish seriously enough) a serious crime surely can be seen as a form of dignitary harm to the victim. Moreover, it is possible that there may be conflicts between dignity and autonomy even if only offenders are considered: an offender might prefer a punishment (a shaming penalty or even execution) that society wishes to reject on dignity grounds, either wholesale or in the case of a particular offender (such as execution for those whose mental illness renders them incompetent to be executed). However, the collective dignity argument in the punishment context is less likely to run into these conflicts partly because punishment (like dignity) runs along a continuum so that there is generally a serious enough punishment available to protect a victim's dignity to replace one that threatens an offender's dignity (and through the offender, collective dignity). Moreover, there are not very many contexts in which offenders would autonomously choose punishments that violate collective dignity. Perhaps most important, the threat to collective dignity is simply greater in the punishment context than in contexts like dwarf tossing or even abortion because the act at issue that is claimed to violate collective dignity (the imposition of criminal punishment) is itself a collective one, not a private one, and thus one that has the power to affect more powerfully our collective life, in the ways I have described above.

The second concern—the about "squishiness" that led Steven Pinker to dismiss appeals to dignity as "stupid"—is also ameliorated in the context of criminal justice. Yes, such claims lie along a continuum that is difficult to gauge. And, yes, it is important to work through the different and potentially conflicting theoretical grounds for appeals to collective dignity in the criminal context. But my hope in this essay has been to show that appeals to the need to protect human dignity in the context of criminal punishment are not mere fig leaves for the importation of unreflective moral preferences, as Pinker asserts they are in the context of bioethics. There is a bounded universe of coherent questions and concerns that are encompassed by the collective strand of dignity arguments in criminal punishment, and, while the answers may be inevitably contested and contestable, these are meaningful and important questions to be asking.

My larger hope has been to show that the nature and scope of our moral and constitutional discourse about criminal punishment shapes not only how we talk about punishment but also how we think about it—that is, that discourse shapes our "punitive imagination." Dignity's relative absence from our current discourse reflects the absence of an imagined identity of each individual with one another and with the collective—the connection that is reflected in the dual location of dignity as residing within each human being as a result of its source in our collective humanity. Thus I close with the quote from William Blake that appears in the title of this essay—the opening line of his mystical masterwork, *Auguries of Innocence*.[70] Blake's poetic invocation of the connection and repetition of each individual part of the universe with the whole of creation evokes an analogous linkage between individual human beings and our collective humanity and suggests the centrality of preserving in our common life the capacity to imaginatively see and feel that connection—the capacity "To see a World in a Grain of Sand."[71]

Notes

I thank Austin Sarat and the participants in the symposium on "The Punitive Imagination," held at the University of Alabama School of Law in September 2012, and I am grateful to Joshua Marcin for excellent research assistance.

1. For the development of human dignity in domestic law, see, for example, Matthias Malmann, "The Basic Law at 60—Human Dignity and the Culture of Republicanism," *German Law Journal* 11 (2010): 9 (German law); Izhak England, "Human Dignity: From Antiquity to Modern Israel's Constitutional Framework," *Cardozo Law Review* 21 (2000): 1903 (Israeli law).

For human dignity in international human rights law, see generally, David Kretzmer and Eckart Klein, eds., *The Concept of Human Dignity in Human Rights Discourse* (The Hague: Kluwer Law International, 2002).

2. Gerald L. Neuman, "Human Dignity in United States Constitutional Law," in *Zur Autonomie des Individuums: Liber Amicorum Spiros Simitis*, ed. Dieter Simon and Manfred Weiss (Baden-Baden: Nomos Verlagsgesellschaft, 2000), at 249, 249.

3. James Q. Whitman, *Harsh Justice: Criminal Punishment and the Widening Divide Between America and Europe* (New York: Oxford University Press, 2003).

4. Jonathan Simon, "Dignity and Risk: The Long Road from *Graham v. Florida* to Abolition of Life without Parole," in *Life without Parole: America's New Death Penalty*, ed. Charles J. Ogletree Jr, and Austin Sarat (New York: New York University Press, 2012).

5. Eva S. Nilsen, "Decency, Dignity, and Desert: Restoring Ideals of Humane Punishment to Constitutional Discourse," *University of California Davis Law Review* 41 (2007): 111.

6. Kyron Huigens, "Dignity and Desert in Punishment Theory," *Harvard Journal of Law and Public Policy* 27 (2003): 33.

7. Neomi Rao, "On the Use and Abuse of Dignity in Constitutional Law," *Columbia Journal of European Law* 14 (2008): 201.

8. Reva B. Siegel, "Dignity and Sexuality: Claims on Dignity in Transnational Debates over Abortion and Same-Sex Marriage," *International Journal of Constitutional Law* 10 (2012): 355.

9. Steven Pinker, "The Stupidity of Dignity," *New Republic*, May 28, 2008: 28, 31.

10. Id. at 28.

11. Dan Kahan, who defends the use of shaming punishments, thinks they are best understood as "degradation penalties." Dan Kahan, "What Do Alternative Sanctions Mean?," *University of Chicago Law Review* 63 (1996): 591, 636. Richard Posner, who opposes the use of shaming punishments, thinks they are more aptly described as "humiliating punishments." Richard A. Posner, "Social Norms, Social Meaning, and Economic Analysis of Law: A Comment," *Journal of Legal Studies* 27 (1998): 553, 557.

12. See, e.g., Kahan, "What Do Alternative Sanctions Mean?," 593–94.

13. James Q. Whitman, "What Is Wrong with Inflicting Shame Sanctions?," *Yale Law Journal* 107 (1998): 1055, 1059.

14. Id. at 1092.

15. Id. at 1090 (emphasis in the original).

16. Id. at 1091–92.

17. Posner, "Social Norms," 557.

18. Id.

19. See Jacques Billeaud, "Joe Arpaio Responds to Ruling Critical of Pink Underwear Policy," *Huffington Post*, March 28, 2012, found at http://www.huffingtonpost.com/2012/03/29/joe-arpaio-pink-underwear-jail_n_1387708.html.

20. Martha C. Nussbaum, *Hiding from Humanity: Disgust, Shame, and the Law* (Princeton, NJ: Princeton University Press, 2004), at 89–90 (citing Freud and expanding on his insights with more recent findings of experimental psychology).

21. Id. at 113. The humiliation entailed by pink underwear and the like reveals the inevitably culturally constructed nature of "dignity" and suggests that a masculine and heterosexual vision may sometimes be asserted as a "universal" account of "human" dignity. This recognition raises the profound issue of how one protects dignity within our current culture without also accepting and even propagating dignity's patriarchal influences, to the detriment of the competing "dignity" of women and sexual minorities.

22. *Wagner v. County of Maricopa*, 673 F.3d 977, 981 (2012).

23. Caleb Smith, "Imprisonment without Justice," in this volume at 88.

24. *Florence v. Board of Chosen Freeholders of County of Burlington*, 132 S.Ct. 1510 (2012).

25. Adam Liptak, "Justices Approve Strip-Search Use For Any Arrest," *New York Times*, April 3, 2012.

26. *Florence v. County of Burlington*, 1526 (Breyer, J., dissenting) (internal quotation marks and citation omitted).

27. Andrew Trees, "Why Can't We Keep Our Clothes On?" *Chicago Tribune*, April 5, 2012.

28. *Johnson v. Phelan*, 69 F.3d 144, 151 (7th. Cir. 1995) (Posner, J., concurring in part and dissenting in part).

29. Id.

30. See Philip Zimbardo, *The Lucifer Effect: Understanding How Good People Turn Evil* (New York: Random House, 2007).

31. See Kahan, "What Do Alternative Sanctions Mean?," 610 ("If the goal is to respect 'individual dignity,' why second-guess offenders about what course of action treats them with the most respect?").

32. See, e.g., Chad Flanders, "Shame and the Meanings of Punishment," *Cleveland State Law Review* 54 (2006): 609 (making a dignity-based argument that "punishment is an institution that is fundamentally at odds with one of liberalism's most basic commitments").

33. *Hope v. Pelzer*, 536 U.S. 730 (2002) (denying qualified immunity to the guard defendants because the constitutional violation was one that was "clearly established" by prior law).

34. Id. at 735.

35. Id. at 745.

36. Id.

37. *Brown v. Plata*, 131 S.Ct. 1910 (2011).

38. Id. at 1927 (quoting lower court).

39. Id. at 1928 (internal quotation marks and citations omitted).

40. Id. (internal quotation marks and citations omitted).

41. *Furman v. Georgia*, 408 U.S. 238 (1972).

42. See *Gregg v. Georgia*, 428 U.S. 153 (1976), and accompanying cases.

43. *Furman v. Georgia*, 287 (Brennan, J., concurring).

44. *Gregg v. Georgia*, 182.

45. See, e.g., Atul Gawande, "Hellhole: The United States Holds Tens of Thousands of Inmates in Solitary Conferment. Is This Torture?" *New Yorker*, March 30, 2009.

46. Jeffrey Smith McLeod, "Anxiety, Despair, and the Maddening Isolation of Solitary Confinement: Invoking the First Amendment's Protection against State Action That Invades the Sphere of the Intellect and Spirit," *University of Pittsburgh Law Review* 70 (2009): 647, 663.

47. See Erica Goode, "Senators Start a Review of Solitary Confinement," *New York Times*, June 19, 2012.

48. Werner Herzog, "Into the Abyss" (Creative Differences Productions, et al., 2011; Sundance Selects, Domestic Theatrical Distributor).

49. Michelle Brown, "'Which Question? Which Lie?' Reflections on *Payne v. Tennessee* and the 'Quick Glimpse' of Life," in this volume at 141 (emphasis added).

50. Jeffrey H. Reiman, "Justice, Civilization, and the Death Penalty: Answering van den Haag," *Philosophy and Public Affairs* 14 (1985): 115, 141

51. Immanuel Kant, *The Philosophy of Law*, trans. W. Hastie (Edinburgh: T & T Clark, 1887), 198.

52. Austin Sarat, "The Cultural Life of Capital Punishment: Responsibility and Representation in *Dead Man Walking* and *Last Dance*," in *The Killing State: Capital Punishment in Law, Politics, and Culture*, ed. Austin Sarat (New York: Oxford University Press, 1999), 226, 227.

53. *Woodson v. North Carolina*, 428 U.S. 280 (1976).

54. *Roberts v. North Carolina*, 428 U.S. 325 (1976).

55. *Woodson v. North Carolina*, 288 (plurality opinion).

56. Id. at 304.

57. Id. (internal citation omitted).

58. Id.

59. David Luban, *Legal Ethics and Human Dignity* (Cambridge: Cambridge University Press 2007), at 70–71.

60. Id. at 71.

61. Id. at 72.

62. *Miller v. Alabama*, 132 S.Ct. 2455 (2012).

63. See Leslie Meltzer Henry, "The Jurisprudence of Dignity," *University of Pennsylvania Law Review* 160 (2011): 169, 220–22.

64. See Carol S. Steiker, "The Death Penalty and Deontology," in *The Oxford Handbook of Philosophy of Criminal Law*, ed. John Deigh and David Dolinko (New York: Oxford University Press, 2011), at 441, 459–61.

65. Austin Sarat, *When the State Kills: Capital Punishment and the American Condition* (Princeton, NJ: Princeton University Press, 2001), at 16–17.

66. Reva B. Siegel, "Dignity and the Politics of Protection: Abortion Restrictions under *Casey/Carhart*," *Yale Law Journal* 117 (2008): 1694.

67. *Manuel Wackenheim v. France*, Communication No. 854/1999, U.N. Doc .CCPR/C/75/D/854/1999 (2002).

68. Id.

69. Compare Jeremy Waldron, "Dignity, Rights, and Responsibilities," *Arizona State Law Journal* 43 (2012): 1107, with Jeffrie G. Murphy, "Human Dignity and the Law: A Brief Comment on Jeremy Waldron's *Dignity, Rights, and Responsibilities*," *Arizona State Law Journal* 43 (2012): 1273.

70. William Blake, "Auguries of Innocence," in William Blake, *Poems and Prophecies* (London: David Campbell Publishers, 1991), at 380.

71. Id.

Injustice, Authority, and the Criminal Law

Stephen P. Garvey

Introduction

In the early morning hours of June 5, 1968, five Marine Corps lieutenants stationed at Quantico, Virginia, were out on the town celebrating: their basic training was almost over.[1] On their way back to the base the five officers (all white) stopped at a hamburger shop in the District of Columbia called the Little Tavern.[2] As they stood at the take-out counter, they noticed three black men—Gordon Alexander, Benjamin Murdock,[3] and Cornelius Frazier—at the end of the counter.

According to prosecution witnesses, one of the officers saw Alexander staring at him. He returned the stare. No words were exchanged. After a time the officer turned and faced the counter. Murdock and Frazier left through the door behind the marines, but Alexander stopped in the doorway. He tapped the marine on the shoulder. When the marine turned around, Alexander poked his nametag: "You want to talk about it more? You want to come outside and talk about it more?" When the marine replied, "Yes," Alexander added: "I am going to make you a Little Red Ridinghood." One of the other marines then stepped forward, saying: "What do you want, you nigger?" Alexander withdrew a long-barreled .38 caliber revolver,[4] pointed it at the marines, and said: "I will show you want I want." In the meantime, Murdock had reentered the shop. As he did so he heard someone say, "Get out, you black bastards." Murdock then withdrew a short-barreled .38 and started to fire.[5]

Murdock emptied his gun. When the shooting stopped, two of the marines were dead. Lieutenant William King was one of them. Alexander, Murdock, and Frazier fled in Alexander's car. As the three drove off, Murdock fired three more shots through the car window at the door of the hamburger shop and at people in the street. Murdock claimed that he acted in self-defense, or at least that he had been provoked.[6] The jury bought none of it and convicted him of murder.[7]

Murdock also claimed he was insane.[8] According to his psychiatric expert, Murdock suffered from an "abnormal mental condition that substantially impaired his behavior controls" such that when he heard the marine call him (or Alexander) a "black bastard," he experienced an "irresistible impulse" to shoot.[9] Moreover, according to Murdock's lawyer, the "reason for that lack of control was a deepseated emotional disorder . . . rooted in his 'rotten social background.'"[10] He grew up "in the Watts section of Los Angeles; . . . his father had deserted his mother, and he grew up in a large family with little money and little love or attention."[11] He was a "man whose bitterness and racial hostility [had] turned into blasting powder which [could] be touched off by a spark."[12] The jury believed he was sane and rejected his claim.[13]

For my purposes Murdock's case raises a more general question: Should it matter that a criminal defendant has been burdened, not only with a rotten social background, but with a rotten social background he was entitled *not* to suffer, or to put it another way, with a rotten social background for which the state is to blame? If it should matter, why and in what way?

But let me begin with a prior question: What makes a social background rotten and, moreover, rotten in ways for which the state is to blame? Alas. Let me count some of the ways: A state can fail to see to it that my life chances depend not upon the color of my skin or my ethnicity or my religion and so on. It can fail to provide me with a place to live free from the violence associated with gangs and drugs. It can fail to afford me adequate access to medical care and educational opportunity. It can fail to foster an economy in which jobs are available to those willing and able to work. And so on. All too often these failures conspire to leave one with a life without hope of a better life. Let me assume for now that the state failed Benjamin Murdock such that it makes sense to say, for example, that the state had "systematically excluded [him] from full participation in the polity,"[14] that it caused him to suffer "deep, systematic social injustice,"[15] that it failed to accord him the "equal concern and respect" to which he was due, and so forth.[16] He was, as I will hereafter describe him, a "second-class citizen."[17]

I can now frame my question as follows: When the state responds to a second-class citizen's crime should its response differ from the way in which it responds when a first-class citizen commits the same crime? If so, how and why should its response differ?

As I see it the answer depends on whether or not the state and its laws (and in particular those laws governing the circumstances under which the state can impose punishment) have authority. If the state lacks authority then the answer depends on the morality of responsibility and the morality of holding another responsible. Is a second-class citizen less responsible for the crimes he commits or perhaps not responsible at all? If he is responsible, does the state nonetheless lack the standing to hold him responsible? The search for answers to these questions has led to protracted disagreement.

If a state has authority then it has the moral power to settle these disagreements. The state gets to decide if a second-class citizen is or is not responsible for his crimes. The state gets to decide if it has standing to hold him responsible. But what the state does not get to decide is what it takes for it to have such authority over its citizens in the first place. Therein lies the rub. A state that treats a citizen as second-class loses the authority to punish him for having committed a crime. It retains authority in a weaker sense to impose a hardship upon him, but this authority permits the state to use coercion only to foster obedience, not to punish disobedience. Indeed, when a second-class citizen defies the command of a state lacking authority over him he cannot be said to be guilty of a *crime* at all. He is at most guilty of what might be called a violation, for which he can be fairly penalized but not punished.

I. Morality

Let me begin with those who believe the state lacks authority such that the state's permission to punish depends on how well it adheres to the demands of morality. I divide my discussion in two. I first take up the *morality of responsibility*: perhaps second-class citizens are not responsible for the crimes they commit, or perhaps they are less responsible compared to first-class citizens. I then take up the *morality of holding responsible*: perhaps the state lacks the standing to hold second-class citizens responsible for the crimes they commit even if they are responsible for having committed them.[18]

Let me set aside cases in which a second-class citizen does no wrong, all things considered, when he commits a (prima facie) crime. For example, we can imagine a state of affairs in which the state's neglect has left a citizen so destitute that theft might well be the lesser of two evils: better to steal than starve. The actor has done nothing wrong, and the law should (and in most jurisdictions would) recognize his necessity as a defense.[19] Such cases seem uncontroversial. The hard cases involve crimes for which no justification exists: crimes no one would contend are not wrongs under the circumstances in which they were committed.

I also want to set aside cases in which a second-class citizen commits a crime under duress or coercion. Duress is commonly described as an excuse: an actor who commits a crime under duress has done something wrong, but he is not responsible for his wrongdoing because it was committed under duress.[20] I nonetheless believe that crimes committed under duress are better understood as nonwrongs. An actor who commits a crime under duress does so because, if he doesn't commit the crime, someone else will wrong him or an innocent third party.[21] The crime he commits might not, so far as the law is concerned, be less wrong than the wrong he thereby avoids, but the crime he commits is nonetheless one a reasonable person would likewise have committed under the same circumstances. Yet if a reasonable person would have committed the crime under the same circumstances, then it stands to reason that a crime committed under duress is one the law should permit, despite the fact that the actor has not in the eyes of the law chosen the lesser wrong.[22]

With the focus thus limited to acts that are plainly wrongs, let me now turn to the morality of responsibility.

A. *The Morality of Responsibility*

An actor is not morally responsible for the choices he makes unless he is in some sense *free* with respect to those choices.[23] But free in what sense? Perhaps the necessary sense of freedom is the capacity to do otherwise: an actor is not morally responsible for what he chooses to do unless he could have chosen to do otherwise.[24] The future must be a garden of forking paths, and moral responsibility requires an actor at the moment of choice to be free to follow any path he chooses, inasmuch as he could have chosen to follow any other.

But if responsibility demands freedom qua capacity to do otherwise then it demands too much. The problem is this: if it turns out that determinism is true, then no one has the freedom it takes to ascribe to him responsibility for the choices he makes because no one has the freedom to choose otherwise. Determinism rules out alternative possibilities. None of our futures is a garden of forking paths; all our gardens have but one path.

So if moral responsibility requires freedom qua the capacity to choose otherwise, then moral responsibility can be ascribed to no one, and no one can bear responsibility for the choices he makes. If we wish to rescue responsibility from determinism and thus from oblivion, the freedom upon which we base it must be something other (and less divine) than the capacity to defy the laws of nature.[25]

It turns out that we do indeed seem prepared to ascribe responsibility in the absence of freedom qua capacity to do otherwise.[26] The freedom we require for such ascriptions is not the capacity to do otherwise. The requisite capacity is more modest. Different writers describe this capacity in different ways. According to what is perhaps the most prominent account, the freedom required for moral responsibility requires the capacity to respond to reasons.[27] It might also be described (in part) as the capacity for self-control inasmuch as the capacity to respond to reasons requires or includes the capacity to resist desires to do as one believes one ought not to do.[28] For present purposes I will refer to this capacity as the capacity to respond to reasons.[29]

Unlike the capacity to do otherwise the capacity to respond to reasons is not hostage to determinism. Even if determinism guarantees that I cannot choose otherwise than I do, I remain responsible for my choices as long as my capacity to respond to reasons is in good working order. We can tell if an actor's capacity to respond is up to snuff with a thought experiment or series of such experiments. All we need to do is ask how the capacity would work under a different set of circumstances: What would happen if the actor's capacity to respond to reasons were (counterfactually) confronted with different reasons? Would the actor respond differently? If so, if he would have made different choices and taken different actions, then he has all the capacity and thus all the freedom needed to ascribe responsibility to him whatever the truth (or not) of determinism.

Under some circumstances, the criminal law will completely or partially excuse an actor whose capacity to respond to reasons is completely or partially diminished.[30] For example, if an actor lacks the capacity (or substantial capacity) to respond to reasons and thus to conform his conduct to the requirements of law due to mental disease or defect, he will (in some jurisdictions) be excused on grounds of insanity. An actor charged with murder whose capacity to respond to reasons is impaired as a result of mental abnormality or reasonable provocation will (in some jurisdictions) have his crime reduced to manslaughter based on the partial excuse of diminished capacity or provocation (respectively). Each of these excuses is limited: insanity is available only if the actor's diminished capacity is the result of a mental disease or defect; diminished capacity and provocation are available only as a partial defense to murder. The criminal law does not recognize a *generic* excuse based on the simple fact that an actor's capacity to respond to reasons was nonculpably undermined or diminished.

But if morality alone has the authority to say when an actor is and is not responsible for what he chooses to do, and if the law derives its authority from that of morality, then the law should (all else being equal) track morality.[31] The law should (all else being equal) mimic morality and do as morality tells it to do. So let's assume that the law is an obedient subject and does as morality would instruct it do to. Let's assume that the law enacts a generic excuse pursuant to which an actor's responsibility for the crime he commits is reduced to the extent that his capacity to respond to reasons is diminished.

What difference would the availability of such an excuse make to Murdock? In layman's terms Murdock "lost it" when one of the marines made a racial insult. The insult ignited a desire to kill and his rotten social background left him with little capacity to keep it at bay. Provocation was no defense for Murdock because under D.C. law words alone could not constitute adequate provocation.[32] Diminished capacity was no defense because D.C. law did not recognize it as a defense.[33] D.C. law did recognize insanity as a defense but the jury failed to see Murdock as someone suffering from a mental disease or defect of the sort needed to support such a defense. If D.C. law embraced the generic excuse of the moral law the result might well have been different. Perhaps Murdock's capacity to respond to reasons *was* impaired when he pulled the trigger.

A generic excuse might have helped Murdock, but it would leave other second-class citizens defenseless because the excuse would extend to anyone whose capacity to respond to reasons was absent or diminished, no matter how the state had treated him. It would extend to first- and second-class citizens alike. Conversely, the defense would not extend to anyone whose capacity to respond to reasons was undiminished. Second-class citizens, whose capacity was intact, would be treated like first-class citizens. The state of one's capacity would be all that mattered. Was it broken or not? If broken, the defense would come to the rescue no matter how it got broken (assuming the actor was not himself responsible for the disrepair). If not, the defense would be unavailable no matter how poorly one had been treated at the hands of the powers that be.[34]

But even if we assume that freedom *qua* sufficient capacity to respond to reasons is all the freedom an actor needs in order to be eligible to bear responsibility for his choices, and even if we assume an actor is equipped with such capacity, he might *still* fail to be responsible for those choices. How? Because it might be that responsibility requires not only freedom but also what we might call *ownership* (or *authenticity* or *authorship*). Freedom may be necessary for responsibility but not sufficient.[35] Ownership may be required too. But what does that mean? Let me explain.

Consider the following story.[36] Professor Plum is a brilliant but extraordinarily greedy man. His lust for mammon is a grave defect of character but his capacity to respond to reasons is in tip-top shape. He suffers no hint of diminished capacity. Ms. White has named Professor Plum as the sole beneficiary of her life insurance policy. Finding himself in need of cash to supplement his sorry salary he decides to kill Ms. White and reap the benefits. He thus forms the intention to kill and follows through on it. He is, without more, guilty of murder. But of course there *is* more. As it happens Professor Plum's character is the creation of an evil neuroscientist (Dr. Strangelove) who has psychosurgically implanted in Plum beliefs and desires such that Plum was causally determined in the circumstances in which he found himself to kill Ms. White. His capacity to respond to reasons was itself working flawlessly. Unfortunately for Plum its flawless working determined that he would choose to take the last act needed to bring about Ms. White's death. If freedom qua capacity to respond to reasons suffices for moral responsibility then Plum is indeed responsible for White's death. The story is naturally meant to challenge that proposition. The odd way in which Plum came to be the sort of person he was is meant to unsettle our confidence. *Is* Plum responsible for White's death?

Consider the following variation. Professor Plum's capacity to respond to reasons remains as before intact. But now the bad guy is not Dr. Strangelove. The bad guy is master hypnotist Svengali. Set aside for now (hard) questions about the actual psychology involved when a person acts under the influence of hypnosis.[37] Set aside too the (likely) possibility that a person under the influence of hypnosis will not do things he regards as repugnant when not under the influence. Assume that Svengali achieves through hypnosis or posthypnotic suggestion what Dr. Strangelove achieved through psychosurgery: he implants in Plum beliefs and desires such that Plum was causally determined in the circumstances in which he found himself to kill Ms. White. Once again the question: Is Plum responsible? Whatever morality would say, the criminal law, for one reason or another, would probably say no.[38] Svengali would be on the hook, but not Plum.

Yet maybe what makes us wonder about the hypnotized Plum's responsibility is not the sense that he acts upon hypnotist-implanted beliefs and desires not his own. Maybe hypnosis doesn't result in implanted beliefs and desires. Maybe being in a hypnotic state or acting under posthypnotic suggestion means that the hypnotized subject acts while in an altered state of consciousness. The beliefs and desires that the will of the hypnotized subject executes into bodily movements may be his beliefs and desires, but the will that does the executing is not a conscious will. But without a conscious will doing the willing, responsibility cannot fairly be ascribed.[39] Perhaps. So let's take the next variation.

Imagine now that Svengali is a brainwasher.[40] He practices his nefarious techniques of coercive indoctrination on Plum such that when Svengali is finished with him Plum can think of nothing else but killing Ms. White. His capacity to respond to reasons once again remains in tiptop shape. When Plum kills White, is he responsible now?

At this point the criminal law becomes ambivalent. In most jurisdictions Plum would be out of luck. No excuse would come to his aid. But, in jurisdictions under the influence of the Model Penal Code, Plum might prevail on a plea of duress.[41] The commentaries to the code's duress provision tell us that the "'brainwashed' actor would not be barred from claiming the defense of duress."[42] According to the code: "The defense of duress may be appropriate in certain circumstances where a defendant was 'so far in the thrall of some power' that the choices he made were not really his."[43] So in a Model Penal Code jurisdiction Plum might well be regarded as a victim of Svengali's thrall such that the choices he made are regarded as Svengali's choices. Svengali owned Plum, not Plum.

You should now be able to see where the argument is headed. So let me carry on. Imagine now that the beliefs and desires that causally determined Plum's choice to kill Ms. White can be traced to no human agency. Instead, Plum simply had the misfortune to have lived a life resulting in his possession of beliefs and desires such that he was causally determined in the circumstances in which he found himself to kill Ms. White. Does the fact that poor Professor Plum had the misfortune to have been taught that money is everything at the tender age of ten undermine his self-ownership? Must we then withhold our blame when he dispatches Ms. White? If so, then causal determinism may be compatible with the freedom needed for responsibility, but not with the ownership needed for it. Causal determinism means that none of us is the true owner or author of our choices, and thus none of us can bear responsibility for those choices.

Persuaded? Some are, others not so much, others not at all. But how is one to avoid falling down the slippery slope that begins with Strangelove and ends with the end of responsibility? The easiest way to avoid a slippery slope is to refuse to take the first step. Is your character the result of psychosurgery? Brainwashing? Too bad. You remain responsible for what you choose to do as long as your capacity to respond to reasons remains operational—even if what you choose to do results from a character not of your own choosing. Responsibility does not depend on history. It depends on, and only on, your capacity to respond to reasons at the moment in time at which you make the choices you make.

Or maybe you are responsible for what you do so long as you identify with,[44] or otherwise take or assume responsibility for,[45] the springs of your actions.[46] Or maybe you are prepared to take the first step down the slope. Maybe you are confident you can find some principled way to stop the fall before you hit bottom. Perhaps you see, as some do, a clear difference between cases in which another agent manipulates someone to do his bidding and cases in which no such agent is in the picture.[47] Manipulation, you might well say, is one thing; causation is another. The two should not be confused. Others see no way to avoid taking the fall all the way down.[48]

My point is that the debate over the relationship between social deprivation and excuse is part of a larger and ongoing debate about the morality of responsibility.[49] Even if we all agree that the freedom responsibility requires is nothing more than the freedom associated with the capacity to respond to reasons, and not the capacity to do otherwise, the question of ownership remains. How far must one be the author of oneself before one can be held accountable for one's choices and actions? If the permissibility of punishment depends on how well the criminal law tracks morality's answer to that question then the race to discover what morality has to say is on. But reasonable minds can and do disagree on what morality has to say. Disagreement over the responsibility of second-class citizens is likely to persist and the state's authority to punish the crimes they commit will therefore remain in doubt.

B. The Morality of Holding Responsible

Maybe Murdock was morally responsible for the murder of Lieutenant King, or maybe not. We disagree on what morality instructs us to believe.

So let's switch gears. What about the morality of *holding* Murdock responsible for his actions? Can we agree on what morality has to say about that? Even if we assume that second-class citizens are responsible for the crimes they commit maybe the state would be wrong to punish them inasmuch it lacks standing to hold them responsible.⁵⁰

Assume that Murdock was morally responsible for killing Lieutenant King. When one person culpably wrongs another he thereby confers standing on others to *hold* him responsible for what he has done: he renders himself liable at the least to blame and censure. But exactly who has such standing? Murdock left himself vulnerable to censure, but from whom? Lieutenant King would surely have such standing (if he were still around), presumably too would those close to him. Indeed, where the wrongdoing involved is as grave as that of Murdock's—intentionally and unjustifiably causing the death of another—we would probably say that (all else being equal) *everyone* has standing to blame him just in virtue of their membership in the moral community of which we are all a part.

But our concern here is not just with liability to blame and censure. Our concern is with liability to blame and censure in the form of *state punishment*. Our concern is with the circumstances under which the *state* has standing to hold someone responsible: to convict him of a crime (thereby censuring him for his wrongdoing) and (perhaps) to punish him for it.⁵¹

According to one influential account a state has standing to declare this or that wrong to be a crime and to punish a citizen's culpable commission of that crime insofar as the wrong is one in which the state can be said to "*share*."⁵² That makes sense. If a state does indeed share the wrong visited upon one citizen at the hands of another, the state itself becomes a victim pro tanto of that wrong. The state does not share *all* the wrongs one citizen visits upon another. Private wrongs are wrongs between the wrongdoer and wronged, but not between the wrongdoer and the state. What makes a wrong a public wrong (on this account) is the fact that it "properly concerns the public": its culpable commission violates the "core values" by which a community "defines itself as a polity."⁵³ Where public wrongs are involved the state has just as much standing to condemn the wrongdoer as does the actual victim. Indeed, all else being equal the state has standing not only to condemn but to punish.

But all else may not be equal. Sometimes an actor can lose his standing to censure another's wrongdoing. Suppose I'm a bank teller and I embezzle two hundred dollars. My employer can rightly regard itself as entitled to blame me for my transgression. So too (I should think) can my coworkers, all else being equal. But when the teller at the next window, who purloined just as much as I did, tries to give me a piece of his mind I could be excused for telling him to shove off. People who live in glass houses should not throw stones. The teller next door is a *hypocrite* and his hypocrisy pulls the rug out from the standing he would otherwise have had to censure me for the wrongdoing of which I am admittedly guilty. My clean-handed coworkers have standing to give me a piece of their minds but my dirty-handed neighbor does not. Get your own house in order before you start condemning others for the sorry state of theirs.

Hypocrisy is one way to lose standing to condemn. Another is *complicity*.[54] Complicity in the criminal law is not a crime: complicity is a theory of liability. Return to the teller example. If I take the two hundred dollars into possession myself I am guilty of embezzlement as a principal. *I* committed the crime. If I help *you* take the two hundred dollars into your possession I'm also guilty of embezzlement (assuming I help with the required state of mind). You are the principal. I am the accomplice: I derive my liability from your liability. Now, if you help me embezzle from the bank, such that I'm guilty of embezzlement as a principal and you as my accomplice, it would be terribly rich if you then started to condemn me for the very crime in which you are complicit.[55] In fact, anyone who condemns a principal for committing a crime with respect to which he is an accomplice is necessarily a hypocrite inasmuch as he is guilty of the very crime he condemns.[56]

What bearing do these observations have on how the state responds to those criminal wrongdoers who the state has itself wronged inasmuch as it has treated them as second-class citizens? According to some it means that the state is guilty of hypocrisy or complicity and as such its standing to condemn is lost or eroded, at least if it does nothing to acknowledge its own culpability.[57] For example, if we agree that the state wronged Murdock insofar as it treated him as a second-class citizen, we might conclude that it has thereby lost its standing to condemn him for Lieutenant King's murder. Condemning Murdock would be hypocritical: The state dirtied its hands when it failed to treat him as it was obligated to treat him and in the bargain lost its standing to condemn him when he dirtied his own hands. King's surviving kin might well have standing to condemn Murdock. Maybe we all do so long as our own hands are clean. But the state does not. Its hands are dirty and condemning Murdock for the dirt on his hands would be hypocrisy.[58] If the state could be charged with complicity in Murdock's crime it would likewise lose its standing to condemn him.

But can the charge of hypocrisy fairly be laid at the state's door? Can the state fairly be described as an accomplice to Murdock's murder of King?

Take hypocrisy. You might say that the state loses its standing to condemn whenever it has dirt on its hands. If so, then the state does indeed lose standing to condemn anyone it has treated as a second-class citizen. But saying that *any* dirt on its hands undermines the state's standing to condemn would set a high bar. If the only one who can cast a stone is someone without sin then good luck finding someone who can cast a stone.[59] If you say more plausibly that the state loses its standing to condemn if its hands are as dirty or dirtier than those of the person it purports to condemn, then the state would lack standing to condemn only if its wrongdoing was the same or bigger than that of the wrongdoer in its sights.[60] Or perhaps you believe that the state never forfeits its standing, or perhaps that a democratic state at least does not.[61]

Complicity avoids the need to compare wrongs inasmuch as a complicit state is necessarily guilty of the same wrong it aims to condemn. The problem with complicity lies in what exactly it takes to make the state (or anyone) complicit. Here are some questions to which any theory of state complicity must attend. First: Does it matter whether the principal would have committed the crime even if he had been treated like a first-class citizen? Second: Does it matter how much aid or encouragement the state provides?[62] Will trivial aid suffice? Third: Does it matter whether the state wants the principal to commit the crime, or does the fact that the state knows (or maybe even just should know) that its neglect fosters crime serve just as well?

Standard criminal-law doctrine says that an accomplice can derive liability for the principal's crime even if the principal would have committed the crime without the aid of the accomplice. Causation is unnecessary for complicity. Nor does it matter how much help the accomplice provides as long as he does *something* that crosses the line from mere presence into assistance or encouragement. Trivial aid will do. But a trivially culpable state of mind will not. An accomplice is not liable for the principal's crime unless he wants the principal to commit the crime with respect to which he provides aid. An accomplice is free from liability even if, when he provides aid, he knows that the putative principal is planning to commit a crime, and he is free a fortiori if he should have known but didn't.[63]

So says standard criminal-law doctrine. But maybe the standard doctrine is wrong. Maybe an accomplice should be liable only if the aid he gives actually causes the principal to commit the crime. If the principal would have committed the crime anyway then maybe the aid-giving party should not be treated as an accomplice after all. Or maybe the necessary aid should be nontrivial. Or maybe the necessary mens rea should be lower. Maybe knowledge or even negligence should suffice. Or maybe an accomplice should be guilty of the principal's crime if he provides substantial aid in the hope that the principal will commit the crime aided and guilty of a lesser crime the less help he gives or the less culpable the mens rea with which he gives it.[64]

Returning to Murdock, has the state lost its standing to punish him either because doing so would be hypocritical or because it can be seen as an accomplice in the murder of Lieutenant King? Assuming that the state has treated Murdock as a second-class citizen and thereby wronged him, does the resulting dirt on its hands mean that it would be hypocritical for the state to condemn him for murder? Does it mean that the state is itself guilty of King's murder as an accomplice? The state's sins do not (for what it's worth) appear to be so grievous as to open it to a charge of hypocrisy. Nor does it make much sense to say that the state should be portrayed as an accomplice in King's murder. I have a hard time seeing how the state's wrongs sabotage its standing to call Murdock to account. But others would disagree, and reasonably so.[65]

The point is the same as before. At the end of the day the state's standing to punish Murdock depends on the conditions under which hypocrisy or complicity undermines such standing, if they undermine it at all. Reasonable minds can and do disagree about what those conditions are and whether or not the state's acts or omissions satisfy those conditions. The morality of holding responsible is just as much a site of disagreement as is the morality of responsibility itself.

II. Authority

So far I've assumed that a state's permission to punish depends on how well its criminal law conforms to the requirements of the moral law. A state has permission to punish if and only if morality says it does. The end to which that assumption has lead is the dead-end of disagreement. Some believe that morality says second-class citizens are not responsible for their crimes. Others disagree. Some believe that morality says the state lacks standing to punish second-class citizens. Others disagree. What to do?

Let's change the assumption and see where it leads. Assume that the state's permission to punish does not depend on how well its criminal law conforms to the moral law. Assume instead that the state and its laws have authority independent of morality: assume that the state has the power (within limits) to decide for itself when it has permission to punish. If the state decides that a second-class citizen is responsible for a crime he commits, then it does no wrong when it punishes him for committing it. Likewise, if the state decides that it has standing to punish a second-class citizen, then it does no wrong when it punishes him for committing it. If a state has authority, then it has (within limits) the power to render permissible that which morality would proscribe if left to its own devices.

Not all states possess this magical power to countermand the demands of morality. Some states never manage to achieve it. Others behave in such a way that they manage to lose it. One way a state can lose its authority is to violate those rights its citizens retain against the state's authority. My suggestion here is that when a state treats a citizen as a second-class citizen, it violates his right not to be so treated and thus can no longer claim to have the authority to punish him for disobedience if and when he commits a crime. The only authority it can claim over him is the weaker authority to coerce him in order to elicit his obedience.[66]

A. Having Authority

Let me begin with an assumption about what it means to say that a state possesses authority. A state with authority is one with the normative power to impose prima facie moral obligations. If such a state says, "Do not φ," then anyone subject to its authority who φs has committed a prima facie wrong, and anyone who culpably commits such a wrong (without a state-sanctioned justification) thereby renders himself liable to censure. Moreover, if such a state says, "Do not φ. If you φ you will render yourself liable to punishment," then anyone subject to its authority who φs has committed a prima facie criminal wrong, and anyone who culpably commits such a wrong (without a state-sanctioned justification) thereby renders himself liable to censure in the form of punishment. Some believe that no state can possess such power.[67] Others believe that a state can possess such power but none actually do,[68] nor is any future state likely to do so. I want to disagree. Let me try to sketch an account of what it would take for a state to have authority.

We should begin with a distinction between that which *justifies* authority and that which *legitimates* it.[69] An authority is justified if and when, through the exercise of its authority, it achieves some good. When we say that a state qua authority is justified, we point to or identify some good that the state achieves though the exercise of its power qua authority to impose prima facie moral obligations. The fact that a state can bring this good into existence is meant to justify its having authority. Indeed, the good to which we point is one that only the state can achieve, and indeed, one it can achieve only if it has authority. An answer to the justification question thus tells us why we would want to have a state with such power in the first place. What good does it do?

An authority is legitimate if and when the exercise of its authority does in fact (prima facie) obligate its subjects to obey.[70] The fact that a state with the power to create and impose obligations may thereby secure some good might justify its existence, but it does not explain how the state's pronouncements come to have the force of (prima facie) moral obligations. It does not explain how those pronouncements come to *bind* those within the state's jurisdiction. I'm subject to the authority of morality—we all are—but what makes me subject to the authority of the state? An answer to the legitimation question thus tells us why we are bound to obey this state or that state. What gives this or that state the power to tell me what to do?

My answer to these two questions is limited to the criminal law. What justifies a state's power to impose obligations the culpable breach of which renders me liable to punishment? What legitimates that power? In other words: What (if anything) justifies the authority of the criminal law? What (if anything) legitimates it? My answer to these questions comes in two parts depending on the nature of the crime at hand.

Some crimes describe actions we should not do no matter what the law has to say about it. Do not cause the death of another human being. Do not cause harm to others. Do not take the property of others, and so on. Doing any of these things culpably will leave you vulnerable to censure. We commonly call such crimes malum in se: they are serious wrongs whether the law says so or not.[71] Then we have malum prohibitum crimes: crimes that are wrongs because the law says so. Do not tear the tag off the mattress. Do not forget to use the correct label on the noxious substance you are transporting from one state to the next. Do not have in your possession this or that substance, and so on.

What justifies a state's authority to criminalize malum in se wrongs such that their culpable commission will render me liable to punishment? What good does it serve to have a state possessed of such power? The simple answer is this: having such a state enables us to stave off the state of nature.

Suppose I intentionally kill you. Suppose too that the state does not exist. Chances are the folks who cared about you will take matters into their own hands and come after me, and if they do, chances are the folks who care about me will come after the folks who cared about you. So it goes. Not a very nice state of affairs: nasty, brutish, and short. Having a state around with the power to impose moral obligations owed *to the state* means that when murder becomes a crime I have wronged not only you but the state as well. Unless I have a state-sanctioned justification or excuse for my actions, I will be liable to the state's punishment. The folks who care about you and the folks who care about me relinquish to the state their standing to punish wrongdoers, but they get the good of social peace in return.

What about malum prohibitum offenses? What justifies a state's authority with respect to them? Once we move beyond the category of malum in se, once we move beyond those actions the prohibition of which is necessary to secure social peace and order, what good can come from a state with the authority to declare this or that a criminal wrong? The answer I would offer is political peace.

We disagree about morality. Does morality say that this should be a crime? What about that? In the absence of some way authoritatively to settle these disagreements the result would be turmoil. We can avoid a social state of nature as long as the state punishes malum in se wrongs. Yet unless we have some way authoritatively to decide whether morality demands or permits the state to punish this or that act outside the malum in se core we will end up in a political state of nature. We need some way to resolve, if only provisionally and for the time being, our otherwise irresolvable disagreements over the demands of morality.[72] In the end the state is worth having because it gives us peace and repose. It saves us not only from a social state of nature. It saves us from a political state of nature as well.[73]

Assuming it would be good for the state to have authority, or at least that a state with authority can secure worthwhile goods, then state authority is justifiable insofar as it does indeed secure the goods it exists to secure. That still leaves us with the legitimation question. Why should I believe that the state's demands bind me? Why should I believe that I am (prima facie) obligated to obey the state such that I would be doing wrong to disobey? This legitimation question turns out to be considerably harder to answer than the justification question. At this point I can do little more than gesture toward an answer I find appealing.

Any functional state can achieve the goods that justify the existence of malum in se and malum prohibitum offenses. A benevolent dictator can rescue us from the chaos of the social and political states of nature. A benevolent dictatorship is in fact fully capable of achieving legitimacy when it comes to malum in se offenses. Why? Because the state's legitimacy in this domain does not rest on the process by which the state decides to criminalize serious moral wrongs. It depends only on the fact that it does indeed criminalize them and thereby delivers us from a social state of nature. I am bound to obey those prohibitions the observance of which fend off the state of nature out of respect for those likewise subject to the state's authority who likewise obey. Fairness to those who forbear and with whom my fate happens to be bound obligates me likewise to forebear or else render myself answerable to the state for my culpable failure to do so. The legitimacy of the state's authority—that which binds me to its demands—comes finally to rest on the respect I owe my fellow subjects.[74]

Respect also grounds the state's legitimacy when it comes to malum prohibitum offenses. But the respect I owe is based not on the fact that my fellow travelers forbear from doing me wrong. A state with the power to declare this or that to be a malum prohibitum offense secures the good of political peace: an end to endless disagreement about what morality requires when it comes to the content of the criminal law outside the core. Yet not just any way of putting an end to disagreement can or should command my respect. The way in which disagreement is resolved must respect my beliefs on the matter as well as the competing beliefs of everyone else. A benevolent dictatorship shows no such respect: only the dictator's opinion counts. The only state that shows the requisite respect is a democratic one and as such the only kind of state to which legitimacy attaches when it comes to resolving disagreement about the content of the criminal law outside the malum in se core is a democratic state. Insofar as I have or am entitled to an equal say in resolving collective disagreements, I am duty bound to respect the democratic answer even if that answer is not my answer.[75]

One final observation before moving on. Some believe that a democratic state's authority has no limits.[76] The state can do whatever it likes so long as the democratic process has been duly observed. But for now I will assume that even a democratic state can only go so far. Its citizens have rights and if the state transgresses those rights its authority comes to an end—or is at least compromised. I will say more below.

B. Losing Authority

Let me now bring the discussion back to the state and crimes of the second-class. What difference does all this talk about authority have to do with Murdock and how the state responds to his murder of Lieutenant King? In order to answer that question I need to say something about the circumstances under which a state that otherwise has the authority to punish—the power to impose obligations the culpable breach of which will render a wrongdoer liable to punishment—can lose or forfeit that authority.

The state can lose its authority to punish in one of two ways. First, it can lose its authority if it fails to deliver the goods that justify its existence in the first place. The raison d'être of any state (democratic or otherwise) is to save us from the social state of nature. Any state that fails to prevent its subjects or some group of them from descending into a state of nature can thus no longer demand their allegiance. I have no reason to obey (let alone an obligation to do so) if the state has for all practical purposes left me to fend for myself.[77]

Likewise, the raison d'etre of a democratic state is to resolve disagreements that inevitably arise over what morality demands and to resolve those disagreements in a way that treats me with equal concern and respect. Insofar as the state has banished me from the democratic process it has consigned me to a political state of nature. A state that has thus disenfranchised me can no longer claim my allegiance with respect to its demands outside the core of malum in se. I may still be obligated not to plunder and kill. I am to that extent still bound to do as I am told even if I have no voice in deciding the terms of collective life. But I am bound not to obey the state when it tells me to do this or that when this or that is not necessary to preserve the social order.

The state can lose its authority in a second way. The problem is not that it fails to deliver the goods. The problem is that it fails to respect the rights its citizens retain against the exercise of the state's authority to determine the circumstances under which punishment is permissible, and when punishment is permissible, how much is permissible. Its failure to honor these rights means that those otherwise subject to its authority are no longer so subject. Now is not the time to say very much about the content of these rights. I have no need to do so in order to make the point I hope to make. So for now I will simply describe in very general terms in what these rights consist.

First, a state has no authority to punish an actor if he has a right to do that which the state purports to criminalize. Second, a state has no authority to punish an actor if he lacks any culpability for the crime he is accused of committing. Finally, a state has no authority to impose grossly disproportionate punishments. Should a state claim to punish me in violation of any of these rights its claim would fall flat: it would have no authority to do so. All it would manage to do if it tried would be to wrong *me*.

Take what is intended as an extreme (and therefore hopefully uncontroversial) example. Suppose a democratic state makes it a crime to sell bumper stickers in support of a candidate for political office. Liability can arise without the actor being aware that what he is selling qualifies as such an item, and punishment for the crime is life imprisonment. I sell a bumper sticker that says "Go Joe Blow!" Joe is a candidate for political office, but I thought he was a soccer player. I had no idea I was committing a crime. I now find myself facing life in prison. The state in this case has authority *ex hypothesi*, but it forfeits that authority over me in this instance because it has violated rights I hold against the exercise of its authority. It purports to punish me for conduct in which I am entitled to engage. It purports to punish me in the absence of any culpability, and the punishment it purports to impose is grossly disproportionate. If the state puts me away for life in the belief that I have done it wrong it has it backward: *I'm* the one being wronged.

Neither of the two ways in which a state can lose its authority to punish are implicated in Murdock's case nor (I will assume) in any case involving a crime of a member of the second-class. The state did not relegate Murdock to the state of nature (social or political). I'm assuming that the state provided him with some adequate level of security against the depredations of others. His life may not (to put it mildly) have been the greatest, but neither (I will assume) could it fairly be described as nasty, brutish, or short. Nor had he been disenfranchised. He may or may not have participated in the political process. We don't know. If he did not, he may well have thought he had better things to do. His right to participate in the democratic process may not have meant a whole lot to him. The option was nonetheless available.[78]

Nor would punishing Murdock for the murder of Lieutenant King violate any of his negative rights. Murdock has no right to cause anyone's death with the intent to do so, except perhaps in self-defense.[79] Nor can he claim to have acted without culpability. He might have liked it if the state had permitted him to raise diminished capacity as a culpability-removing or -reducing defense, but it would be hard to say that the state violated his rights if the state refused to recognize such a defense. Nor can we say that the punishment the state imposed on him for killing Lieutenant King—fifteen years to life—was grossly disproportionate.[80] Murdock might have believed that a lesser sentence would have been more fitting. He might have been right. Saying with any precision when a sentence goes from proportionate to disproportionate to grossly disproportionate is not easy. Does a term of fifteen years to life for murder cross the line? For the time being I will assume not.

At the risk of repetition: Murdock neither found himself reduced to a social or political state of nature, nor did the state violate any negative right he possessed when it sent him to prison for fifteen years to life for killing Lieutenant King. The state nonetheless *did* wrong Murdock when it failed to give him his fair share of the fruits of social cooperation. The state's wrongful failure in this regard did not reduce him to a state of nature, nor did it violate any negative right it was required to respect. It did nonetheless fail to respect those positive rights the guarantee of which is meant to protect him and others from becoming second-class citizens. There comes a point at which a citizen goes from being a second-class citizen to one inhabiting the state of nature,[81] but reasonable minds can disagree about when that point has been reached. We are for now simply assuming that Murdock's life, bad as it was, was not so bad that he would have been no worse off without the state.

What follows? What difference does the fact that the state treated Murdock like a second-class citizen make when it responds to his crime? My answer is this: When a state treats a citizen as a second-class citizen without abandoning that citizen to a state of nature or violating any of his negative rights, what changes is the *nature of its authority*. I have so far assumed that a state with authority is one with the power or capacity to impose (prima facie) moral obligations on those subject to its authority where the obligations it imposes are owed *to the state*. A crime is thus just what it has long been said to be: a wrong against the state. Moreover, a crime in a democratic state is a wrong against those in whose name the state claims to act: the people. When the culpable violation of a state-imposed obligation renders an actor liable to punishment, he is guilty of what we call a crime. Punishment, however, is not to be confused with coercion. Punishment is coercive: inherent in it is an imposed hardship or suffering. Yet what transforms coercion into punishment—what turns hardship or suffering vel non into punishment—is the intent to condemn or censure that accompanies its imposition.

With respect to those it relegates to second-class status the state no longer possesses such authority. It no longer possesses the power to impose obligations. It continues to possess authority, but only in a weaker sense. Its authority is limited to making demands and backing them up with hard treatment in the event those subject to its authority culpably fail to comply. The coercion it applies to back up its demands is justified inasmuch as such coercion is needed in order to secure the goods for which the state exists. Yet inasmuch as its demands lack the force of obligations an actor who culpably disobeys the state's demands does no wrong against the state. His defiance constitutes no crime.

We might say instead that it constitutes a *violation* to which the state can justifiably respond with coercion or a penalty.[82] What we cannot say is that it constitutes a crime to which the state can justifiably respond with punishment. A state that wrongs those within its jurisdiction inasmuch as it treats them as second-class citizens forfeits its authority to declare crimes and to punish their culpable commission. It nonetheless retains the weaker authority to coerce or penalize what must then be named something other than a crime. In other words: crimes of second-class citizens are second-class "crimes," which is to say that they are not really crimes at all.[83]

Here is another way to look at it. What happens when the state treats you like a second-class citizen is that it changes the nature of its relationship with you.[84] The relationship is no longer a moral one; it no longer defines or constitutes what might fairly be called a moral community. It is instead more akin to the relationship between an occupying power and those within the territory it occupies. Those subject to its demands give their obedience based on nothing more than fear. In this connection it should come as no surprise that when second-class citizens describe their relationship with the state, the language they sometimes use is the language of one subject to the supervision of an occupying power: remote, threatening, alienated, alienating.

Conclusion

If we assume that the state has treated Murdock unjustly—but not so unjustly as to return him to a state of nature—what difference does this sorry fact make when the state responds to his murder of Lieutenant King? It has long seemed to many thoughtful observers that it must somehow matter. The harder question has been how.

The most common set of replies assumes that the state's permission to punish Murdock in response to his crime depends on what morality has to say. Was Murdock responsible for the murder of Lieutenant King in the eyes of the moral law? If not, then the state is not permitted to punish him. Does the state have standing to punish Murdock in the eyes of the moral law? If not, then the state is not permitted to punish him. It all depends on what morality says because morality is the only authority we have. The central problem with this line of reply is that different people reasonably read the moral law in different ways. The only way we can authoritatively settle the disagreement to which such different readings lead is to turn to the state.

Once we make that turn we can see that what changes when a citizen who the state has treated as a second-class citizen commits a crime—any crime—is the nature of the state's authority over that citizen. No longer can the state claim to enjoy with respect to him the type of authority constitutive of a moral community. No longer can it call what he has done a crime. No longer can it punish him. The state does not abandon all authority over him, but the authority it retains is pale and pallid: the authority a justified occupier enjoys over those within the territory it occupies. It can justifiably issue demands and enforce those demands with coercion. But it can do no more. If such a state imagines otherwise, it must plead guilty to mistake or self-deception.

Notes

I thank Mark Chen for his helpful research assistance. I also thank the University of Alabama Law School, Dean Kenneth Randall, and Austin Sarat for inviting me to participate in the symposium on "The Punitive Imagination" for which this paper was prepared.

1. *United States v. Alexander*, 471 F.2d 923, 928 (D.C. Cir. 1973) (per curium) (Bazelon, C.J.). Barbara Kelly, a friend of one of the marines, was also present and wounded in the fray.

2. Id. at 957.

3. Murdock's correct name was Murdock Benjamin. The court of appeals continued to refer to him as Benjamin Murdock for the sake of consistency. Id. at 926n1.

4. Alexander was charged with and convicted of assault. He did not testify at trial but claimed to have drawn his weapon in self-defense. Id. at 936. Frazier was not charged. Id. at 927n2.

5. Id. at 929.

6. The surviving marines testified that they stood still after Alexander drew his weapon. Murdock testified that the "[m]arines were advancing fast, and he felt they were going to kill him." Id. Murdock apparently challenged neither the instructions on self-defense nor the sufficiency of the evidence on

which the jury rejected that claim. He did challenge the sufficiency of the evidence with respect to the jury's decision to reject his provocation claim. The court nonetheless concluded that the "jury was presented with sufficient evidence to find that Murdock was not adequately provoked to justify the deadly force with which he retaliated," id. at 941 and 942n49, no doubt in large part because Murdock did not "attack the traditional rule that 'mere words standing alone, . . . no matter how insulting, offensive, or abusive, are not adequate to reduce a homicide from murder to manslaughter.'" Id. at 941n48.

7. Id. at 927.

8. He also claimed that the trial judge erred when he refused to instruct the jury on the so-called mens rea variant of the doctrine of "diminished responsibility." The majority affirmed the trial judge: "[T]he rejection of this instruction [on diminished responsibility] was clearly within the terms of the law as it has been thus far conceived to be by this court." Id. at 967 (McGowan, J.). The D.C. Circuit had also rejected the so-called partial responsibility variant of that doctrine pursuant to which liability for what would otherwise be murder is reduced to manslaughter. Id. at 951 (Bazelon, C. J., dissenting).

9. Id. at 957–58. The D.C. Circuit at the time defined insanity according to the so-called *Durham* rule. It defined the "mental illness" needed to support a claim of insanity as "any 'abnormal condition of the mind that substantially affects mental or emotional processes and substantially impairs behavior controls.'" Id. at 958 (citing *McDonald v. United States*, 312 F.2d 847, 851 [D.C. Cir. 1962] [en banc]). The psychiatrist who testified on Murdock's behalf offered evidence that supported a finding that Murdock suffered from what the law regarded as a "mental illness," even though the psychiatrist himself believed that the term "mental illness" should be limited to "major psychos[e]s." Id. at 958. Chief Judge Bazelon likewise noted that if Murdock were acquitted on grounds of insanity, he would "automatically have been committed to St. Elizabeth's Hospital for further examination . . . [but that] [p]lainly, the Hospital would find it difficult to justify holding [him] on the grounds that he was insane in any conventional sense." Id. at 961.

10. Id. at 959 (Bazelon, C.J., dissenting) (referring to Murdock's trial counsel's closing argument). The phrase "rotten social background" has become part of the vernacular of the criminal-law literati thanks to Richard Delgado, "'Rotten Social Background': Should the Law Recognize a Defense of Severe Environmental Deprivation?," *Law and Inequality* 3 (1985): 9. For Delgado's most recent thoughts on the subject, see Richard Delgado, "The Wretched of the Earth," *Alabama Civil Rights and Civil Liberties Law Review* 2 (2011): 1.

He now prefers to emphasize "severe environmental deprivation" rather than "rotten social background."

11. *Alexander*, 471 F.2d at 958 (Bazelon, C.J., dissenting).

12. Id. at 962 (Bazelon, C.J., dissenting). Murdock's claim might today be described in terms of "black rage," a term attributed to William H. Grier and Price M. Cobbs, *Black Rage* (New York: Basic Books, 1968). See generally Patricia Falk, "Novel Theories of Criminal Defense Based upon the Toxicity of the Social Environment: Urban Psychosis, Television Intoxication, and Black Rage," *North Carolina Law Review* 74 (1996): 731.

13. Judge Bazelon would have reversed Murdock's conviction on the ground (among others) that one of the trial court's instructions in connection with the insanity defense was reversible error. *Alexander*, 471 F.2d at 959–60 (Bazelon, C.J., dissenting). The majority disagreed. Id. at 968 (McGowan, J.). Judge Bazelon expanded upon the ideas he expressed in his *Alexander* dissent in his J. Edgar Hoover Foundation lecture delivered at the University of Southern California Law School. See David L. Bazelon, "The Morality of the Criminal Law," *Southern California Law Review* 49 (1976): 385. For a critical response to that lecture, see Stephen J. Morse, "The Twilight of Welfare Criminology: A Reply to Judge Bazelon," *Southern California Law Review* 49 (1976): 1247. The exchange continued with David L. Bazelon, "The Morality of the Criminal Law: A Rejoinder to Professor Morse," *Southern California Law Review* 49 (1976): 1269, and Stephen J. Morse, "The Twilight of Welfare Criminology: A Final Word," *Southern California Law Review* 49 (1976): 1275.

14. R. A. Duff, *Answering for Crime: Responsibility and Liability in the Criminal Law* (Oxford: Hart Publishing, 2007), 191.

15. Roberto Gargarella, "Penal Coercion in Contexts of Social Injustice," *Criminal Law and Philosophy* 5 (2011): 21, 22.

16. The state of affairs I have in mind is dire but not *so* dire that we would describe it as a return to the state of nature. I want to set aside questions about the state's *culpability* for creating and sustaining a class of second-class citizens. The conditions I have in mind are meant to be so egregious that the state can fairly be said to be aware (or willfully ignorant) of the fact that it stands in breach of its moral obligations or at the very least negligent with respect to that breach.

17. Are some citizens of the United States today second-class citizens? Some say yes; others say no. For present purposes I will simply assume that Murdock was indeed a second-class citizen. I leave it to others to argue whether such a class of citizens exists in the United States today and whether

the state can fairly be held accountable for creating it or for tolerating its continued existence. See generally Michael Tonry, *Punishing Race: A Continuing American Dilemma* (Oxford: Oxford University Press, 2011); Bruce Western, *Punishment and Inequality in America* (New York: Russell Sage Foundation, 2006).

18. I leave aside a third line of reply (which appears to be fairly popular): the state is permitted to punish crimes of the second-class, but for one reason or another the hardship it imposes in so doing should be less than the hardship it would impose on a first-class citizen who committed the same crime. Second-class status should mitigate punishment if and because, for example, second-class citizens who commit crimes suffer from unfairly diminished opportunities (or what might be called economic duress) or deserve less suffering in the form of retributive punishment inasmuch as they have previously endured undeserved suffering in other forms.

For what I take to be arguments to this effect, see Gertrude Ezorsky, "The Ethics of Punishment," in *Philosophical Perspectives on Punishment* (Albany: State University of New York Press, 1972), xi, xxiv-xxvii (mitigation based on "whole life" perspective on criminal desert); Martha Klein, *Determinism, Blameworthiness, and Deprivation* (Oxford: Clarendon Press, 1990), 4 (mitigation based on the offender having "paid-in-advance" for his offense); Richard L. Lippke, *Rethinking Imprisonment* (Oxford: Oxford University Press, 2007), 100 (mitigation based on the offender's having had unfairly diminished opportunities to conform to the law); Andrew von Hirsch and Andrew Ashworth, *Proportionate Sentencing: Exploring the Principles* (Oxford: Oxford University Press, 2005), 68 (mitigation based on the offender having been placed in a "more troubled situation" as a result of having been "denied ... social supports" such that the "temptations to offend become harder to resist"); Peter Chau, "Poverty, Distributive Justice, and Punishment," *Canadian Journal of Law and Jurisprudence* 25 (2012): 39, 40 (mitigation based on the offender having been a victim of distributive injustice such that mitigation will "improve distributive justice"); Jules Holroyd, "Punishment and Justice," *Social Theory and Practice* 36 (2010): 78, 102 (mitigation based on the offender's "context of deprivation or disadvantage" having provided him with "significantly different reasons for action") (emphasis omitted); Barbara Hudson, "Beyond Proportionate Punishment: Difficult Cases and the 1991 Criminal Justice Act," *Crime, Law and Social Change* 22 (1995): 59, 76 (mitigation [or nullification] based on "economic duress or similar circumstantial constraint"); Okeoghene Odudu, "Retributive Justice in an Unjust Society," *Ratio Juris* 16 (2003): 416,

427 (mitigation based on the offender's "lawful opportunities" to conform to the law having been "reduced"); Jeffrey Reiman, "The Moral Ambivalence of Crime in an Unjust Society," *Criminal Justice Ethics* (2007): 3, 13 (mitigation based on the offender's "weaken[ed] . . . obligation[] to obey the law" as a result of having been a victim of distributive injustice). Joshua Dressler has expressed sympathy for this mitigation approach in Joshua Dressler, "Reflections on Excusing Wrongdoers: Moral Theory, New Excuses and the Model Penal Code," *Rutgers Law Journal* 19 (1988): 671, 714–15. For responses to von Hirsch and Ashworth's rendition of this argument, see Peter Chau, "Temptations, Social Deprivation and Punishment," *Oxford Journal of Legal Studies* 30 (2010): 775, and Richard L. Lippke, "Social Deprivation as Tempting Fate," *Criminal Law and Philosophy* 5 (2011): 277.

These accounts (as I understand them) do not challenge the state's authority to punish. What they all seem to say in the end is that because an offender has suffered distributive injustice or because his having suffered distributive injustice has caused something else to be true of him, the state should reduce the punishment it otherwise would have imposed on him. As I see it a state is permitted to entertain whatever considerations it wishes when deciding to exercise its permission to punish and to entertain whatever considerations it wishes when deciding how much to punish if it chooses to exercise that permission. However, the state cannot legitimately impose on an offender a grossly disproportionate punishment or otherwise violate rights he retains against the state's exercise of its authority. Reducing an offender's punishment because he has suffered distributive injustice or some effect thereof may or may not be what morality says a state should do, but it would not (all else being equal) result in a grossly disproportionate punishment.

19. See, e.g., Stuart P. Green, "Just Deserts in Unjust Societies: A Case-Specific Approach," in *Philosophical Foundations of the Criminal Law*, ed. R. A. Duff and Stuart P. Green (Oxford: Oxford University Press, 2011), 352, 356–58 (discussing the applicability of the necessity defense to disadvantaged defendants).

20. See, e.g., Joshua Dressler, "Duress," in *The Oxford Handbook of Philosophy of Criminal Law*, ed. John Deigh and David Dolinko (Oxford: Oxford University Press, 2011), 269.

21. The criminal-law defense of duress is commonly limited to threats one person makes to another. See, e.g., Model Penal Code § 2.09 (1980). This limitation would naturally be an obstacle in most cases in which a second-class citizen commits a crime. Most commentators, but not all, believe that

this limitation lacks principle. See Peter Westen and James Mangiafico, "The Criminal Defense of Duress: A Justification, Not an Excuse and Why It Matters," *Buffalo Criminal Law Review* 6 (2003): 833.

22. A fair number of commentators have endorsed this proposition or something like it. See, e.g., Larry Alexander, Kimberly Kessler Ferzan, with Stephen Morse, *Crime and Culpability: A Theory of Criminal Law* (Cambridge: Cambridge University Press, 2009), 138 ("[M]uch of the debate over whether duress is a justification can be better understood by recognizing that duress captures within it instances of personal justification."); Alan Brudner, *Punishment and Freedom: A Liberal Theory of Penal Justice* (Oxford: Oxford University Press, 2009), 257 (arguing that duress is a defense when the actor has "showed no less fortitude or self-restraint than the character of reasonable firmness and self-love would have shown"); Michael Moore, *Placing Blame: A Theory of Criminal Law* (Oxford: Oxford University Press, 1997), 561 (describing the "unfair opportunity" branch of the choice theory of excuse [and thus duress] as the "'failed justification'" idea of excuse); Alan Wertheimer, *Coercion* (Princeton, NJ: Princeton University Press, 1987), 168 (describing duress as "agent-relative" justification); John Gardner, "The Gist of Excuses," *Buffalo Criminal Law Review* 1 (1998): 575, 597 (arguing that "[o]ne is under duress . . . only if one's fear of the threats one is subject to was rationally adequate, in one's own eyes as well as according to the applicable standards of character, for one to commit the wrong one committed"); Dan Kahan and Martha Nussbaum, "Two Conceptions of Emotion in Criminal Law," *Columbia Law Review* 96 (1996): 269, 337 (in cases of duress "it will often seem that the actor did the only morally right thing for her"). The lesson to be learned from the debate over whether to categorize duress as an excuse or justification is probably a simple one: the justification-excuse dichotomy is procrustean.

23. I should mention that neither is an actor morally responsible for the choices he makes unless he satisfies certain epistemic conditions (assuming those conditions are not properly encompassed within the requisite freedom conditions). See Alfred Mele, "Moral Responsibility for Actions: Epistemic and Freedom Conditions," *Philosophical Explorations* 13 (2010): 101 (questioning whether and to what extent the epistemic conditions for responsibility are separate and distinct from the freedom conditions). These epistemic conditions have tended to get less attention than the freedom conditions but they are subject to no less disagreement. For example, some argue that an actor is not morally responsible for any wrong he does unless he is aware of the fact that what he is doing is wrong. See, e.g., Michael J. Zimmerman, *Living with Uncertainty: The Moral Significance of Ignorance* (Cambridge: Cambridge Uni-

versity Press, 2008). Others argue in favor of less demanding conditions. See, e.g., George Sher, *Who Knew? Responsibility without Awareness* (Oxford: Oxford University Press, 2009).

I should perhaps also mention that some writers who defend what has been called attributionism believe that responsibility does not require freedom in any sense. It requires only that an actor's choice be appropriately attributable to him. See, e.g., Angela Smith, "Control, Responsibility, and Moral Assessment," *Philosophical Studies* 138 (2008): 367. For criminal-law theorists who defend attributionism or at least something in the same ballpark, see, for example, R. A. Duff, Intention, *Agency and Criminal Liability* (Oxford: Basil Blackwell, 1990), 154; Kenneth W. Simons, "Culpability and Retributive Theory," *Journal of Contemporary Legal Issues* 5 (1994): 365. It seems to me that the hard question for attributionism is whether it can really support ascriptions of responsibility sufficiently robust to permit censure qua punishment. See, e.g., Neil Levy and Michael McKenna, "Recent Work on Free Will and Moral Responsibility," *Philosophy Compass* 4 (2009): 96, 118.

24. The need for this capacity is commonly said to derive from the principle of alternative possibilities (PAP): alternative possibilities must be open to an actor at the moment of choice in order for an actor to be morally responsible for the choice he makes. He must have the capacity to choose some possibility other than the possibility he chooses.

25. The theory described in the text is one brand of what is often described as contemporary or new compatibilism. According to this theory responsibility is compatible with the truth of determinism inasmuch as responsibility does not require freedom qua capacity to do otherwise, and the freedom it does require is compatible with the truth of determinism. See Michael McKenna, "Contemporary Compatibilism: Mesh Theories and Reasons-Responsive Theories," in *The Oxford Handbook of Free Will*, 2nd ed., ed. Robert Kane (Oxford: Oxford University Press, 2011), 175. I focus on it because it would appear to constitute the theory most criminal-law theorists embrace insofar as they embrace any theory. Other theories with more or less currency among contemporary philosophers include: 1) alternative-possibilities incompatibilism, according to which responsibility requires the capacity to do otherwise but the truth of determinism is incompatible with that capacity; 2) libertarianism, according to which responsibility requires the capacity to do otherwise, and agents possess that capacity such that determinism is to that extent false (see, e.g., Randolph Clarke, *Libertarian Accounts of Free Will* [Oxford: Oxford University Press, 2003]); 3) dispositionalism, according to which responsibility requires the capacity to do otherwise, and agents possess such capacity, despite

the truth of determinism inasmuch as that capacity is understood in terms of a sophisticated conditional analysis (see, e.g., Michael Fara, "Masked Abilities and Compatibilism," *Mind* 117 [2008]: 843; Michael Smith, "Rational Capacities, or: How to Distinguish Recklessness, Weakness, and Compulsion," in *Ethics and the A Priori: Selected Essays on Moral Psychology and Meta-Ethics* [Cambridge: Cambridge University Press, 2004], 114; Kadri Vihvelin, "Free Will Demystified: A Dispositional Account," 32 *Philosophical Topics* 32 [2004]: 427). For criticism, see Randolph Clarke, "Dispositions, Abilities to Act, and Free Will: The New Dispositionalism," *Mind* 118 (2009): 232; Ann Whittle, "Dispositional Abilities," *Philosophers' Imprint* 10 (2010): 1.

26. So-called Frankfurt examples are meant to demonstrate the existence of this intuition. Whether Frankfurt examples prove that freedom and responsibility do not require the capacity to do otherwise has of course generated an exceptionally large amount of literature. See generally David Widerker and Michael McKenna, eds., *Moral Responsibility and Alternative Possibilities: Essays on the Importance of Alternative Possibilities* (Burlington: Ashgate Publishing Company, 2006); John Martin Fischer, "Recent Work on Moral Responsibility," *Ethics* 110 (1999): 93, 109–25; Levy and McKenna, "Recent Work," 98–102. The circumstances under which we actually ascribe responsibility, together with the circumstances under which we withhold such ascriptions, likewise suggest that responsibility does not depend on the capacity to do otherwise. See R. Jay Wallace, *Responsibility and the Moral Sentiments* (Cambridge: Harvard University Press, 1996).

27. See John Martin Fischer and Mark Ravizza, *Responsibility and Control: A Theory of Moral Responsibility* (Cambridge: Cambridge University Press, 1998); D. Justin Coates and Philip Swenson, "Reasons-Responsiveness and Degrees of Responsibility," *Philosophical Studies* (forthcoming) (arguing that the capacity to respond to reasons is a matter of degree). The capacity to respond to reasons consists in the capacity to recognize those reasons as reasons and the capacity to react to those reasons. The first capacity deals with cognition, the second with volition. See John J. Davenport, "Fischer and Ravizza on Moral Sanity and Weakness of Will," *Journal of Ethics* 6 (2002): 235, 246. Stephen Morse argues that the capacity needed to underwrite responsibility is (or perhaps should be understood as) exclusively cognitive: it consists in the capacity for rationality and excludes the possibility of diminished responsibility based on claims of an impaired or nonexistent capacity for self-control. See, e.g., Stephen J. Morse, "Against Control Tests for Criminal Responsibility," in *Criminal Law Conversations*, ed. Paul Robinson, Stephen P. Garvey, and Kimberly Kessler Ferzan (Oxford: Oxford University Press, 2009), 449.

28. See Alfred R. Mele, *Backsliding: Understanding Weakness of Will* (Oxford: Oxford University Press, 2012).

29. The leading compatibilist alternative to the reasons-responsiveness account is Frankfurt's hierarchical account. See Harry G. Frankfurt, "Freedom of the Will and the Concept of a Person," in *The Importance of What We Care About: Philosophical Essays* (Cambridge: Cambridge University Press, 1988), 11; "Identification and Wholeheartedness," in id. at 159.

30. Consistent with the conventional wisdom at the time, Delgado understood duress as an excuse resting on an actor's impaired or nonexistent capacity to conform his conduct to the requirements of law. Delgado, "Rotten Social Background," 49 ("[D]uress is one of the better defenses available to an RSB [rotten social background] defendant . . . because living in stressful, impoverished circumstances may . . . push[] his or her breaking point").

31. See Stephen P. Garvey, "Dealing with Wayward Desire," *Criminal Law and Philosophy* 3 (2009): 1. Stephen Morse has also argued in favor of a generic diminished capacity defense, but whereas I have suggested such a defense based on impaired or nonexistent volitional capacity, Morse would base such a defense on impaired or nonexistent cognitive capacity. See Stephen J. Morse, "Diminished Rationality, Diminished Responsibility," *Ohio State Journal of Criminal Law* 1 (2003): 289.

32. *Alexander*, 471 F.2d at 941n48.

33. Id. at 951.

34. Stephen Morse made this point several years ago. See Stephen J. Morse, "Deprivation and Desert," in *From Social Justice to Criminal Justice: Poverty and the Administration of Criminal Law*, ed. William C. Heffernan and John Kleinig (Oxford: Oxford University Press, 2000), 114, 144–45. For a recent reprise, see Stephen J. Morse, "Severe Environmental Deprivation (AKA RSB): A Tragedy, Not a Defense," *Alabama Civil Rights & Civil Liberties Law Review* 2 (2011): 147, 150–51. See also Sanford H. Kadish, "Fifty Years of Criminal Law: An Opinionated Review," *California Law Review* 87 (1999): 943, 962 (Children brought up in "deplorable conditions of life . . . are more likely when they grow up to commit certain crimes [street crimes especially], . . . [b]ut it doesn't follow that the child once grown who commits a crime has been disabled from making a responsible choice").

35. See, e.g., Fischer and Ravizza, *Responsibility and Control*, 170; Ishtiyaque Haji, *Moral Appraisability: Puzzles, Proposals, and Perplexities* (Oxford: Oxford University Press, 1998), 124–25. Others have described this requirement as the "condition of Ultimate Responsibility, or UR." Robert Kane, *A Contemporary Introduction to Free Will* (Oxford: Oxford University Press, 2005), 121.

36. The story is based on Derk Pereboom, *Living Without Free Will* (Cambridge: Cambridge University Press, 2001), 112–17 (four-case argument). Other prominent variations on the story can be found in Robert Kane, *The Significance of Free Will* (Oxford: Oxford University Press, 1998), 64–65 (CNC cases); Alfred Mele, *Autonomous Agents* (Oxford: Oxford University Press, 1995), 145–46 (Beth and Ann); Alfred Mele, *Free Will and Luck* (Oxford: Oxford University Press, 2006), 189 (zygote argument). The argument in which the story and others like it feature is generally known in the philosophical literature as the "manipulation argument." See, e.g., Ishtiyaque Haji, *Incompatibilism's Allure: Principal Arguments for Incompatibilism* (Ontario: Broadview Press, 2009), 119. The argument has produced an exceptionally large literature trying either to defend or deflate it. The general problem the manipulation argument raises can also be cast in terms of luck and the ways in which luck can undermine an actor's responsibility for his choices. See Neil Levy, *Hard Luck: How Luck Undermines Free Will and Moral Responsibility* (Oxford: Oxford University Press, 2011).

37. According to one group of theories (dissociation theories) the phenomena associated with hypnotism can be explained inasmuch as the hypnotized subject occupies a dissociative or altered state of consciousness. According to a competing group of theories (social cognitive theories) the phenomena associated with hypnotism can be explained inasmuch as the hypnotized subject unwittingly fulfills a particular social role: they unwittingly conform to the expectation that they will do as the hypnotist suggests. Compare Erik Z. Woody and Pamela Sadler, "Dissociation Theories of Hypnosis," in *The Oxford Handbook of Hypnosis*, ed. Michael R. Nash and Amanda J. Barner (Oxford: Oxford University Press, 2008), 81, with Steven Jay Lynn, Irving Kirsch, and Michael N. Hallquist, "Social Cognitive Theories of Hypnosis," in id. at 111.

38. Although I have not found a reported case involving a defendant who claimed to have committed a crime under the influence of hypnosis, the law and the commentators agree that such a defendant should not be convicted. According to some a hypnotized defendant fails to satisfy the voluntary act requirement. See, e.g., Model Penal Code § 2.01(2)(c) (Philadelphia: American Law Institute, 1985) ("[C]onduct during hypnosis or resulting from hypnotic suggestion . . . [is] not [a] voluntary act[]."); Michael Moore, *Act and Crime: The Philosophy of Action and Its Implications for Criminal Law* (Oxford: Oxford University Press, 1993), 257–59; Robert F. Schoop, *Automatism, Insanity, and the Psychology of Criminal Responsibility: A Philosophical Inquiry* (Cambridge: Cambridge University Press, 1991), 154. According to others a "very plausible case . . . can be developed for the proposition that acts under hypnosis or as

a result of hypnotic suggestion are voluntary" and that "[i]t may be better . . . to deal with [a hypnotized defendant's] culpability, if any, as a potential excusing defense." Joshua Dressler, *Understanding Criminal Law* § 9.02[3][a] (LexisNexis, 6th ed. 2012), 91.

39. See Moore, *Act and Crime*, 257.

40. See Kathleen Taylor, *Brainwashing: The Science of Thought Control* (Oxford: Oxford University Press, 2006).

41. Model Penal Code § 2.09. See generally Thomas D. Nolan III, "The Indoctrination Defense: From the Korean War to Lee Boyd Malvo," *Virginia Journal of Social Policy & Law* 11 (2004): 435.

42. Model Penal Code § 2.09, cmt. 3, 376.

43. Id. at 376n40. For the well-known debate between Richard Delgado and Joshua Dressler on the merits of incorporating a "brainwashing" defense into the criminal law, see Richard Delgado, "Ascription of Criminal States of Mind: Toward a Defense Theory for the Coercively Persuaded ('Brainwashed') Defendant," *Minnesota Law Review* 63 (1978): 1; Joshua Dressler, "Professor Delgado's 'Brainwashing' Defense: Courting a Determinist Legal System," *Minnesota Law Review* 63 (1979): 335; Richard Delgado, "A Response to Professor Dressler," *Minnesota Law Review* 63 (1979): 361. Paul Robinson brings the debates surrounding brainwashing and those surrounding rotten social background together in the suggestion that the latter might be analogized to the former such that if the former should constitute an excuse then so too should the latter. See Paul Robinson, "Are We Responsible for Who We Are? The Challenge for Criminal Law Theory in the Defenses of Coercive Indoctrination and 'Rotten Social Background,'" *Alabama Civil Rights & Civil Liberties Law Review* 2 (2011): 53. Morse rejects the analogy: brainwashing blurs into indoctrination, which blurs into education, which blurs into causation, which spells the end of responsibility. See Morse, "Severe Environmental Deprivation," 159–64.

44. See, e.g., Harry G. Frankfurt, "Three Concepts of Free Action," in *The Importance of What We Care About*, 47, 54; Harry Frankfurt, "Reply to John Martin Fischer," in *Contours of Agency: Essays on Themes from Harry Frankfurt*, ed. Sarah Buss and Lee Overton (Cambridge: MIT Press, 2002), 27; Daniel Haas, "In Defense of Hard-Line Replies to the Multiple-Case Manipulation Argument," *Philosophical Studies* (forthcoming); Michael McKenna, "A Hard-Line Reply to Pereboom's Four-Case Manipulation Argument," *Philosophy & Phenomenological Research* 77 (2008): 142; Micheal McKenna, "Moral Responsibility, Manipulation Arguments and History: Assessing the Resilience of Nonhistorical Compatibilism," *Journal of Ethics* 16 (2012): 145; Matthew Tal-

bert, "Implanted Desires, Self-Formation and Blame," *Journal of Ethics & Social Philosophy* 3 (2009): 1; Manuel Vargas, "On the Importance of History for Responsible Agency," *Philosophical Studies* 127 (2006): 351.

45. See Fischer and Ravizza, *Responsibility and Control*, 207.

46. What if the desire to identify with, or otherwise take or assume responsibility for, the springs of one's actions was itself the product of responsibility-undermining manipulation?

47. See Mele, *Free Will*, 170; Haji, *Incompatibilism's Allure*, 124–39; Gideon Yaffe, "Indoctrination, Coercion and Freedom of Will," *Philosophy & Phenomenological Research* 67 (2003): 335 (distinguishing between manipulators and "neural causal mechanisms"); Alfred R. Mele, "Moral Responsibility and History Revisited," *Ethical Theory & Moral Practice* 12 (2009): 463. Some empirical evidence exists to the effect that most people see this difference as a relevant one. See Chandra Sekhar Sripada, "What Makes a Manipulated Agent Unfree?," *Philosophy & Phenomenological Research* (forthcoming). If so, then perhaps one's reaction to the case of the second-class citizen who commits a crime rests in some measure on whether one sees the state as a manipulator or not.

48. See Pereboom, *Living without Free Will*, 115 (arguing that the fact that the action is not "in the last analysis brought about by other agents . . . is [not] a relevant difference"); Derk Pereboom, "A Hard-Line Reply to the Multiple Case Manipulation Argument," *Philosophy & Phenomenological Research* 77 (2008): 160. For a sympathetic treatment in the recent criminal-law literature, see Anders Kaye, "Objectifying and Identifying in the Theory of Excuse," *American Journal of Criminal Law* 39 (2012): 175.

49. The work of two famous thinkers—Judge Bazelon and Norval Morris—can be understood as part of this debate. Both thought hard about the responsibility of those who would not have committed the crimes they committed but for the fact that they suffered from a mental disease or defect or from the burdens of social deprivation. But they reached diametrically opposed conclusions. Bazelon would not only have retained the insanity defense: he would have extended it to include those who would not have committed a crime but for the effects of a rotten social background. Morris would have refused to extend any defense to a defendant suffering from the effects of a rotten social background, but lacking any way to distinguish such a defendant from one who would not have committed a crime but for the effects of a mental disease or defect, he would have abolished the insanity defense. See Norval Morris, *Madness and the Criminal Law* (Chicago: University of Chicago Press, 1984). In short, while Morris would have refused to take the first step down the slope,

Bazelon was prepared to follow it almost all the way down. For a recent endorsement of Judge Bazelon's proposal that "testimony be permitted in appropriate cases concerning the influence of deep disadvantage on behavior and that the jury be directed 'that a defendant is not responsible if at the time of his unlawful conduct his mental or emotional processes or behavior controls were impaired to such an extent that he cannot justly be held responsible for his act,'" see Michael Tonry, "Can Deserts Be Just in an Unjust World?", in *Liberal Criminal Theory: Essays for Andreas von Hirsch*, ed. Andrew P. Simester, Ulfrid Neumann and Antje du Bois-Pedain (Oxford: Hart Publishing, forthcoming 2014), manuscript at 21.

50. The idea that the state has standing to hold a citizen responsible for committing a crime and the idea that it has authority to do so are sometimes treated synonymously. See, e.g., R. A. Duff, "'I Might Be Guilty, But You Can't Try Me': Estoppel and Other Bars to Trial," *Ohio State Journal of Criminal Law* 1 (2003): 245, 247. Treating them as such does no injury to ordinary language, but I nonetheless believe the two concepts should be kept distinct. Standing seems more apt outside a relationship of authority. Authority seems more apt within such a relationship.

51. For an argument that "responding to unwelcome blame by claiming that the critic lacks standing is usually . . . utterly beside the point," see Macalester Bell, "The Standing to Blame," in *Blame: Its Nature and Norms*, ed. D. Justin Coates and Neal A. Tognazzini (Oxford: Oxford University Press, 2013), 263, 264–65.

52. See Duff, *Answering for Crime*, 140–146; R. A. Duff, "Towards a Modest Legal Moralism," *Criminal Law & Philosophy* (forthcoming). Duff originally advanced this account in Sandra Marshall & R. A. Duff, "Criminalization and Sharing Wrongs," *Canadian Journal of Law & Jurisprudence* 11 (1998): 7.

53. Duff, *Answering for Crime*, 141. Michael Moore is skeptical of any reliance on the elusive public-private distinction to define that which the state can and cannot legitimately criminalize. See Michael Moore, "Liberty's Constraints on What Should Be Made a Crime," unpublished manuscript (Sept. 9, 2011): 21–23. Perhaps he is right to be skeptical. It seems to me in any event that if the Duff-Marshall account of that which makes a wrong a public wrong is the right account, then criminal cases should be captioned *People ex rel. Smith v. Doe* or *State ex rel. Smith v. Doe* (or something along similar lines) in order to emphasize that the real victim is Smith, not the People or the State. They share the wrong but are not themselves wronged.

54. On the law of complicity, see generally Dressler, *Understanding Criminal Law*, § 30.02, 458–59; Christopher Kutz, "The Philosophical Foundations of

Complicity Law," in *The Oxford Handbook of Philosophy of Criminal Law*, ed. John Deigh and David Dolinko (Oxford: Oxford University Press, 2011), 147, 151–54.

55. I ignore for now in what hypocrisy consists and why it can undermine or erode the hypocrite's standing to hold another responsible for wrongdoing. For helpful thoughts on these questions, see, for example, G. A. Cohen, "Casting the First Stone: Who Can, and Who Can't Condemn the Terrorists?," in *Finding Oneself in the Other*, ed. Michael Oysuka (Princeton, NJ: Princeton University Press, 2013), 115; G. A. Cohen, "Ways of Silencing Critics," in id. at 134; T. M. Scanlon, *Moral Dimensions: Permissibility, Meaning, Blame* (Cambridge: Harvard University Press, 2008), 166–79; Béla Szabados and Eldon Soifer, *Hypocrisy: Ethical Investigations* (Ontario: Broadview Press, 2004); Angela M. Smith, "On Being Responsible and Holding Responsible," *Journal of Ethics* 11 (2007): 465, 478–80; R. Jay Wallace, "Hypocrisy, Moral Address, and the Equal Standing of Persons," *Philosophy & Public Affairs* 38 (2010): 307; Victor Tadros, "Poverty and Criminal Responsibility," *Journal of Value Inquiry* 43 (2009): 391. I do the same for complicity.

56. Is the power of complicity to undermine one's standing to blame parasitic on that of hypocrisy?

57. See R. A. Duff, "Blame, Moral Standing and the Legitimacy of the Criminal Trial," *Ratio* 23 (2010): 123; Tadros, "Poverty and Criminal Responsibility." For criticism of Duff's argument, see Peter Chau, "Duff on the Legitimacy of Punishment of Socially Deprived Offenders," *Criminal Law & Philosophy* (forthcoming); Matt Matravers, "'Who's Still Standing?' A Comment on Antony Duff's Preconditions of Criminal Liability," *Journal of Moral Philosophy* 3 (2006): 320. For a response to Chau's critique, see Jeffrey Howard, "Punishment, Socially Deprived Offenders, and Democratic Community," *Criminal Law & Philosophy* 7 (2013): 121. Morse refers to this theory (which he rejects) as the "social forfeit" theory. See Morse, "Deprivation and Desert," 152–53; Morse, "Severe Environmental Deprivation," 153.

Duff and Tadros believe that a state that has lost its standing to punish can regain it if it somehow owns up to or answers for its own wrongdoing. See Duff, id. at 139; Tadros, id. at 400–401. According to Duff: "[W]hat is needed is the development of fora in which unjustly disadvantaged citizens can pursue their legitimate grievances; but also (especially when those fora do not yet exist) provision within the criminal process of a space in which such issues can be addressed: not because this might affect the verdict or sentence ... but because only then could the trial claim to have legitimacy." Duff, id. at 139–40.

58. The facts were in fact more complicated. Remember that Lieutenant

King racially insulted Murdock. Does that insult mean that King (had he survived) would lose standing to condemn Murdock for attempting to kill him? The question raises another one: Why is provocation a defense?

59. See Moore, *Act and Crime*, 114. But see Jeffrie G. Murphy, "Moral Epistemology, the Retributive Emotions, and the 'Clumsy Moral Philosophy' of Jesus Christ," in *Punishment and the Moral Emotions: Essays in Law, Morality, and Religion* (Oxford: Oxford University Press, 2012), 21.

60. I don't think Duff pays enough attention to this problem. See Duff, "Blame, Moral Standing and the Legitimacy of the Criminal Trial," 127n8.

61. See Morse, "Deprivation and Desert," 153 ("In a working democracy, the majority of citizens will not believe that the society is sufficiently unjust to compromise its legitimacy").

62. Although the language of "aiding" or "encouraging" is commonly used to characterize the actus reus of accomplice liability a person can (at least according to the Model Penal Code) be an accomplice if "having a legal duty to prevent the commission of the offense, [he] fails to make proper effort to do so." Model Penal Code § 2.06(3)(iii). The idea here is that the state can be liable as an accomplice all else being equal if it has "fail[ed] to make proper effort" to satisfy the obligations justice imposes upon it.

63. See Dressler, *Understanding Criminal Law*, §§ 30.01-.05, 457–76; Kutz, "Philosophical Foundations of Complicity Law," 154–64.

64. See Joshua Dressler, "Reforming Complicity Law: Trivial Assistance as a Lesser Offense?," *Ohio State Journal of Criminal Law* 5 (2008): 427; Joshua Dressler, "Reassessing the Theoretical Underpinnings of Accomplice Liability: New Solutions to an Old Problem," *Hastings Law Journal* 37 (1985): 91.

65. For example, Victor Tadros argues that the "poor can deny that the state is entitled to hold them responsible on the grounds that the state has created unjust conditions in which their responsible criminal offending becomes more likely. As a consequence it bears responsibility for their crimes." Tadros, "Poverty and Criminal Responsibility," 409.

66. What I have to say about authority here is discussed in a little more detail in Stephen P. Garvey, "Was Ellen Wronged?," *Criminal Law & Philosophy* 7 (2013): 185. Jeffrie Murphy has (as I read him) famously argued that a citizen whom the state has treated unjustly in the domain of distribution has no obligation to obey the state, and the state has no authority to punish the disobedience of a citizen it has so treated. See Jeffrie G. Murphy, "Marxism and Punishment," *Philosophy & Public Affairs* 2 (1973): 217, 240–42. For criticism of Murphy's theory, see Green, "Just Deserts in Unjust Societies," 360–62 (describing Murphy's theory as a "broken social contract" theory).

When I say that a state has (or does not have) the "authority to punish," I mean to describe a state to which authority is properly ascribed and where that authority consists in the power to impose obligations the culpable breach of which confers on the state a permission to punish. When I say in contrast that a state (merely) has (or does not have) the "authority to coerce" I mean to describe a state to which authority is properly ascribed and where that authority consists (only) in the power to make demands the culpable breach of which confers on the state a permission to coerce.

67. See, e.g., Robert Paul Wolff, *In Defense of Anarchism* (New York: Basic Books, 1970).

68. See, e.g., A. John Simmons, *Moral Principles and Political Obligations* (Princeton, NJ: Princeton University Press, 1979).

69. See A. John Simmons, "Justification and Legitimacy," in *Justification and Legitimacy: Essays on Rights and Obligations* (Cambridge: Cambridge University Press, 2001), 122. Most of the traditional theories of political obligation—consent, fair play, natural duty, and so forth—are efforts to give answers to the legitimation question.

70. When I say obey I mean (more precisely) conform in contrast to comply. I conform if I do as I'm told for whatever reason; I comply if I do as I'm told because I'm told to do it. See Scott Hershovitz, "The Authority of Law," in *The Routledge Companion to Philosophy of Law*, ed. Andrei Marmor (New York: Routledge, 2012), 65.

71. I limit the category of malum in se wrong to serious wrongs, i.e., wrongs the culpable commission of which threaten the social order and the criminalization of which is needed to secure our escape from the state of nature. I would therefore assign trivial malum in se wrongs to the category of malum prohibitum. I hope this slightly unconventional rendering of the distinction between malum in se and malum prohibitum is not unduly confusing.

72. Although I have so far emphasized the need for the state to resolve disagreement over what morality says about the scope of the criminal law, i.e., whether or not this or that should be a crime, disagreement invariably arises over two other questions the criminal law must answer. First: What does it take to make an actor culpable for the crimes he commits such that he loses the immunity he would otherwise enjoy to the state's censure? Does culpability rest on an actor's free choice to do wrong, on the fact that what he does reflects a character worthy of condemnation, or something else? Second: What good is to be achieved when the state accompanies such censure with hard treatment (i.e., punishment) such that its imposition would be morally permissible? Is the good of doing retributive justice sufficient to render pun-

ishment permissible, must punishment achieve some other good as well, or something else? We need the state to reach an authoritative settlement on each of these questions.

73. The distinction between a social state of nature and a political state of nature may map on to the different ways in which Hobbes and Locke imagine what the state of nature would look like. The problem in the state of nature as Hobbes imagined it was the war of all against all. The problem as Locke imagined it was disagreement in the application of the basic moral code to which all would adhere despite the state's absence. See, e.g., Reiman, "The Moral Ambivalence of Crime in an Unjust Society," 6; Matt Zwolinski, "States of Nature," *Journal of Value Inquiry* 45 (2011): 27, 34.

74. It may seem that I am here endorsing the so-called fair-play or fairness theory of punishment. See Herbert Morris, "Persons and Punishment," in *On Guilt and Innocence: Essays in Legal Philosophy and Moral Psychology* (Berkeley: University of California Press, 1976), 31; Richard Dagger, "Playing Fair with Punishment," *Ethics* 103 (1993): 473; John Finnis, "Retribution: Punishment's Formative Aim," *American Journal of Jurisprudence* 44 (1999): 91. Richard Dagger has emerged as the most prominent proponent of this theory. See Richard Dagger, "Punishment as Fair Play," *Res Publica* 14 (2008): 259.

The problem is figuring out what the fair-play theory is a theory of. My current thinking is that the fair-play theory of punishment is best understood as an application of the fair-play theory of political obligation in which the latter theory is limited to those laws that proscribe the commission of malum in se offenses. The fair-play theory of political obligation justifies state authority based on its capacity to secure the general good of social cooperation with fairness to one's fellows being that which legitimates state authority. The fair-play theory of punishment justifies state authority based on its capacity to secure the good of social cooperation to the extent needed to achieve and maintain social peace with fairness to one's fellows being that which legitimates state authority. So understood the fair-play theory of punishment does not portray itself as a justification for the state to exercise its permission to impose punishment. It portrays itself as an answer to the justification and legitimation questions that any putative authority must answer before those subject to it would do wrong to disobey its directives. It explains the conditions (all else being equal) under which state punishment is permissible, not why the state would be justified to exercise that permission. See Dagger, id. at 265 ("One can hold . . . that the state's right to punish is grounded in fair play without concluding that the agents of the state can consider nothing but unfair benefits when deciding how or how much to punish offenders"); Zachary

Hoskins, "Fair Play, Political Obligation, and Punishment," Criminal Law & Philosophy 5 (2011): 53.

If the fair-play theory of punishment is portrayed as a theory meant to explain why the state would be justified in exercising its permission to punish the answer it offers is that doing so would restore the balance of benefits and burdens the offender experiences: crime gives him a benefit; punishment imposes a burden that takes it away. So portrayed the theory is subject to objections that need overcoming. For some of these see, for example, Shawn J. Bayern, "The Significance of Private Burdens and Lost Benefits for a Fair-Play Analysis of Punishment," New Criminal Law Review 12 (2012): 1.

75. See, e.g., Thomas Christiano, *The Constitution of Equality: Democratic Authority and Its Limits* (Oxford: Oxford University Press, 2008).

76. See, e.g., Jeremy Waldron, *Law and Disagreement* (Oxford: Oxford University Press, 1999).

77. One reviewer fairly wanted me to say more about the content of the positive rights a citizen has against the state. I'm afraid I will need for now to defer. My argument depends on a distinction between those the state has treated as second-class citizens inasmuch as it has failed to secure for them the conditions of a minimally decent life and those the state has relegated to a state of nature. Spelling out in any detail where the line between the two is to be drawn will take more time and thought.

78. If a state provides a person with protection against the state of nature but disenfranchises him, he would remain obligated to obey the state with respect to malum in se offenses but he would have no obligation to obey with respect to prohibitions outside that core. The state would lose all authority—to punish and coerce—a disenfranchised actor for the culpable commission of acts in violation of those prohibitions. For example, if the state has disenfranchised me, I would have no obligation to obey its prohibitions on drug possession (assuming such prohibitions are outside the malum in se core), nor would the state have the authority to punish or coerce me in response to my possession of drugs in violation of its prohibition.

79. See Claire Oakes Finkelstein, "On the Obligation of the State to Extend a Right of Self-Defense to Its Citizens," *University of Pennsylvania Law Review* 147 (1999): 1361. Murdock raised self-defense as a bar to conviction but the jury didn't buy it.

80. *Alexander*, 471 F.2d at 927n2.

81. See Matravers, "Who's Still Standing?," 327 ("There is a point at which the state fails to function to such a degree that its citizens can properly think of themselves as having returned to a state of nature").

82. See Joel Feinberg, "The Expressive Function of Punishment," in *Doing and Deserving: Essays in the Theory of Responsibility* (Princeton, NJ: Princeton University Press, 1970), 95, 96 (distinguishing "mere" penalties from punishment). For the Model Penal Code's definition of an "offense" constituting a "violation," and not a "crime," see Model Penal Code § 1.04(5).

83. What does this mean for those who are the victims of such noncrimes? It means that although the state can impose hardship on those who have victimized them, it cannot punish the victimizers. Nor can the victim himself: only that state has that privilege. Thus in the end it means that the victimizer will go unpunished, and the victim will accordingly go without the vindication that punishment alone can bring. First-class and second-class citizens alike are obliged to pay this price for tolerating a state that treats some of its members as second-class citizens. For what I take to be a kindred observation, see R. A. Duff, *Punishment, Communication, and Community* (Oxford: Oxford University Press, 2001), 199

84. One reviewer wanted to know what was really "at stake in drawing the line between imposing a hardship in order to punish and imposing a hardship in order to coerce obedience." In one sense, nothing is at stake. A culpable offender is carted off to prison (or whatnot) either way. But in another sense something quite important is at stake: If the state has the authority to punish, it has the authority to condemn or censure those subject to its authority for the culpable wrongs they do. If the state lacks such authority, and possesses merely the authority to coerce, then it has no authority to condemn or censure. It lacks that authority because it can no longer legitimately claim to stand in a relationship with the offender in which the reactive emotions that motivate such condemnation or censure make sense. In other words, what's at stake is our understanding of precisely what the state is doing when it imposes the burdens associated with the criminal law: Is it punishing, or merely coercing?

Imprisonment without Justice
Caleb Smith

I've taken an ambiguous phrase for my title. What does it mean to speak of imprisonment without justice?

Two possibilities come quickly to mind. First, the phrase might refer to the imprisonment of a wrongfully convicted defendant. The incarceration of the innocent, almost everyone would agree, is imprisonment without justice. Second, imprisonment without justice might refer to a sentence that is technically valid, according to the letter of the law, but contrary to some nonlegal ideal, some moral standard, of fairness or of right. In preparing to address an audience at the University of Alabama Law School on the punitive imagination, I thought of Martin Luther King Jr.'s detention in the state fifty years earlier, in 1963. "One has not only a legal but a moral responsibility to obey just laws," King wrote in his famous letter from the Birmingham Jail. "Conversely, one has a moral responsibility to disobey unjust laws." Since the 1960s, many others condemned to incarceration in America have identified themselves as political prisoners, living martyrs to a corrupt, racist, or imperialist state. With a haunting eloquence, they have described American prisons as zones of dispossession and dehumanization.

In "How We Carry Ourselves" (1979), a poem dedicated "To Others in Prisons," Jimmy Santiago Baca recalls, "We sought to remain human." The prison is a place where humanity is dispossessed. The poet observes how inmates' bodies, his own among them, are mauled and welded into the machinery of the institution:

> We are steel hunks of gears and frayed ropes,
> our hands the toolsheds,

our heads the incessant groan
of never ending revolving wheels,
in an empty, gaunt warehouse
our blood dripping from steel joints
like grease and oil onto granite floors.[1]

Baca's lines develop an image of the prison system, but they do not open themselves up to the styles of interpretation that Law and Literature critics have most often brought to bear on the punitive imagination. There is no individual character or lyric subject; there is a collective entity, a kind of population or mass. Even consciousness has been displaced: "our heads the incessant groan." The lines do not easily yield to the critique of the disciplinary subject or to the ethical recognition of the speaker's agency. Moreover, the poem is not a narrative. There is no plot, no progression through events; there is an arrested present. The phrase "We are," composed of a single predicate and verb, holds the action in suspension. The lines are not readily available to allegorical reading. And finally, although the poem represents a scene of imprisonment, it does not dramatize punishment as the enforcement of justice in a normative sense. The lines do not invite us to measure the ideological justification of violence against some other, more human standard.

In other words, the punitive machinery on display in "How We Carry Ourselves" does not legitimate itself in the conventional ways that we know how to deconstruct. Baca's prison is not a stage for an injured sovereign's ritualized vengeance against the body of the offender, and it is not an apparatus for the reformation of the unruly soul. It is a warehouse, a space of mere containment. There is violence in this prison, but it is justified neither as retribution nor as rehabilitation. It is a wasting away. Here, Baca glimpses a third prospect, the one I wish to focus on in the rest of this chapter: *imprisonment without justice* might mean something other than *unjust imprisonment*; the phrase might signify, instead, a regime of incarceration that has detached itself, more or less explicitly, from any claim to justice at all.

Such an institution would be a bizarre novelty. From its beginnings in the late eighteenth century through the riots and struggles of the 1970s, perhaps, the penitentiary system in the United States was mainly understood as the concrete manifestation of some theory of justice, either retributive or rehabilitative. Over the past forty years or so, though, the ideological connection between imprisonment and justice has worn thin. In

"The New Penology" (1992), Malcolm Feeley and Jonathan Simon made this point with perfect clarity: "The new penology is neither about punishing nor about rehabilitating individuals. It is about identifying and managing unruly groups."[2] The traditional justice system had concerned itself with the individual offender, with determining fault and imposing an appropriate penalty. Rehabilitation meant assessing character and attempting to transform it, and even retributive punishment took as its target the guilty subject, one who deserved to suffer. The new penology left those ways of thinking behind. It shifted its focus away from the particular offender, toward target populations; away from guilt, toward security; away from the execution of a just sentence, toward the smooth functioning of its own institutional machinery.[3]

According to Feeley and Simon, penology in the late twentieth century was closing itself off from the rest of the world. It was becoming a self-regulating, self-contained system, less and less concerned with norms drawn from such external spheres as law, politics, and popular culture. Although the same era had witnessed "the 'tough on crime' rhetoric" of right-leaning politicians disenchanted with the notion of rehabilitation, for instance, such macho talk disclosed little about penology's own logic; no single "master narrative for the system" could be identified.[4] Feeley and Simon's view can be understood as a formal institutionalization of the conceptual distinction laid out in Friedrich Nietzsche's *Genealogy of Morals*, where the "act" of punishment bears no substantive relation to the "meaning" or "purpose" assigned to that act. As Nietzsche argues, any number of justifications for punishment might be offered—vengeance, rehabilitation, deterrence, incapacitation, and so forth—and these are fluid, shifting over time, but beneath these transitions in meaning, the real violence of punishment goes on and on, untouched and unchanged.

It is not clear that the prison system, massive and self-reproducing as it has become, really requires legitimacy in the form of active public assent. Yet I would not quite wish to concede, as Feeley and Simon seem to, that there is no longer *any* substantive relationship between the prison system and the rest of the social world. I would like to explore another possibility: that the policies and police strategies contributing to mass incarceration exploit a generalized fantasy of secure and sanitary public space. In recent years, the talk in the policy-oriented public sphere tends to be of population management rather than personal transformation, of incapacitation rather than moral education, of "broken windows" and "secure communities" rather than disciplined souls. To be sure, there has been plenty of "tough on crime" bluster, but I am going to maintain that such noise is inessential. The analytic problem for a critique of mass incarceration is not only to expose its ceremonies of spectacular self-justification. It is to grasp something more nebulous but more fundamental, to analyze the half-conscious patterns of thought that Michel Foucault called "the conditions of acceptability of a system."[5]

I want to ask whether the concept of justice, so crucial both to legitimation and to dissent, has occluded our view into the quieter, less sensational but perhaps more profound place of security in fortifying the acceptability of the prison system. The ideology of the penal state may not be composed entirely of moral narratives about transgression and penitence. It may also include certain modes of picturing and enjoying the built environment. What calls the warehouses of abjection into being might be the spatial imaginary of our time.

The novelty of imprisonment without justice, if that is what we are seeing, therefore poses some difficult methodological problems. The new system has been called by several names—mass incarceration, the prison-industrial complex, the New Jim Crow—and it is arguably the most conspicuous and world-changing development in the American legal system over the past forty years. As it turns out, these same four decades saw the rise of the interdisciplinary constellation known as Law and Literature. The two are almost exact contemporaries. And yet, as I have tried to suggest, by way of Baca's poem, the styles of interpretation practiced in Law and Literature have sometimes made it difficult for us to think about such large-scale transformations. While we know how to analyze the exceptional case, especially the drama of the violent crime and the trial, it is everyday policing and plea-bargaining that keeps the warehouse prisons overcrowded. While we know how to think about the motives and reasons of the one who chooses to break the law, the criminal justice system identifies whole social classes for surveillance, exclusion, and control. While we frame our arguments about vengeance and mercy, the criminal justice system imposes mere incapacitation. While we consider justice and injustice, it operates on logics of security.

How might those of us in the critical humanities or our friends in critical legal studies, accustomed as we are to thinking in terms of justice and injustice, begin to analyze the imaginative aspects of a prison system that legitimates itself less and less by invoking any familiar discourse of retribution or of rehabilitation? How might our interpretive practice, so long preoccupied with allegories of innocence and martyrdom, address a system that takes so little interest in the individual case? In the first part of this paper, I'll lay out the challenges posed by two recent studies of mass incarceration in the social sciences, each of which suggests, in its way, the waning into obsolescence of the old narratives of guilt and redemption, of vengeance and reform, that were central to the ideology of the penitentiary for almost two centuries. In the second part, I'll sketch the outline of a critical research program that would respond to these challenges by shifting its focus from narrative to image, from allegorical stories of unjust imprisonment to the ways of imagining space that undergird mass imprisonment without justice.

One thing I will not offer, here, is a normative argument against the present system. Carol Steiker's contribution to this volume, with its theory of collective dignity as a jurisprudential value, is a beautiful and compelling exercise in that genre. For my part, I take it for granted that the vast regime of violence and dispossession that we call mass incarceration, among other names, is an intolerable disaster. I also take it for granted that those of us who oppose such a regime do so for many reasons, out of many different kinds of ethical and social commitments. One of my premises is that invocations of justice (or of humanity or of dignity), in the face of so much imprisonment, lose some of their force when the penal system no longer makes any serious claim to be just. But another is that the work of opposition needs the broadest possible coalition, maximally pluralist in its norms. For now, my endeavor is to begin excavating some of the ways of thinking about space, about the geographies of social life, which contribute to the acceptability of incarceration without justifying it in moral or ethical terms at all.

I. The Insecure Imagination

Over the past few decades, the United States has built the largest prison system in the world—inhuman not only in its violence but also in its scale. How did this happen? Scholars of mass incarceration, or what some call the "penal state," trace its origins back to the late 1960s and 1970s. In those years, both the material form and the ideological function of imprisonment began to change. At one level, the transformation was provoked from within the prisons, as the widely publicized riots at Soledad, Attica, and elsewhere brought the existing system into crisis, and authorities responded with a reactionary crackdown. More broadly, there was the social and economic instability of deindustrialization, the backlash against the radicalizing civil rights and antiwar movements, and a political turn to the right that culminated in the Reagan presidency and the triumph of a neoliberal consensus. By the early 1980s, the prison boom was underway, and it has continued and accelerated up to the present, in red states and blue states, under the direction of officials from both political parties.[6]

As many studies of penal ideology have pointed out, the rise of mass incarceration was animated—and perhaps legitimated, in the public sphere—by an increasingly harsh rhetoric about crime and punishment. Since the late eighteenth century, the American penitentiary system had been associated with a humanitarian reform movement that represented the cell not only as a site of punishment but also as a scene of rehabilitation and redemption. The ministers and officials who oversaw the building of the first penitentiaries routinely defined them against the public tortures and tomb-like dungeons of a despotic past. Many drew a contrast, as well, with the dehumanizing violence of southern slave discipline in their own Jacksonian present—a distinction which had to be reconsidered after emancipation and the Civil War amendments, when convict leasing put black labor back in chains and state-run "prison farms" came to occupy the grounds of the antebellum plantations.[7] To be sure, the promises of compassion and rehabilitation were often betrayed by realities of wounding and killing, and these realities were not always kept secret; the prison could easily be represented to a restless public as an instrument of harsh justice. But in the liberal vision that animated much American statecraft, at least from the New Deal through the early 1960s, the prison system was most commonly imagined in terms of *correction*.[8]

By 1981, that vision was fading fast, and the legal scholar Francis Allen announced the "decline of the rehabilitative ideal."[9] Punishment in America, Allen argued, no longer sought to explain itself as a technique of correction. Instead, what Allen called a "war theory" of punishment, incompletely buried in the distant past, had returned with a vengeance. In the propaganda of harsh justice, offenders were not depicted as lost souls to be reclaimed. They were stigmatized as enemies of society to be captured, humiliated, and broken down. James Q. Whitman's *Harsh Justice* (2003) confirmed Allen's dark prophecies, arguing that America's criminal justice empire, with its distinctive vastness and cruelty, rests on an ideology of punitive degradation.[10]

"The measure of the explosive power of mass politics," Whitman proposes, "can indeed be taken from the law of punishment, where the push for a tough retributivism has had an extraordinary effect."[11] Perhaps, then, mass incarceration today is justified in the public sphere by stories and images that conjure up old-fashioned nightmares of crime. Perhaps the system disseminates its ideology in mass culture by unearthing long-buried fantasies of vengeance. Even the most casual observer of politics or the popular media can see it happening: right-wing pundits ranting against dangerous "predators"; celebrity sheriffs inviting decent citizens to laugh at the humiliation of their inmates; an endless spectacle of monstrous criminals and hero crimefighters, all of it more or less explicitly organized along the lines of race and class. The so-called War on Crime is a war of good against evil, a battle to defend the sovereign community against a malign presence that threatens the peace, and there will be no mercy for the enemy.

Strange to say, there is something almost comforting about this picture. I don't mean only that its familiar moral categories soothe the anxieties or excite the fantasies of an uncritical mass public. I mean that the critical analysis itself comes around to an oddly reassuring conclusion. In many of these accounts of the punitive imagination, a terrible novelty—the largest, most expensive, and arguably the most punitive prison system in the history of the world—is explained as the latest manifestation of old flaws in the American character. For two centuries, so the story goes, the pendulum of penal ideology has been swinging back and forth between two ideals of justice, between retribution and rehabilitation. It has swung back, for now, to the side of vengeance. But the tradition of liberal critique knows how to respond: with humanizing stories, with calls for mercy and understanding, with efforts to restore the project of reform. So many protests against mass incarceration inherit the ideals of mercy and redemption on which the penitentiary system was first erected; they call American criminal justice to live up to its own highest ideals.

Meanwhile, however, a less consolatory picture is being drawn by social scientists studying the penal system in structural terms, analyzing the function of the prison boom with reference to the large-scale social and economic transformations of the late twentieth century. "No doubt, a new and more punitive attitude toward the proper role of punishment has emerged in recent years," Feeley and Simon acknowledge—and yet, "looking across the past several decades, it appears that the pendulum-like swings of penal attitude moved independently" of the new penology, with its depersonalized, managerial logic.[12]

Here I will consider the work of two social scientists who make serious efforts to communicate, across the disciplinary divide, with the critical humanities. Significantly, these two have conducted their research not on the Deep South or the Old West, but on California and New York, states often seen as relatively progressive in politics and culture. In *Golden Gulag*, the cultural geographer Ruth Wilson Gilmore describes California's metastasizing prisons as "partial geographic solutions to political economic crises, organized by the state, which is itself in crisis."[13] In *Prisons of Poverty* and *Punishing the Poor*, the sociologist Loïc Wacquant explores the structural link between neoliberal politics and the massive expansion of the prison system.

Gilmore does not focus her attention on what happens in particular trials. She is interested in mapping the movements of people and resources on a much larger scale. Her account begins with the virtually simultaneous disintegration of California's industrial and agricultural economies in the 1970s. In responding to this crisis, she argues, state officials discovered a partial solution in a prison system that seemed capable of reconfiguring the relationship between the city and the countryside. Driven by tough sentencing laws like the famous "three strikes" policy, one of the signature inventions of harsh justice, mass incarceration in California took underemployed people, especially young men of color, out of the urban centers. It promised to clean up and secure the streets of the decaying cities by removing this troublesome population. It made people disappear. At the same time, new prison construction in California brought state investment and the promise of high-paying and secure jobs to rural zones, whose mostly white populations had sagged into poverty. Naturally, as Gilmore acknowledges, "the successful political promotion of fear of crime as *the* key problem, and the ideological legitimacy of the U.S. state as the institution responsible for defense at all levels, allowed California to act."[14] But the real project was to mobilize capital toward the restructuring of social space on a massive scale.

Gilmore emphasizes that California's prison system, the largest state system in the country, has discarded most of the conventional justifications for punishment—the reformist ideal of rehabilitation, of course, but also the vengeful fantasy of retribution and the mission of governance through fear which is called *deterrence*. In California, as elsewhere, the logic of incarceration has been stripped down to its simplest form, the practice of mere containment, of warehousing, which is known as *incapacitation*. As a conceptual justification for punishment, Gilmore observes, incapacitation "is not ambitious in a behavioral or psychological sense." It has no designs on refashioning the inmate's character or teaching the public a moral lesson. But "it is, ironically the theory that undergirds the most ambitious prison-building project in the history of the world."[15]

Incapacitation is a peculiar idea. The term is routinely placed in a sequence of concepts—retribution, deterrence, rehabilitation, and incapacitation—each of which can give penal violence a kind of legitimacy. But incapacitation is distinctive in that it does not justify itself in relation to the offender's crime. Instead, incapacitation is putatively about preventing the prisoner from committing some unspecified *future* transgression. This is the lynchpin of the new penology: "Incapacitation promises to reduce the effects of crime in society not by altering either offender or social context, but by rearranging the distribution of offenders in society. If the prison can do nothing else, incapacitation theory holds, it can detain offenders for a time and thus delay their resumption of criminal activity."[16] Incapacitation needs no reference to a past event; it is anxiously prospective. From one point of view, then, incapacitation is not really a theory of punishment at all. It is a policy for the management of social instability and social space. It does not require a vengeful memory. Its signature affects are insecurity and fear.

Gilmore's emphasis on incapacitation begins to open up an alternative to Allen's account of the "war theory" behind the prison boom. Allen took the rhetoric of the War on Crime seriously, showing how it targeted criminals as enemies to be destroyed. Gilmore's spatial analysis, by contrast, suggests that inmates in the warehouse prisons, as they are understood by the system, have less in common with active enemies on the battlefield than with prisoners of war—figures who have been removed from the scene of combat so that they can do no further harm. The legal scholar Sharon Dolovich has linked the recent expansion of life without parole sentencing to the rise of supermax prisons, arguing that these two developments work together to solidify, as the central imperative of today's penology, "the exclusion from the shared public space of those deemed a threat to public order and security, and the exercise of state control to keep those marked out for such exclusion separate and apart from society for the duration of their sentences."[17] The point is simply to detain them, to hold them in suspension, into an indefinite future.[18]

To describe the prison as a geographic solution to social and economic crises, as Gilmore does, is not to say that no other solution was (or is) possible. One of the unhappy ironies of the prison boom is that it is a massive expansion of state power, demanding huge capital investments and ballooning public debt, which was devised mainly by politicians who came into office on promises of smaller government and greater individual liberty. This paradox is a critical opportunity for Wacquant, who shows the direct correlation between the dismantling of the welfare state and the construction of the penal state.[19] "Incarceration," Wacquant writes, "has de facto become America's largest government program for the poor."[20] As the ascendant neoliberals (Republicans and Democrats alike) took apart the midcentury's institutions of welfare and public health, and as the industrial economy gave way to a postindustrial order, characterized by a heightened instability and the erosion of workers' rights, governments began using prisons to manage a whole range of social problems—mental illness, drug addiction, vagrancy, and above all poverty itself—which had previously been addressed by other means.

Wacquant is not the only critic to locate the contemporary prison system within material economies of money and power. Comparisons to the industrial factory and to the antebellum plantation have become commonplace. But Wacquant argues that the new regime is best understood neither according to an outmoded logic of industrial exploitation, nor as a reinvention of slavery by another name. Rather, the prison boom must be seen as a part of neoliberalism's reorganization of both the economy and the state. The benefits to capitalism, such as they are, come through the closing down of the alternatives to low-wage, low-stability employment for the poor: on one hand, the destruction of welfare programs; on the other hand, the harsh criminalization of the illegitimate economy, even of joblessness itself. The state redefines its mission, including the business of policing crime, and appears before the public in a new form. It abandons the lexicon of education and uplift with which penal rehabilitation had long been associated; it addresses social insecurity as it addresses so many other problems, with targeted securitization and neglect.

Wacquant also has his own view of the punitive imagination. He seeks to combine a Marxian, materialist analysis of incarceration with a symbolic one adapted from Emile Durkheim and Pierre Bourdieu: "The prison," he writes, "symbolizes material divisions and materializes relations of symbolic power; its operation ... fuses domination and signification."[21] Thus his work offers provocations not only for policymakers but also for critics of culture. Like Gilmore, Wacquant recognizes that the radical expansion of the prison system has been accompanied by "a new cultural industry of the fear and loathing of (lower-class and dark-skinned) offenders."[22] Like other scholars, he perceives the continuities between the mass incarceration of the present and the Jim Crow order of the past.[23] But Wacquant's most original insights belong to another movement in today's critical prison studies, a kind of spatial turn.

Wacquant tells a story that begins with Rudolph Giuliani's New York

City in the 1990s. His critique targets the myth that Giuliani and his police chief, William Bratton, rescued the city from crime by instituting so-called zero tolerance or "broken windows" policies that aggressively punished such minor offenses as vandalism, panhandling, and trespassing. Giuliani and Bratton made their names by going after "petty drug retailers, prostitutes, beggars, the homeless, drifters, and perpetrators of graffiti and other urban depredations.... In short, the enemy is the subproletariat that mars the scenery and menaces or annoys the consumers of urban space."[24] The poor, especially poor people of color, experienced zero tolerance as an intensifying harassment, intimidation, or worse. But for affluent whites, the city under Giuliani began to feel like a safer place to work and shop.

Can the same be said of the cities of Gilmore's California? Los Angeles, the battleground where the War on Crime has been pursued with the most spectacular militarism, has also become a zone of resegregation and neoliberal gentrification. Writing of the City of Angels in the 1980s, Mike Davis tells a story that, in many ways, anticipates Wacquant. "The defense of luxury lifestyles is translated into a proliferation of new repressions in space and movement," Davis argues. "This obsession with physical security systems, and, collaterally, with the architectural policing of social boundaries, has become a zeitgeist of urban restructuring."[25] Los Angeles–based geographer Edward J. Soja concludes in *Seeking Spatial Justice* that the animating force behind the shape of today's cities is a "security-obsessed urbanism."[26] California, like New York, is living through an era not only of harsh justice but also of the restructuring of the landscapes of social life.

What might be the consequences of these arguments for the study of the punitive imagination—of literature, the arts, and culture at the margins of a policy-oriented public sphere? They could easily support the critique of mass-media texts which demonize the subproletariat, above all impoverished black and brown men, as so many predators stalking the streets of the cities. There are echoes of the Frankfurt School in Wacquant's references to a mystifying, fear-mongering "cultural industry." At one point he goes so far as to compare the media spectacles generated by the penal state to the redundant titillations of pornography. As a critic of the punitive imagination, Wacquant remains the descendant of Durkheim and Bourdieu; he thinks of the spectacles of criminal justice as ritualized reaffirmations of the state's legitimacy, calling the mass public to assent to the exercise of penal violence.

Even more unsettling and provocative, however, is Wacquant's account of urban geography. A major implication of the spatial turn in critical prison studies is that the penal state is operative in sites where we might not be accustomed to looking for it. Its influence is felt not only within the prison interior—nor quite, as Foucault famously argued, in the interior life of every modern subject.[27] Mass incarceration is at work also in cities that seem to have been emptied of their "troublesome poverty" and transformed into smooth, clean zones for the enjoyment of "consumers of urban space." To take the readiest example, it becomes possible to think of the shops, museums, and parks of Manhattan in the early twenty-first century as sites violently carved out of the urban landscape by the penal state. And thus it might be argued that the American public assents to mass incarceration not only in the obvious way, by rallying like a lynch mob to the side of tough-on-crime politicians, but also by its eager participation in the securitization of public space.

From Gilmore's research, then, we get an account of a state that responds to economic and social crisis by rearranging bodies in the landscape. From Wacquant, an analysis of the refashioning of governance—the deconstruction of most welfare programs (which, in the United States, had never been as robust as their European counterparts) and the rise of a penal state whose warehouse prisons become the only alternative to the kinds of low-wage, unstable jobs that are available to the poor in the neoliberal economy. Both of these social scientists acknowledge that new penal institutions and policies sometimes justify themselves, in the arenas of popular politics and culture, with fear mongering about subhuman criminals or with narratives of a merciless vengeance. Yet the total picture that emerges from their work is one of a system whose real business is the management of territory and populations on a vast scale. The problem to be addressed is not the criminal violation of the social compact; it is economic and social instability. And the fantasy to be peddled is not so much one of retribution against the terrible few as one of greater stability for the rest of us—in particular, the fantasy of urban space as a smooth, clean zone of circulation and consumption.

II. Notes Toward a Critique of Spatial Fantasy

Perhaps, then, the system of mass incarceration legitimates itself today by appealing not only to a punitive imagination but also, more subtly, to an *insecure* one. These two critiques are not mutually exclusive, of course, and it would probably be too much to suggest that there is anything really new about insecurity. What we are seeing, instead, is the emergence into prominence of features that have long been present, but subordinate, in the ideology of criminal justice. Still, certain important shifts can be observed in the way that imprisonment is imagined and justified. There is a turn from the moral economy of justice to material economies of capital and power. There is a waning interest in the mentality or character of the particular offender and a greater focus on the designation of target populations, often in terms of race or class. And there is a movement away from narratives of transgression, toward a picture-based imaginary that conceives of public space as either secure or insecure, either contaminated by troublesome poverty or polished clean for smooth circulation.

Consider, for instance, a popular detective show—*Crime Scene Investigation: Miami* or *NCIS: Los Angeles* or *NYPD Blue*. It would be easy to show how the plots endlessly rehearsed by these programs contribute to a punitive imagination. Depicting offenders as sociopaths and subtle villains, they focus on the highly individuated malefactor whose psychology is complex and whose motives are personal. These monstrous figures, the critic might argue, obscure the public's vision into the social and structural causes of ordinary crime. Similarly, the sophisticated forensic technologies and morally ambiguous interrogation strategies on display in these shows might be said to distract viewers from the everyday realities of mundane police work—emergency response and stop and frisk—that keep the warehouses of mass incarceration stocked with petty offenders.

Yet it would not be quite right to say that television crime dramas are interested only in the individual, to the exclusion of the social or the structural. Note how obsessively, how lovingly they represent urban space. Almost every cop show calls attention to its setting, often naming a city in its title. The typical opening sequence is a view of the skyline from a helicopter or a panning shot of the streets from the window of a cruiser. Those of us who are trained in the analysis of narrative genres tend to see these sequences as background. We wait for the introduction of characters and the movements of plot, where the real action is to be found. But if social scientists like Gilmore and Wacquant are right, if the penal system is most of all a machine for the transformation of public space, then we might need to retrain our eyes to see the image as primary and the setting, not the character or the plot, as the bearer of ideological weight. To study the punitive imagination, then, would require a critical research program into cultural representations of the geographies of contemporary life. In the rest of this chapter I will sketch, in a preliminary way, a few of the directions toward which this line of inquiry might lead.

As a cultural-historical project, research on the insecure imagination might begin with the period of rapid urbanization in the nineteenth century. It would reconstruct the patterns of settlement and segregation, but it would pay special attention to the genres of imaginative culture, the fictions that expressed and refashioned the meaning of public space. It might begin, for instance, with the tales of Edgar Allan Poe. Remembered as the inventor of the modern detective story, the genre whose descendants today include our endless forensic fantasies, Poe was also one of the first American chroniclers of the cityscape; his representations of urban society and the mental states of its members anticipated, in significant ways, the theories developed decades later by sociological theorists. The mysterious character he calls "the man of the crowd," a wanderer whose movements through the cityscape allow Poe to map its gathering places and its corridors—this otherwise inscrutable figure is also "the type and the genius of deep crime."[28]

It was not until the last decades of the nineteenth century, though, that sociologists and reformers—writers like Jacob Riis, W. E. B. Du Bois, and William Dean Howells—made the case for thinking about crime as an effect of ill-conceived urban geographies. Earlier generations had fixed their attention on innate depravity or the aberrant mind. The modern school adapted the analytic methods of the social sciences and the technology of the camera to expose the overcrowded, neglected slums of the swelling cities as breeding grounds of crime. "They are shiftless, destructive, and stupid," Jacob Riis wrote of New York's impoverished slumdwellers in 1890; "in a word, they are what the tenements have made them."[29] Riis and his contemporaries argued that crime was best understood as an effect of structural conditions, not of character. The history of this thesis is more than familiar to social scientists and historians, and literary scholars have long understood its connection to the rise of realism in the arts. But if critics have said almost all there is to say about urban sociology and realism, as diagnostic discourses, what remains to be explored is their negative image—the fantasies of hygienic spaces that were inspired by these encounters with decay.

From every depiction of a crime scene there rises, like an angel, an idealized picture of what this space had been before its violation, or of what it could become if it were scoured clean: an inviolate, secure home, a cheerful public meeting place for friends and neighbors, a street humming with the circulation of traffic and goods. Riis proposed that charity and wiser neighborhood planning could solve the crisis of the tenements. Indeed,

Riis looks like the most moderate of reformers, even a conservative, when his proposals are compared to those of the urban planners of the first half of the twentieth century—Ebenezer Howard in England, Le Corbusier in France, Daniel Burnham and, later, Robert Moses in the United States—who took the conditions of crime and social disintegration as the occasion to dream up their "garden cities," their "radiant cities," their "cities beautiful." Although they disagreed profoundly on matters of style, all of these men envisioned building a safer, more sanitary society through the vast reorganization of urban geography. Their designs have been called "spaces of negation which seem the promise of freedom."[30] They called for opening up the city's dark zones to light and air. They drew up schemes for the rationalization of traffic. They razed clutter. They partitioned and segregated the urban world. In all these ways, their projects for "urban renewal" prompted governments and developers to try out spatial and architectural approaches to the problem of crime.[31]

The plans didn't work. Instead, things only seemed to be getting worse. By the middle of the twentieth century, the large-scale reorganization of urban space by modernist designers had itself come to be identified as the source of crime. In *The Death and Life of Great American Cities* (1961), Jane Jacobs charged the city planners with having created vacant, unwelcoming urban spaces where violence was sure to fester. The utopianists behind urban renewal, Jacobs argued, had attempted to impose order on the city from above, to force its intricate and subtle form into an abstract elegance; they had been so preoccupied with urban decay that they had never taken the trouble to study how a healthy city sustained itself. "To build city districts that are custom made for easy crime is idiotic. Yet that is what we do."[32] The radiant city of Le Corbusier, Jacobs wrote, was like "a wonderful mechanical toy"— charming in its design but of no practical value in the living, working world. Severing the manifold connections that sustained the city's life, planners like Moses had created great voids, where nothing but crime was likely to happen.

Perhaps no writer has so eloquently expressed the consequences of large-scale urban planning on affective life at street level:

> The first thing to understand is that the public peace—the sidewalk and street peace—of cities is not kept primarily by the police, necessary as police are. It is kept primarily by an intricate, almost unconscious network of voluntary controls and standards among the people themselves, enforced by the people themselves. In some city

areas . . . the keeping of public sidewalk law and order is left almost entirely to the police and special guards. Such places are jungles. No amount of police can enforce civilization where the normal, casual enforcement of it has broken down.[33]

Hoping to preserve what remained of an older cityscape, Jacobs foresaw that, as it disappeared, more and more police, more and more elaborate systems of surveillance and enforcement, more and more naked force would be required to do the work of safekeeping that had once been done organically and semiconsciously by ordinary citizens.

There is some nostalgia in Jacobs's vision of the self-policing neighborhood, perhaps even a touch of imperialism in her invocations of "civilization" and the "jungle," but Jacobs and the new urbanists, who developed her ideas into models of city planning, were no reactionaries. Like the turn-of-the-century sociologists, they rejected the view that crime expressed the racial inferiority or cultural vices of minority populations. And Jacobs laughed off Riis's Prohibitionist anxieties about rum houses and stale beer dives, too; she described the famous White Horse Tavern in New York's Greenwich Village, for instance, as a warm gathering place that kept the street safe by keeping it full of people. Showing no respect for those who associated crime with secularization, Jacobs compared the White Horse to a church. This kind of urbanism loved the lively diversity of the modern city.

For all of its cultural progressivism, though, Jacobs's critique of large-scale, government-directed planning turned out to have something in common with the neoliberal assault on the welfare state. The building and management of urban space, Jacobs had argued, was best handled not by government bureaucrats or central planners but by the "casual," organic forces of social interaction. Jacobs, drawing from the lexicon of democracy, would invoke the self-governing power of "the people themselves." The neoliberals would look instead to the capitalist marketplace, with its invisible hand. Within just a few years, the right-wing economist Martin Anderson, in *The Federal Bulldozer* (1964), would be aligning himself with the attack on urban renewal projects in order to make his case for "free enterprise" solutions to the urban crisis.[34] Jacobs is not to blame, of course. As David Harvey argues, the actual transformation of the cityscape in the postmodern period involved "pandering to the rich and the private consumer rather than to the poor and to public needs" in ways that "scarcely [favored] an outcome that meets Jacobs's objections" to modernism.[35] She could hardly have foreseen how her arguments would be absorbed into policies that cut funding to virtually all institutions of urban welfare and waited for the market to save the city—a story whose dismal ending has been written in recent obituaries for urban life like Carlo Rotella's *October Cities*, Mike Davis's *Dead Cities*, and Charlie LeDuff's *Detroit: An American Autopsy*.[36]

Meanwhile, the deregulation of the economy and the dismantling of the midcentury welfare state would be accompanied by the construction of a vast prison network, which, while unperceived by the casual consumer of urban space, came to seem necessary to the preservation of unbroken windows and storefront commerce. When the modernist planners of the welfare state were chased from the scene, and when the city failed magically to police itself, Giuliani, Bratton, and a militarized New York Police Department stepped into the breach. From the sanitizing destruction of the tenements to the vast housing projects that turned the resources of architectural modernism to the purposes of the welfare state—all of this would be a part of the prehistory of mass incarceration. Today's warehouse prisons, often erected in rural zones hundreds of miles away from the urban center, are the true successors to midcentury urban renewal's housing projects and monuments to civic life.

The crucial endeavor for a critique of the system's urban-spatial imaginary, then, would be to understand how the ongoing urban crisis of the neoliberal era, from the late 1970s up to the very recent past, came to be seen most of all as a problem of crime, a condition of insecurity in public space to be addressed by police and prisons. The problem would be to understand, in other words, how governments and publics came to think about crime less as a transgression against divine law or the social contract to be met with just punishment, less as an effect of poverty to be managed by the welfare state, and more as a disturbance in the landscape, especially the cityscape—to analyze how the concept of crime was expanded so that institutions designed for criminal justice could serve the much broader program of spatial reorganization. This line of inquiry would lead away from narrative, which for a quarter century or more has served as the key link in the interdisciplinary configuration known as Law and Literature. It would turn away from a Durkheimian model of punishment as a ritual for the reparation of community and the legitimation of state authority, away from the Frankfurt School's critique of a hegemonic culture industry. Its business, instead, would be to excavate ways of thinking about the spaces of social life that are hardly present to consciousness. Ultimately it would seek to explain how the vagrant in the park or the dealer on the corner came to be imagined as a disturbance that could best be eliminated through the construction of warehouses of incapacitation on a vast scale.

These are serious changes in critical orientation, but if the social scientists are right in their argument that the prison system has transformed the very character of the state, then some deep reconsideration is probably in order. In particular, it seems unlikely that this new system, redefining the missions of government in relation to populations and territories, would leave intact an earlier period's public sphere. Today, the prison is sensationally visible in popular culture as it has never been before. Cable television offers a continuous stream of documentaries, dramas, and other genres ranging in seriousness from *The Wire* to *Lockdown* and *Orange Is the New Black*. And yet, as Michelle Brown has argued with great ethical force, these representations tend to function as spectacle; they participate in a kind of sensationalism that reinforces the spectator's moral distance from the realities of pain and the political economies of state violence.[37] Those of us who wish to protest the prison confront a system so vast, so ingrained in the common sense of life under neoliberalism, that it requires no ritual reaffirmation—so uncontroversial that it can permit almost any representation of itself, including stories of wrongful imprisonment and martyrdom, as it continues its quiet and inexorable expansion.

I am not arguing that the prison system is *not* propped up, now and then, by the propaganda of harsh justice. Nor am I rehearsing Foucault's well-known critique of humanitarian reform, which showed how the ideals of mercy and rehabilitation served, paradoxically, to reinforce and expand the prison regime. What I am suggesting is that the prison system may no longer need to legitimate itself by appeal to either vengeance or rehabilitation—that it no longer depends on any theory of justice at all. In a profound sense, the prison is not an instrument of punishment anymore. It is a warehouse, as Jimmy Santiago Baca says. Perhaps, then, dissent from the ideology of harsh justice can be joined to the analysis of spatial injustice, a critical research program into the image-world of urban insecurity.[38] If we want to see how mass incarceration works its way into the social imaginary, how it takes hold in such a fundamental way that there almost seems to be no alternative, we will need to do more than critique the speeches of tough-on-crime politicians, the rants of reactionary pundits, or the sensational representations of crime and vengeance in the latest blockbuster. The insecure imagination is to be discovered, instead, in the background: in every nightmare of broken windows, in every fantasy of secure communities.

Notes

1. Jimmy Santiago Baca, *Immigrants in Our Own Land* (Baton Rouge: Louisiana State University Press, 1979), 43.

2. Malcolm M. Feeley and Jonathan Simon, "The New Penology: Notes on the Emerging Strategy of Corrections and Its Implications," *Criminology* 30:4 (1992) 449–74, 455.

3. Some scholars have raised doubts about the "new penology" thesis. For a critique, see Leonidas K. Cheliotis, "How Iron Is the Iron Cage of New Penology?: The Role of Human Agency in the Implementation of Criminal Justice Policy," *Punishment and Society* 8:3 (July 2006): 313–40.

4. Feeley and Simon, "The New Penology," 451.

5. Michel Foucault, "What Is Critique?," in *The Politics of Truth*, ed. Sylvère Lotringer, trans. Lysa Hochroth and Catherine Porter (Los Angeles: Semiotext[e], 2007), 41–81, 62.

6. There is, by now, a substantial scholarly literature on the rise of mass incarceration. My account is informed by Christian Parenti, *Lockdown America: Police and Prisons in the Age of Crisis* (London: Verso, 1999); Marie Gottschalk, *The Prison and the Gallows: The Politics of Mass Incarceration in America* (Cambridge: Cambridge University Press, 2006); Jonathan Simon, *Governing through Crime: How the War on Crime Transformed American Democracy and Created a Culture of Fear* (New York: Oxford University Press, 2009); and Robert Perkinson, *Texas Tough: The Rise of America's Prison Empire* (New York: Picador, 2010).

7. On the transition from plantation to prison farm, see especially David M. Oshinsky, *Worse than Slavery: Parchman Farm and the Ordeal of Jim Crow Justice* (New York: Free Press, 1996).

8. The concepts of correction and vengeance in imprisonment, associated with images of the imprisoned self as either a rehabilitated subject or an object of dehumanizing violence, are at the center of my cultural history of the penitentiary system, *The Prison and the American Imagination* (New Haven, CT: Yale University Press, 2009).

9. Francis Allen. *The Decline of the Rehabilitative Ideal: Penal Policy and Social Purpose* (New Haven, CT: Yale University Press, 1981).

10. James Q. Whtiman, *Harsh Justice: Criminal Punishment and the Widening Divide between America and Europe*. (Oxford: Oxford University Press, 2003).

11. Id. at 56.

12. Feeley and Simon, "The New Penology," 454.

13. Ruth Wilson Gilmore, *Golden Gulag: Prisons, Surplus, Crisis, and Opposition in Globalizing California* (Berkeley: University of California Press, 2007), 26.

14. Id. at 114.

15. Id. at 14.

16. Feeley and Simon, "The New Penology," 458.

17. Sharon Dolovich, "Exclusion and Control in the Carceral State," *Berkeley Journal of Criminal Law* 16:2 (2011) 259–339, 260–61. Dolovich draws a contrast between this "exclusion and control" penology and older strategies of retribution and rehabilitation.

18. On the legal and ideological connections between inmates in the contemporary prison system and indefinite detention in American war prisons, see Colin Dayan, *The Story of Cruel and Unusual* (Boston: Boston Review Books/MIT Press, 2007). On the proliferation of war metaphors in the rhetoric of criminal justice, see Simon, *Governing through Crime*.

19. Loïc Wacquant, *Prisons of Poverty*, expanded edition (Minneapolis: University of Minnesota Press, 2009), and *Punishing the Poor: The Neoliberal Government of Social Instability* (Durham, NC: Duke University Press, 2009). I offer a more extended discussion of Wacquant's interventions in critical prison studies in my "Spaces of Punitive Violence," *Criticism* 55:1 (Winter 2013): 161–68.

20. Wacquant, *Prisons*, 69.

21. Wacquant, *Punishing*, xvi.

22. Wacquant, *Prisons*, 5.

23. See Michelle Alexander, *The New Jim Crow: Mass Incarceration in the Age of Colorblindness* (New York: New Press, 2010), and Khalil Gibran Muhammad, *The Condemnation of Blackness: Race, Crime, and the Making of Modern Urban America* (Cambridge, MA: Harvard University Press, 2011).

24. Wacquant, *Prisons*, 16.

25. Mike Davis, *Cities of Quartz: Excavating the Future in Los Angeles* (New York: Verso, 1990), 223.

26. Edward W. Soja, *Seeking Spatial Justice* (Minneapolis: University of Minnesota Press), 2010.

27. Michel Foucault, *Discipline and Punish: The Birth of the Prison*, trans. Alan Sheridan (New York: Vintage, 1977).

28. The starting point for this discussion might be Walter Benjamin's examination of Poe, Baudelaire, and urban space in *Charles Baudelaire: A Lyric*

Poet in the Age of High Capitalism (London: Verso, 1983). On the emergence of New York as a major urban and industrial center in the antebellum period, see Edward K. Spann, *The New Metropolis: New York City, 1840–1857* (New York: Columbia University Press, 1981). On the popular discourses of urban transformation in the same era, see Paul Boyer, *Urban Masses and Moral Order in America, 1820–1920* (Cambridge, MA: Harvard University Press, 1978).

29. Jacob A. Riis, *How the Other Half Lives* (1890; New York: Penguin, 1997).

30. Richard Sennett, *The Conscience of the Eye: The Design and Social Life of Cities* (New York: Knopf, 1990), 173.

31. See Samuel Zipp, *Manhattan Projects: The Rise and Fall of Urban Renewal in Cold War New York* (New York: Oxford University Press, 2010).

32. Jane Jacobs, *The Death and Life of Great American Cities* (1961; New York: Vintage, 1992), 23, 31.

33. Jacobs, *Death and Life*, 31–32.

34. Martin Anderson, *The Federal Bulldozer: A Critical Analysis of Urban Renewal, 1949–1962* (Cambridge, MA: MIT Press, 1964). On Jacobs and Anderson, see Zipp, *Manhattan Projects*, 367–68. On Jacobs and neoliberalism more generally, see Brian Tochterman, "Theorizing Neoliberal Urban Development: A Genealogy from Richard Florida to Jane Jacobs," *Radical History Review* 112 (Winter 2012): 65–87.

35. David Harvey, *The Condition of Postmodernity: An Enquiry into the Origins of Cultural Change* (Cambridge, UK: Blackwell, 1990), 77.

36. Carlo Rotella, *October Cities: The Redevelopment of Urban Literature* (Berkeley: University of California Press, 1998); Mike Davis, *Dead Cities and Other Tales* (New York: New Press, 2002); Charlie LeDuff, *Detroit: An American Autopsy* (New York: Penguin, 2013).

37. Michelle Brown, *The Culture of Punishment: Prison, Society, and Spectacle* (New York: New York University Press, 2009).

38. Here, again, I draw from Soja, *Seeking Spatial Justice*.

Punishment as an Act of the Imagination

Leo Katz

American prison sentences are long—longer than most judges would like them to be, whatever their political stripe. Or so it has seemed to me when I have talked to them at judicial seminars. Occasionally a judge makes public his disapproval; sometimes by telling the defendant how much he hates to be doing it. But for the most part the judges submit; they see it as their role obligation. Rarely do they think to resign to avoid having to impose these sentences.

How confident should they feel that they are doing the right thing by suppressing their unease and doing what the law demands of them? How worried should they be that they might someday somehow find themselves called upon to answer for their actions? In a practical sense, they probably do not worry at all. But perhaps in some other sense? What exactly I mean by that question—whether they should be worried about what they are doing, at least in some other than the practical sense—will become clearer once I try to answer it.

I approach the question in a decidedly old-fashioned, law-professorial style by looking at it through the lens of a very specific case.[1] The case arose in post–World War II West Germany and involved the prosecution of a former judge from Communist East Germany who had fled to the West. We are not told his name: he is merely referred to as "the Accused." Let's therefore call him "A." While serving as a judge in Communist East Germany, A. was asked to pass judgment on several Jehovah's Witnesses, who had, claiming the status of conscientious objectors, refused to do their obligatory military service in the East German People's Army. They were charged with various treason-related offenses: espionage, incitement to war, and something else one might best translate as seditious libel. The gist of the charge was of course quite simply that they were dissenters. As was customary, the judge presiding over this case received very firm and specific instructions from Communist Party higher-ups as to the sentences he was to mete out, which he did. The sentences ranged from three-and-a-half to ten years. Not too long after doing all of this, the judge decided he had had enough of living in East Germany. Not much is known about the nature of his disenchantment. But the West German court's opinion suggests that his distaste for what he was asked to do as an East German judge had at least something to do with the falling-out and with his decision to flee to the West, which was then still easy to do since the Berlin Wall was not yet up. Once in the West, however, he was surprised to find himself the subject of a prosecution by West German authorities for his actions as an East German judge, specifically for imposing those draconian sentences on Jehovah's Witnesses.

How can one legally and morally justify the West Germans' prosecution of this East German judge? And are there any interesting lessons the case holds for the situation of an American judge who finds himself imposing sentences that he too finds too draconian? Should an American judge be worried, even if not in a practical sense, but at least in a moral sense, and as a matter of legal theory as it were, that his position is perhaps not so different from that of this East German judge?

There are, I think, chiefly three grounds why one might balk at the idea of prosecuting this East German judge for the harsh sentences he imposed on those Jehovah's Witnesses—and three reasons why an American judge is likely to scoff at the idea that he could even in theory be held accountable for imposing excessively harsh sentences on criminal offenders. Each is interesting in its own right. Let us examine what they are and how they stand up to scrutiny.

I.

The first and simplest ground for balking at the judges' prosecution is that there seems to be no legal basis for it. What sort of law would one base oneself on? The judge was applying the law of the state in which he lived, which seems the only relevant law under the circumstances. And even if one felt free to impose the law of the state to which he fled, West Germany, it still isn't clear what sort of crime he should then be charged with if all he did was impose the law of the state he happened to be serving?

What the former East German judge was in fact charged with were two offenses. The first offense was something that might best be translated as false imprisonment, which seems at least comprehensible if perplexing. To be sure, what he did was imprison his victims, but on what basis can we call it *false* imprisonment, when it was pursuant to East German law? The second offense he was charged with will seem even more perplexing because it simply does not exist in Anglo-American law. It is called *Rechtsbeugung*, literally, "bending the law." The offense of false imprisonment in fact was prosecuted as a special instance of *Rechtsbeugung*. But what in the world is *Rechtsbeugung*? The translation I gave, bending the law, does not seem to shed much light on it. In what sense was this East German judge guilty of bending the law?[2]

Rechtsbeugung is a crime that has been part of the German criminal code for several centuries. What it was primarily intended to cover was something quite straightforward: a judge's willful misapplication of law. We don't really have such an offense in the United States, but there is nothing patently absurd about the idea of such an offense. An example offered by one of the law's leading commentators is that the municipal supplier of electricity brings an action against a customer who has refused to pay his electric bill. The customer argues to the court that he does not need to pay his bill because the energy is supplied from a nuclear power plant, and nuclear power plants were immoral. The judge presiding over this case turns out to be a thorough-going eccentric and sides with the customer. Nuclear power is immoral, he agrees, and the customer does not have to pay his bill. Naturally the electric company will have no trouble getting this decision reversed. But the matter need not end there. A prosecution for the willful misapplication of law, *Rechtsbeugung*, could easily be pursued here.[3] Now clearly the case of the East German judge is not like this at all. So how could he be found guilty of *Rechtsbeugung*?

The crime of *Rechtsbeugung* was expanded in scope in the wake of World War II. At that time the authorities were casting about for a way to prosecute former Nazi judges and prosecutors who had enforced particularly immoral laws, having to do with miscegenation, involuntary euthanasia of the feeble-minded, and of course the infamous Nuremberg race laws. The way in which they did this was to interpret *Rechtsbeugung*, misapplication of law, to cover not just cases like that of the electric company but also cases in which the law was being faithfully applied but in which the law that was being so faithfully applied was an extremely immoral one, such as the Nuremberg race laws. Such laws were deemed not to have been valid laws in the first place. Hence their enforcement was a misapplication of law. This was the theory under which the East German judge was being prosecuted as well. The draconian sentences, though consistent with East German law, involved such a sufficiently immoral act that they ceased being legal.

However sympathetic an American judge might feel, purely at a gut level, to the prosecution of former Nazi or Communist judges, this theory of liability is going to leave him nothing short of horrified. Lots of people feel that way. This is what is sometimes known as the problem of transitional justice. After the defeat of the Third Reich, but even more after the collapse of Communism, many commentators thought that the very idea of going after those who enforced the extremely unjust laws of those extremely unjust regimes could not really be given a proper legal or moral justification. With regard to the Third Reich, this was probably a minority view, but with regard to Communism, it became the majority view, bordering on consensus.

But there have been a few very vigorous and very thoughtful dissenters from that near consensus, two of which I want to briefly discuss. The first of these dissents, by Eric Posner and Adrian Vermeule, appeared in an article in the *Harvard Law Review*, revealingly titled "Transitional Justice as Ordinary Justice."[4] The second appeared in a compact, pamphlet-like book by the German criminal law scholar Wolfgang Naucke whose unwieldy German title roughly translates as "the doctrinal privileging of state-sponsored criminality."[5]

The heart of Posner and Vermeule's argument is that situations of transitional justice are not as extraordinary as they appear at first. The transition from one kind of legal regime to another, from Nazi or Communist justice to Western style democracy, is just an extreme case of the kind of changes all legal regimes are undergoing all the time. Law never stays the same, and it is an everyday event in all legal regimes that yesterday's key decision makers are being judged by standards that were only created today. In other words, according to Posner and Vermeule,

> [The] theorists of transitional justice commonly err by treating regime transitions as a self-contained subject, thereby denying the relevance or utility of comparisons and analogies between regime transitions, on the one hand, and the wide variety of transitions that occur in consolidated democracies, on the other. Sometimes this error ap-

pears as an explicit claim, as when Judith Shklar writes of Nuremberg and other transitional trials that "all analogies drawn from municipal law . . . are unconvincing." Sometimes it takes the form of an implicit but necessary assumption in an argument, as when Jon Elster examines the "moral dilemmas" of transitional justice without reference to obvious analogies from domestic law. Against this view, we claim that legal and political transitions lie on a continuum, of which regime transitions are merely an endpoint.[6]

Let's make this more concrete. Those who object to condemning yesterday's judges under laws newly minted today do so on several grounds. Most importantly, there is the norm against retroactive laws. But there also is a slew of more practical worries, having to do with the fact that any effort to rectify the wrongs of deceased unjust regimes would deprive the state of much needed skilled personnel, that it would unduly unsettle property rights and wreak havoc in the market place as a result, that it would congest the courts, that it would cast a pall over the reputations of many innocents who would likely find themselves the targets of unjustified prosecutions, not to mention blackmail, and that it was bound to result in an indefensibly selective choice of prosecution targets. To this Posner and Vermeule reply that the identical problems arise every day, as a result of legal changes that no legal regime can avoid.

Start with retroactivity in criminal cases, where ostensibly it is most frowned upon. Yet "[e]ven in the criminal setting," note Posner and Vermeule, "legislatures and courts have ample leeway to adjust the ex post facto prohibition in pragmatic style. Legislatures may retroactively extend criminal statutes of limitations so long as the limitations period has not already run." Criminal defenses are often narrowed or expanded without regard to the prohibition. Or the government might skirt the prohibition by declining "to describe the prescribed sanctions as 'penal', or by describing the new law as 'procedural' rather than substantive.'"[7] Perhaps the bluntest, simplest, and commonest way of dodging the prohibition is for a court to declare that something has been the law all along, but just not been properly recognized as such, in other words by the very quotidian practice of engaging in law making under the guise of law finding.

Retroactivity in *non*criminal cases is even more commonplace. Take the way property rights are handled. Respect for property rights, which amounts to a respect for certain kinds of settled expectations, is a kind of antiretroactivity norm, but one which is mostly honored in the breach, because property rights are in fact far more uncertain than the official rhetoric about them acknowledges. As Posner and Vermeule note,

> [i]n domestic law, property rights are always uncertain; their precise contours are unknown and cannot be determined at reasonable cost. An owner's title to personal property is vulnerable to a potential claim by a prior owner from whom the property was stolen. Title in real estate is vulnerable to adverse possession if the owner does not occupy the property. Title to land in many parts of the United States is vulnerable to a potential claim by an Indian tribe whose land was taken from them illegally by state governments or by the federal government. Title—or, more accurately, the value of property under title—is vulnerable to uncompensated regulatory takings or ordinary takings that are inadequately compensated under the law. Indeed, nothing prevents the federal government and state governments from raising property taxes or any other general taxes to an extent that would undermine the value of holding particular kinds of property. Title would be preserved, but as an empty form; the value of property is qualified by the risk of changes in the tax law, as well as in regulatory laws.[8]

In short, the quasi-retroactive character of prosecuting someone for *Rechtsbeugung* when he enforced a law we now judge to have been egregiously immoral is not too different, argue Posner and Vermeule, from what we do every day in the course of ordinary, supposedly nonretroactive justice. But,

> [i]f transitional justice is continuous with ordinary justice, then there is no reason to treat transitional justice measures as presumptively suspect on either moral or institutional grounds, unless we are to treat the justice systems of consolidated liberal democracies as suspect as well. . . . The dominant instinct among academic commentators on transitional justice is to condemn transitional justice measures wholesale, either on the ground that transitional measures are retroactive and thus inherently illiberal, or on the closely associated ground that new regimes should reserve their energies exclusively for forward-looking measures of state building, economic growth, and the development of political cohesion. . . . But this posture is

no more coherent than would be a parallel condemnation of all the measures that legal systems ordinarily use to manage change.⁹

Consider next Wolfgang Naucke's argument in support of prosecutions for *Rechtsbeugung*. He makes an argument that is broadly similar and yet distinct from Posner and Vermeule's. He draws attention to the fact that our criminal law is a far less monolithic structure than it appears at first. In fact criminal law divides itself rather naturally, he points out, into several "tracks" (*Spuren*), each of which is subject to a variety of rather different norms, and the norm against retroactivity is entirely irrelevant to many of these tracks. The main track of the criminal law, the one we immediately think of when we think of the subject, is indeed governed by a strong retroactivity norm, the prohibitions against murder, rape, theft, and their more modern variants, securities fraud, insider trading, and so on. But there is also the track that deals with crimes by minors or the criminally insane, which is governed by a rather different set of norms than the first track. Yet a third track deals with the use of illegal drugs, which in Germany is a distinct body of law, most conspicuously distinguished by its procedural rules, as well as some more minor tracks, such as the one dealing with premature abortions, or the one dealing with crimes calling for "restorative justice" style remedies. Why then be so reluctant, Naucke asks, to create a new track for wrongdoers who utilized the machinery of state for their criminal actions? Moreover aren't there in fact excellent reasons for ignoring the retroactivity norm in this context since it seems so singularly ill suited for this kind of wrongdoing? It would allow those making criminal use of the machinery of state to essentially bootstrap themselves into protection that they don't deserve by making legal what so clearly should not be legal.

I don't really want to claim that I find either Posner and Vermeule's or Naucke's arguments persuasive from beginning to end. They both suffer from the problem that the very type of argument they present can easily be run in reverse and be used to present a quite powerful case against punishing the officials of a wicked regime. This is especially true of Posner and Vermeule's version of the argument. They say that cases of retroactive punishment in the transitional context are only variations on retroactive justice in nontransitional contexts. Now suppose we took as our starting point some uncontroversial instance of a retroactive punishment we disapprove of. Suppose that a new statute suddenly declared the consumption of alcohol illegal and that all who consumed alcohol in the recent past were found guilty of violating it, even though the statute had not yet been enacted when they did their drinking. No one would want to support *that*. Now we can argue, Posner/Vermeule style, that what we are doing to that East German judge is perfectly continuous with this, only less egregious for a variety of reasons, but that that basic of the two cases similarity establishes at least a presumption against holding him liable for something that was legal in the place and at the time that he did it. I don't consider this a knockdown rebuttal of Posner and Vermeule, but it does suggest caution in drawing sweeping conclusions from such continuity-type arguments.

Where does this leave our East German judge and his American counterpart? I believe with a lot weaker ground for complaining about the lawlessness or immorality of being held liable for imposing draconian sanctions that are mandated today and may be decried tomorrow than one might have thought at first glance.

II.

There is a second reason why an American judge is going to look askance at the idea of punishing that East German judge for meting out disproportionate punishment, and it has to do with the very concept of disproportionate punishment. How much concrete content does the idea really have, he will ask. He will distrust the German court's confident judgment that a three- to ten-year sentence for conscientious objectors is so draconian as to render its imposition automatically unlawful. Where do these disproportionality judgments come from, he is likely to ask. Why is ten years too much, whereas six months would not be? He would more readily understand the court's taking the position that punishing the conscientious objectors *at all* is automatically unlawful (if, that is, he can set aside the objections discussed in the previous section), but a quantitative judgment about the appropriate amount of punishment will seem to him inherently unprincipled.

And yet, what he is almost surely overlooking is that we have far more precise intuitions about just deserts than he realizes. This is something first shown by two sociologists, Marvin Wolfgang and Thorsten Sellin, who had the ingenious idea of using the tools of a somewhat obscure branch of psychology known as psychophysics to uncover our intuitions about penal desert. The initial concern of psychophysics was to lay bare our perceptions of various physical dimensions, like weight, size, color, taste, and so on. It was inspired by the observation that when you ask someone to assess the relative weights of several objects, the first of which might weigh one pound, the second two pounds, the third three pounds, and so on, most people will not judge the second object to be twice as heavy as the first, the third to be three times as heavy, and so on. Typically, they will judge the second object a little less than twice as heavy and the third object a little less than three times as heavy. This is known as Weber's law. (The Weber in question is not the German sociologist Max Weber, but the psychologist Eugen Weber, also incidentally German.) In the process of getting people to express their judgments about perceived increases in weight, size, and so on, psychophysicists developed various rating tools. In addition to just asking for a numerical assessment (Is it twice as heavy? Three times as heavy?), they would ask subjects to adjust the intensity of the light of a lamp as an alternative way of expressing the perceived weight differences. Or they might ask them to press something called a dynamometer with the degree of effort corresponding to the increase in weight or size of the objects being evaluated, as well as other tricks of the same type.[10]

Wolfgang and Sellin were interested in getting a sense of people's perceived severity of a crime and to compare it with the law's treatment of the criminals who had committed those crimes. They would therefore ask the subjects to rate the severity of the offense on a scale of one to one hundred. "Sometimes they asked them to compare every offense to some standard offense and state whether it was twice, ten times, or perhaps only half or one-tenth as serious as that standard. Sometimes they asked them to press a 'dynamometer' with the degree of intensity that best expressed how strongly they felt."[11] They were in this way able to assign a severity score to each offense and to compare it with the actual punishment typically given in such cases. What they found is that if one rank orders offenses according to their severity score, one ends up with a list that almost perfectly matches the rank ordering of the sentences actually meted out for such cases. We can therefore see that we seem to have rather extensive intuitions about just penal desert and that these intuitions are in fact reflected in our laws.

Now there is a further interesting wrinkle to all this. One thing that troubled psychologists in looking at Wolfgang and Sellin's results was the fact that although the rank ordering of the offenses by their severity score matched rather closely the rank ordering of the offenses according to the actual punishment they received, there was a certain bothersome mismatch as well. If offense x received a severity score that was two and a half times as severe as offense y, that did not mean that the punishment was therefore two and a half times as severe. It simply meant that x would typically be punished more severely than y. That suggested a certain disturbing imprecision in our judgments about penal desert.

But then it occurred to someone that it was actually a mistake to simply compare the increase in the severity score of an offense with the increase in punishment. What really should be compared was the increase in the severity score of an offense with *our perception* of the increase in severity of the actual punishment. In other words, we need to apply the same tools used to assess the perceived seriousness of a crime to assess the perceived seriousness of the punishment meted out. Once one does this and assigns a severity score for a given amount of punishment, one will then discover that the two severity scores match up with startling precision. In other words, if crime x is judged two and a half times as severe as y, then the punishment typically given for x will turn out to be judged two and a half times as severe as the punishment typically given for y. Punishments turn out to fit their crimes like a glove, though as I noted elsewhere, more like a glove that is purchased off the rack as opposed to one that is tailor made.[12]

This particular worry about the West Germans' assessment of disproportionate character of the East German judge's punishment thus turns out to be ill founded. Desert judgments are not vacuous or conclusory. They build on widely shared and surprisingly robust intuitions.

III.

There is at least one more ground on which one might question the rightness of prosecuting the East German judge, and this is the ground the West German court took most seriously. For a crime to really be a crime, the defendant must have the right mental state, or mens rea, in the common law's terminology, and the West German court acknowledged that there were problems with that in regard to this defendant. Arguably, said the court, he lacked the requisite consciousness of wrongdoing.

This is going to sound very odd to American ears, because Anglo-American law generally does not require anything like a consciousness of wrongdoing for someone to be guilty of a crime. That, after all, is what the precept about ignorance of law not being a defense is all about: One need not understand the illegality, or immorality, of what one has done to be liable so long as one acted with the requisite intention (or knowledge or recklessness or negligence, as the case may be) with regard to the various actions that constitute the conduct portion (or actus reus, in the common law's terminology) of the crime. If someone intends to take another person's property, we are not interested in whether he thought he was doing the right thing or not, only whether he realized he was taking someone else's property and did so with the intention of keeping it. German law however is different. Ignorance of law is a defense there. If for some reason the thief believes he is doing the right thing, perhaps even for as outrageous seeming a reason as that he believes private property is immoral, that will often exonerate him. To be sure, even in Anglo-American law there are exceptions to the ignorance-of-law-is-no-defense principle, but none of those are likely to apply here.

Now the West German court eventually concluded that the former East German judge did in fact have the requisite consciousness of wrongdoing, ironically, on the ground that he decided to flee to West Germany. He did so, surmised the court (but left it for further exploration by the trial court), because he felt qualms about all the dirty stuff he had been asked to do by the East German regime, of which the punishment of Jehovah's Witnesses was probably the most disturbing instance.

But the court is making the mens rea problem much too easy for itself. While there is in fact a mental state problem here with convicting the judge, it is much more complicated than merely whether one wants to recognize ignorance of law a defense and whether this defendant was in fact ignorant of the law. Mental states operate in a much trickier fashion than is commonly acknowledged, and they do so especially with regard to the issue posed by this case, namely whether the defendant really engaged in (what the West German court essentially saw as) the crime of excessive punishment.

The best way to get at the deep issue raised here is with the help of some hypothetical cases posed in a seminal article by Larry Alexander, "The Doomsday Machine: Proportionality, Punishment and Prevention." Alexander begins by "asking the reader to consider an example commonly used by retributivists to demonstrate the concept of excessive punishment as violative of the principle of proportionality—the example of hanging pickpockets in Victorian England." Actually, he adds, "I don't really know or care if they did hang pickpockets, or cut off their hands, or what, but the example is a good one, fictitious or not."[13] Such punishment by common consensus is disproportionate, and many people would therefore regard it as off limits. Certainly retributivists would. And I suppose the German court that regarded a lengthy sentence for Jehovah's Witnesses as disproportionate would have a similar reaction to hanging pickpockets.

Alexander next asks us to consider a somewhat bizarre system of punishment that looks at first like the pickpocket scheme generalized to the point of absurdity: "Assume there is a super-sophisticated satellite that can detect all criminal acts and determine the mental state of the actors.... If the satellite finds that the actor knew his act was a crime, that he has no recognized excuse or justification for committing it, that he was not acting in the heat of passion or under duress, and that he was not too young, enfeebled, mentally unbalanced and so forth to be deemed without capacity to commit a crime—zaps him with a disintegration ray. Once the satellite detects the crime, it is impossible to prevent punishment of the criminal, no matter how merciful the authorities might feel.... The entire population is informed of the existence of the satellite and what it does."[14]

Alexander then makes the following observation: "At first the reader might feel that the Doomsday Machine [Alexander's term for the satellite] is indistinguishable from the practices of Victorian England, and so, for consistency's sake, answer that its punishment is excessive."[15] However, he claims, on closer consideration, it will turn out to be quite difficult to sustain the intuition that there is anything objectionable about such a Doomsday Machine.

To see why objections to the Doomsday Machine are not so easy to sustain, Alexander next asks us to consider the case of a

> man who keeps a moat to protect his castle (or an electric fence to protect his house); [one day] he receives a letter from someone who says that the first time the castle (house) is deserted he will attempt to enter it; and because he cannot swim (is not shockproof) his death will be on the owner's hands if the moat is not drained (the current is not turned off). Is there a duty to drain the moat (shut off the current) in order to avoid excessive punishment? And what if one hides his jewels on top of an unscalable cliff after having been told that the latter would attempt to climb it if the jewels were placed there? ... I might go on in my hypotheticals to drag out vicious dogs, crocodiles, and spring guns to protect persons from petty crimes, and pit these devices against petty criminals, whose common denominator is that they all know of certain consequences of their acts, know that their acts are illegal, are determined to proceed with them anyway, and are acting premeditatedly without any recognized legal excuse, justification or incapacity.... [The point of these examples is that most people] will not feel that these examples involve excessive punishment. Indeed, many are probably unsure whether the examples involve punishment at all. Perhaps only a few readers

will maintain that in these examples one has a duty to render a violation of one's rights reasonably safe in the face of a violator's threat of, in effect, suicide.[16]

But isn't that what the Doomsday Machine is like? Alexander continues: "[I]f these examples do not involve excessive punishment, then the Doomsday Machine does not mete out excessive punishment either. The structure of the Doomsday Machine hypothetical and the other hypotheticals is the same. A person bent on violating another's moral rights is fully aware of a condition that renders such an attempt life-threatening to him but not to others who might have an excuse or justification or who might be unaware of the dangerous condition. There is a trap, but it is only one for the wary. And once the violation occurs or reaches a certain stage, no human intervention will be effective to prevent the threat from being carried out."[17] The larger lesson Alexander draws from these examples is this:

> Once it is clear that it makes no difference whether the disproportionate harm befalls the criminal before or after he succeeds in violating another's rights, so long as he is threatened with the harm before he acts, we can see that the electric fence, the moat, the cliff, and so forth, on the one hand, and harsh criminal punishment administered by human beings on the other, as well as the Doomsday Machine programmed for either instantaneous zapping, are all related phenomena. They are all instances of the enterprise of prevention, an enterprise that I maintain appears to be morally justifiable when conducted according to certain principles, among which is NOT the principle of proportionality. The principles which are germane to proper conduct of the enterprise of prevention are the principle that requires that the person threatened with the harm have no right to engage in the conduct which triggers the harm (the wrongful act principle) and the principle that requires adequate notice of the threat before it may be carried out (the notice principle).[18]

Punishment, he says, needs to respect the proportionality principle, but the enterprise of prevention does not.

That prompts the question: What determines whether one is engaged in punishment or prevention? That would seem to largely depend on the mental state of the person inflicting this treatment. Does he consider himself to be engaged in the one or the other? Does he think of himself as meting out retribution or does he think he is simply preventing harm by installing a mechanism that inflicts harm on someone who tries to infringe on his rights? This would suggest that as long as the East German judge viewed himself as being engaged in the preventive enterprise, he might be entitled to avoid guilt because the proportionality principle simply does not apply to him.

To be sure, someone might well quarrel about the applicability of Alexander's lesson this way on several grounds, which on closer examination will not however turn out to hold much water. One might object, for instance, that the East German regime did not give adequate notice to wrongdoers about what might happen to them if they did not obey the law. But that's not very plausible. Admittedly, the rule of law, and the notice requirement more generally, were not held to be terribly important from a moral point of view, but in point of fact the regime wanted obedience and found that advertising its wishes very clearly and accompanying that with very palpable threats was the most effective way of doing so. Jehovah's Witnesses surely did have notice about what might be done to them if they did not comply. Moreover, I am not entirely sure that the notice requirement is in fact a prerequisite for Alexander's conclusion. Suppose the owner of the jewelry hid it in a snake pit but did not warn potential thieves about the presence of the snakes. It is not clear to me that that would make him liable so long as they were not entitled to go after those jewels.

One might also object that the East German regime was not simply seeking to protect its rights. But that is not so clear either. As even the West German court acknowledged, there was nothing inherently immoral about the East German conscription law. The only issue was the disproportionality of the sanction imposed for noncompliance.

One might object further that it makes a difference whether we install a Doomsday Machine or build a moat or electric fence and then let things take their course when the wrongdoer decides to trigger them or whether instead we actually fire and kill the wrongdoer when he has performed his wrong, *making ourselves act the part of the Doomsday Machine, the moat or the electric fence.* The timing, or sequencing, may well make more of a difference than Alexander acknowledges. Be that as it may, however, it does not affect the liability of the judge because he is not himself carrying out the execution. He is having his impact as indirectly as the owner of the electric fence or the moat.

Punishment as an Act of the Imagination 117

Now there is something quite strange about the fact that the way in which the judge conceptualizes his own actions should determine whether he was acting immorally, or illegally, or not. The philosopher who has most clearly pinpointed the oddity involved is Frederick Schick, in a book simply titled *Understanding Action*. Schick opens his book with a story involving George Orwell and the Spanish Civil War. Orwell "had gone out to a spot near the Fascist trenches from which he thought he might snipe at someone. He waited a long time without any luck. None of the enemy made an appearance. Then, at last, some disturbance took place, much shouting and blowing of whistles followed, and a man 'jumped out of the trench and ran along the parapet in full view. He was half-dressed and was holding up his trousers with both hands, as he ran. I refrained from shooting at him. . . . I did not shoot partly because of that detail about the trousers. I had come here to shoot Fascists; but a man holding up his trousers isn't a Fascist, he is visibly a fellow creatures, similar to yourself, and you don't feel like shooting at him.'"[19] Schick then asks, "Why did Orwell put down his gun? We have a general theory of action that ought to be of use to us here. The theory says that people's actions issue from their beliefs and desires, that to explain what someone did we need to know only what he believed and what he wanted. Suppose that some person wanted *this* and believed that to get it he had to do *that*. The belief and desire together were his reason, and the reasons a person has lead him to do what he does."[20] The Orwell story does not fit this theory.

> As Orwell tells it, he was ready to shoot. What he believed and what he wanted prompted him to do it, and he would in fact have fired if the man's trousers hadn't been down. Yet seeing the man half naked changed no beliefs that Orwell had. He had known all along that, under their pants, Fascists were like himself, that they were "fellow creatures." Nor did it change what he wanted. He had not wanted to shoot fellow creatures and he didn't now cease to want to shoot Fascists. But if his beliefs and desires were such as to lead him to shoot if it weren't for those pants, some other factor, neither a belief nor a desire, must be brought in to explain why he didn't. His reason for refraining from shooting can't just have been some belief and desire.[21]

The usual understanding of mens rea in the criminal law does not comport with this either. Instead it follows the traditional belief-desire theory so succinctly stated by Schick. The only thing that affects liability is a mistake that affects the beliefs and desires of a defendant. Not his "understanding" or "seeing" of what he is doing, which if Schick is right does in fact greatly affect what he will do. And Alexander's example is a nice morally relevant example of how this might happen. There is a relevant change in mens rea if the judge sees himself as engaged in the enterprise of prevention rather than retribution, and if he does, then the principle of proportionality becomes irrelevant.

This is an exceedingly peculiar state of affairs: a defendant is only guilty of an offense if he thinks of what he is doing in one way—as punishment—but not if he conceives of it in another way—as being part of the enterprise of prevention. Is this peculiarity peculiar to Alexander's example, or is there something more general going on here?

Let's begin by trying to see whether something like this can be found if we look beyond the enterprise of prevention. Are there, for instance, other quasi-punitive practices that operate like the enterprise of prevention: if the defendant thinks of them as being an instance punishment, he is guilty, but if he thinks of them in some other way, he is not. What might be candidates for this sort of thing? To search more efficiently, let's try to be clear what constitutes a quasi-punitive practice. Presumably any context in which disfavored conduct by one party legitimates painful repercussions by or in behalf of the other party might qualify. Let's examine a few such possibilities.

(1)Informal sanctions. We hold people responsible and subject them to sanctions outside the law through criticism and ostracism. Could this realm of informal sanctions function like the enterprise of prevention, such that if someone thinks of himself as being engaged in this particular enterprise, he becomes subject only to the norms of this particular enterprise by virtue of the fact that that is what he thinks he is doing?

Let's first note that the realm of informal sanctions is indeed interestingly different from the realm of formal sanctions. The norms that govern the attribution of responsibility in this context have been explored in an area of psychology known as attribution theory, whose foundational text is Fritz Heider's *The Psychology of Interpersonal Relations*.[22] Perhaps the most familiar finding from this area of psychology is the much-cited Fundamental Attribution Error,[23] which is our tendency to explain someone's actions by imputing to him certain dispositions rather than recognizing that the situation was one in which most people would act as he did. Now notice that lurking behind the idea of the Fundamental Attribution Error is an unarticulated assumption about the attribution of responsibility: namely that if the situation is one in which most people would misbehave as the defendant did, then that diminishes the responsibility we should attribute to him. The Fundamental Attribution Error is considered an error because most people make an erroneous factual assumption about how most folk would behave in certain situations. This of course is completely different from the norms of the criminal law, where the fact that the defendant acted as most people would under the circumstances does not count for much. To be sure, it is not entirely irrelevant. When someone pleads duress he can argue that a reasonable person would not have been able to resist and that involves an implicit appeal to the way in which most people would react to a situation. But that kind of argument only flies if the person making it was threatened with death or some approximation thereof. Simply yielding to temptation, when most people would have, will not suffice. (The exception may be certain cases of governmental entrapment, but those again are very special and circumscribed.)

We could say of the East German judge that he thought himself within this realm. He thought that the only criticism he was vulnerable to was that of informal, nonlegal sanctions, and hence probably judged himself to not have behaved so badly inasmuch as he did what most, or at least many, people in his situation would have done. Does this exonerate him? The argument has some force though not nearly as much as the preventive enterprise argument. So we have here at least a weak analogue to Alexander's phenomenon.

(2) Operant conditioning. Certain kinds of psychological treatment have an obvious quasi-punitive character, the kind of operant conditioning that employs negative reinforcers—the token economies that are used in reform schools and other places of rehabilitation. Rehabilitation is subject to its own sets of norms, restrictions on the circumstances in which someone may be subjected to rehabilitation and on the severity of the negative reinforcers that may be used. These are presumably the norms that govern what Naucke refers to as one of the nontraditional penal tracks, the one used to deal with minors and the insane.

What if the East German judge thought of himself as being engaged in this kind of rehabilitative enterprise? What if he viewed the treatment to which he subjected Jehovah's Witnesses as being this kind of reeducation? We still might disapprove, indeed we probably would, because our norms of rehabilitation probably would allow that kind of a sentence, but we would now be evaluating him differently and probably more leniently. Here then we may have a closer analogue to Alexander's pheneomon.

(3)Other legal contexts: contracts. Certain legal contexts have an obviously quasi-punitive structure. Consider the law of contracts. If someone does not do what the contract requires, he is "punished" by being subjected to the appropriate remedies, typically the obligation to pay expectation damages. The law of contracts, like the enterprise of prevention, has its own set of norms, by which this quasi-punishment is administered, norms that are not the same as those of the criminal law. For instance, the person who breaches a contract need not have exhibited fault to become liable. Whether his breach of the promise was intentional, knowing, reckless, or negligent is typically irrelevant. He promised something but did not perform. Hence he is liable. There are exceptions, to be sure. There are the defenses of impossibility, changed circumstances, frustration of purpose, duress, and others. But they are far more limited than the fault requirements of the criminal law. There are subtler differences too between contractual and punitive norms: the causation doctrine operates somewhat differently. Foreseeability plays a much more prominent role in assessing contract damages than in setting the appropriate punishment in the criminal law. Assisting in a breach is not treated in the same way as assisting someone with a crime. The former can sometimes, in the rare case, be reached via something like the interference with contractual relations doctrine but far more rarely than one is able to apply the doctrine of complicity in the criminal law.

Could the East German judge have avoided liability by simply thinking of himself as engaged in the enforcement of a contract? He would have had to think of Jehovah's Witnesses as breaching a social contract to which they are a party. That brings with it some familiar difficulties, since they never formally entered into such a contract. But there are familiar answers to that. Reaping the benefits of living in a certain society is enough for some to consider this a species of assent. It is after all not that different from buying a share in a corporation and then automatically being subject to the terms of the corporation's charter, its own form of social contract.

There are other difficulties. One might argue that the social contract they entered into is one that incorporates the terms of a humane criminal code, including incidentally the East German law on the books, as opposed to in application. But it is not clear that that is the appropriate yardstick.

Or one might argue that they never had much of a choice about whether to enter into that social contract. But contract law often dispenses with the voluntariness requirement. No peace treaty concluding a war would ever get off the ground if we insisted on too much voluntariness before a contract is valid. Most peace treaties, after all, are signed at the point of a gun.

Then there is the fact that contracts trying to provide for penalties other than monetary damages are typically not enforceable by way of an injunction. Sending someone off to jail is enforcement of the sort that we generally frown upon. But whether we really have good reasons for objecting to it is subject to controversy.

So it is possible for the East German judge to argue that inasmuch as he thought he was dealing with breakers of a social contract, he was entitled to give out the disproportionate penalties that are often meted out in contracts cases.

(4) Other legal contexts: the necessity doctrine. There are specific legal doctrines that could be thought of as analogues to the enterprise of prevention. Take the doctrine of necessity, which says that under extreme circumstances infringement of someone's rights is legitimate for the sake of the larger public good. The East German judge could have thought of himself as covered by that doctrine. He would presumably get less solace from this than most of the foregoing because it is not a case where merely thinking so will make it so. We might forgive him his mistake, but he would then simply get off on the familiar ground that he lacked the mens rea for the offense, thinking he had a defense he does not have, not on the more interesting ground that his perception of the situation actually changes it.

(5) Other legal contexts: rules abstractly considered. All legal doctrines considered from a sufficiently abstract point of view have of course a quasi-punitive character in that certain adverse consequences follow from certain kinds of disfavored actions. The action need not even be disfavored. You work, earn an income, and have to pay taxes on that income. Earning the income, though not disfavored, is an action with a quasi-punitive consequence. If the East German judge considered himself as engaged in one of those practices, as doing something on the order of imposing a tax, could he get off? That depends on whether it is at all conceivable that he might have viewed himself as falling under such a doctrine. But that is not entirely implausible. Tax law pure and simple would not serve our purpose here, but there is an analogue: the law of conscription. Suppose he took himself to simply be imposing an alternative conscription obligation: An alternative to actually serving in the army, he might say, is doing certain kinds of tasks in other buildings, which happen to be called prisons. To be

sure, there may be norms of humanity, which he violated, but notice that, yet again, the standards by which we judge him have changed from those of proportionality mandated by the criminal law.

Does what I will now call the "Alexander phenomenon" extend beyond the punishment context? In other words, are there other contexts in which what someone is doing changes its moral character depending on how he conceives of it? A natural place to look because it is so similar to the punitive context is positive, as opposed to negative, desert. I am thinking here of situations in which we judge someone to be deserving of a prize, or even a material reward, in return for some positive, as opposed to negative, action.

The norms of positive desert are similar—though not identical—to those of negative desert. Just how similar is not generally appreciated. Let's begin by briefly listing the rules governing the attribution of negative responsibility, and then let's note that most of these in fact carry over to the attribution of positive responsibility: we hold people responsible for negative consequences if they acted either intentionally, knowingly, recklessly, or negligently. Those negative consequences must not be too remote but rather must have followed proximately, as the common law's term has it, from the defendant's actions. Moreover, the defendant must have performed an act to bring about those consequences, as opposed to merely allowing them to happen by way of omission. This at least is required to hold him liable as a principal. If he cannot be held liable as a principal, he might still be held liable as an accomplice, for helping a criminal consequence to be brought about. And if he cannot be held liable either as a principal or an accomplice in the successful execution of a crime, he might yet be held liable for the unsuccessful attempt to carry out a crime. Finally, even if he meets these so-called prima facie requirements for liability, he might yet escape liability, or have it reduced, if he is able to qualify for certain defenses, such as necessity, duress, self-defense, insanity, and others.

All of this carries over to a remarkable extent to the attribution of positive responsibility, that is, responsibility for positive outcomes. To see this clearly, let's consider what we would say about a group of soldiers fighting valiantly for a just cause. Here we have consequences identical in kind to those we usually punish—deaths of human beings—but we attach positive value to them because they are enemy soldiers. We would say about each soldier that he gets credit for an enemy death if he brought it about intentionally, but not if he did so inadvertently (and there are intermediate degrees of credit depending on the degree of advertence, corresponding to

Punishment as an Act of the Imagination 123

recklessness and negligence in the blaming context). Moreover, for such credit to accrue the death must have resulted proximately from his actions. In addition, his conduct must indeed involve an act, as opposed to a mere omission (such as not interfering with another soldier who actually carried out the successful killing of the enemy soldier). This at least is what would be required to credit him as a principal in the killing of the enemy soldier. He might also receive credit, albeit to a lesser extent, if he merely contributed as an accomplice to someone else's killing of the enemy soldier. And he might receive some lesser credit if he attempted, but failed, in a difficult mission intended to bring about enemy deaths. Finally, if he acted out of necessity, duress, or self-defense that might well diminish the credit he gets for his actions. Insanity, interestingly does not operate in such a symmetrical fashion. It will not diminish the credit he gets for a valiant action, even though it will diminish the blame he gets for a blameworthy action. As I said the rules of positive desert are similar but not identical to those of negative desert.[24]

Consider now a negotiation between an academic who claims to have access to a major discovery—a major cancer treatment breakthrough, to be very concrete—for which he asks his dean to award him a special chair and a large raise. I said "has access to a major discovery" because he did not actually himself make the discovery, at least not in the traditional sense. Rather, I will imagine he contributed to it in a way that would not ordinarily lead us to accord him all that much credit. Imagine for instance that he reports that the discovery is actually the work of an unemployed, publicity-shy, depressed friend who only was able to complete the work because the academic put him up and gave him the material and psychological support necessary for him to finish the project. Or imagine that the breakthrough was the result of pure chance, one extraordinary coincidence after another conspiring to make our academic the beneficiary of this crucial insight, his role being a little like that of Chauncy Gardiner in Jerzy Kozinski's well-known novel. In other words, he does not meet the criteria according to which we ordinarily give credit for a major breakthrough to someone. Yet somehow he has managed to be in a position where he now controls access to this discovery. Is it right that he should get his chair and accompanying material benefits? The answer I think is that it depends on how he and the dean think of their transaction. If they think of it like a simple contract, analogous to a mere salary negotiation, there is no problem. But if they think of the chair and the salary as being in the nature of a prize, which needs to be deserved, then it is an entirely different story. Then the academic's insistence on his terms comes close to being blackmail because he is extracting a benefit from the dean to which he is not entitled. But notice that whether or not he is acting wrongfully here entirely depends on how they conceive of the transaction, which was the hallmark of Alexander's "preventive enterprise."

IV.

In the end, then, a judge who subjects a criminal to excessive punishment might escape sanction—both legal and moral sanction—not for the reasons we might at first think of: not because doing so would involve violating the norm against retroactive laws or because proportionality is too vague a concept. Instead, the judge can escape punishment *because punishment, like the award of rewards and prizes, is to an unappreciated extent an act of the imagination.* If the judge imagines himself to have been engaged in a nonpunitive, or merely quasi-punitive practice, then that is in a sense a self-legitimating act, as a result of which he can no longer be considered to have engaged in punishment[25] because punishment seems to depend to an unappreciated extent on the way in which the person meting it out conceptualizes what he is doing. If he thinks of it as something other than punishment, then sometimes by virtue of that it *becomes* something other than punishment.

Can that really be true? Could the judge's blameworthiness, his eligibility for punishment, really depend in this peculiar and unusual way on how he conceives of what he is doing? Not only does this seem like an exceedingly strange, downright paradoxical state of affairs, but it has at least one further paradoxical implication. Let's think for a moment about the state of mind of the court that passes judgment on the East German judge. It would seem that what *that* court is entitled to do to him will in turn depend on how *that* court conceives of its role, whether it thinks of itself as being in the business of prevention, rehabilitation, the enforcement of implicit social contracts, or the pursuit of any number of nonpunitive practices rather than that of retribution. To be sure, the general social consensus, as to how what the court is doing should be characterized, might constrain the court's ability to decide on its own how to conceive of what it is doing. But since the social consensus will often be shaped by what the court decides to do—in other words, society at large will often conceive of the court in whatever way the court decides to conceive of itself—even that constraint is less significant than it might seem at first.

Notes

This essay benefited greatly from the vigorous comments of Austin Sarat and my fellow symposiasts, as well as the enthusiastic engagement of the faculty and student audience of the University of Alabama Law School, which convened this event.

1. Bundesgerichshof [BGH] [Federal Court of Justice] Feb. 16, 1960, Neue Juristische Wochenschrift [NJW] 974, 1960.

2. Strafgesetzbuch [STGB] [Penal Code], Aug. 19, 1997, Bundesgesetzblatt [BGBl. I] 2040, § 339 (Ger.).

3. Gunter Spendel, § 336 paragraph 60 in *Leipziger kommentar*, 10th ed., ed. Hans-Heinrich Jescheck (Berlin: Walter de Gruyter, 1989).

4. Eric A. Posner and Adrian Vermeule, "Transitional Justice as Ordinary Justice," *Harvard Law Review* 117 (2004): 761.

5. Wolfgang Naucke, *Die strafjuristische privilegierung staatsverstaerkter kriminalitaet* (Frankfurt am Main: Vittorio Klostermann, 1996).

6. Posner and Vermeule, "Transitional Justice," 762–63.

7. Id. at 799.

8. Id. at 785–86.

9. Id. at 764–65.

10. Marvin Wolfgang and Thorsten Sellin, *The Measurement of Delinquency* (New York: John Wiley and Sons, 1964); William James, chapter 13 in *The Principles of Psychology* (New York: Henry Holt & Co., 1890), 483–549.

11. Leo Katz, *Ill-Gotten Gains* (Chicago: University of Chicago Press, 1996), 150.

12. George A. Gescheider, *Psychophysics*, 2nd ed. (Hillsdale, NJ: Lawrence Erlbaum Associates, 1985), 227–67.

13. Larry Alexander, "The Doomsday Machine: Proportionality, Punishment and Prevention," *Monist* 63 (1980): 199.

14. Id. at 209.

15. Id. at 209.

16. Id. at 210.

17. Id. at 210.

18. Id. at 213.

19. Frederick Schick, *Understanding Action* (New York: Cambridge University Press, 1991).

20. Id. at 1.

21. Id. at 2.

22. Fritz Heider, *The Psychology of Interpersonal Relations* (Hillsdale, NJ: Lawrence Erlbaum Associates, 1958).

23. Adam Benforado, Jon Hanson, and David Yosifon, "Broken Scales: Obesity and Justice in America," *Emory Law Journal* 53 (2004): 1657.

24. See Katz, *Ill-Gotten Gains*, part 3; Michael J. Zimmermann, *Essay on Moral Responsibility* (Totowa, NJ: Rowman and Littlefield, 1988).

25. As Carol Steiker nicely put it, the practice of punishment is at least in part about "meaning creation."

"Which Question? Which Lie?"
Reflections on *Payne v. Tennessee* and the "Quick Glimpse" of Life
Michelle Brown

> When interpreters have finished their work, they frequently leave behind victims whose lives have been torn apart by these organized, social practices of violence.
> —Robert Cover

In the case of capital punishment, death penalty advocates and opponents routinely generate oppositional claims centered upon the worth of the lives and deaths of perpetrators and victims. Questions circulate as unavoidable reminders of the tragic underpinnings of cultural violence and punitive practice: Whose life counts? Whose does not? These questions, while profoundly important, are not the only ones. As legal philosopher Martha Minow writes, "The contemplation of death reminds us that what we ask frames what we answer" and the lies we countenance.[1] Here, in the "dialectic or tension between disclosure and dissembling,"[2] other kinds of questions about capital punishment squeamishly persist below the surface of public and legal discourse about pain, death, and the law, periodically breaking the surface. One problem far more deeply submerged in the cultural life of capital punishment might be posed this way: What if no one—neither the perpetrator nor the victim—really counts? To discuss the questions raised and the questions ignored about the death penalty is also to discuss the "choice of lies"—and the levels of deception that are rendered culturally acceptable in these inquiries.[3] This chapter seeks then "to raise to visibility the social meanings that are taken for granted"[4] in our questions—and to engage the kind of punitive imaginings that are available for legal interpreters to choose between when they seek to leave the limits of life and death uncontested.

Such a project is grounded in a central but unattended question for sociolegal studies, one that asks what it means to take up a jurisprudence of life and death. The problems of living and dying and of killing and being killed span an ever-increasing range of legal categories: charges of manslaughter and murder, wrongful death litigation, personal injury lawsuits, estate planning, abortion and reproductive rights, end-of-life decision making, and life without parole and death sentences, to name only a few. The role of law in moderating life and death, however, extends further and deeper than, at first glance, we might imagine. From the mundane to the spectacular, legal interpretation centered upon life and death problematizes categories of recognition and personhood foundational to citizenship and state sovereignty. Interstitial zones of social abandonment that follow neoliberal trajectories and center upon dislocation and dispossession reveal the vast cultural, political, and sociolegal work of defining what and who is inside and outside the configuration of life when confronted with indigence, transience, migration, terrorism, statelessness, punitiveness, and violence. As political philosopher Giorgio Agamben writes, "Bare life is no longer confined to a particular place or a definite category. It now dwells in the biological body of every living being," and any one of us who might find ourselves facing conditions of precarity.[5] A jurisprudence of life and death entails marking a path of inquiry across the spaces where law finds itself embroiled in cases where there is none to little agreement on the language of pain or life or death and a marked cultural aversion to addressing that very ambiguity. It takes seriously the fragility of life and the problematic line between life and death that increasingly materializes as a "moving threshold," a "zone of indistinction" in which what constitutes "alive" and what constitutes "dead" are increasingly contested.[6] I argue that such ambiguity necessitates a conversation about empathy in the everyday world of law and society as part of the cultural imaginary—a discussion of the "sides" we take in our intersubjective alliances. Even as pain and death undergird the foundations of law, where "bodies are everywhere,"[7] we have yet to fully address the questions of life and death and the incomplete efforts at identification that drive law's efforts at sense making in these realms. In taking up a jurisprudence of life and death, we may begin to understand law and empathy's most dangerous, necessary, and fragile formations. The ongoing practice of capital punishment in the United States marks a striking site from which to do this work.

The possibilities and predicaments of such jurisprudence achieve stark visibility in a contemporary re-reading of the landmark capital case of *Payne v. Tennessee* (1991), where imaginings about the worth of perpetrators and victims, the living and the dead, assume center stage. Pervis Tyrone Payne, an African American male, was convicted of murdering Charisse Christopher, a single white mother, and her two-year-old daughter, Lacie, with a butcher knife, stabbing Charisse over forty times in her west Memphis apartment. He was also found guilty of assault with intent to commit first-degree murder for attacking Christopher's three-year-old son, Nicholas, who survived. Although the state of Tennessee had no guidelines for the inclusion of victim impact evidence in capital trials and the Supreme Court had recently ruled in two cases, *Booth v. Maryland* (1987) and *South Carolina v. Gathers* (1989), that victim impact evidence was inadmissible, *Payne* nevertheless incorporates the victim's voice of grief and loss. The case hinges upon two key moments in court proceedings. In the first instance, during the sentencing phase, Nicholas's grandmother testified briefly about the psychological effects of the murders on her grandson. "He cries for his mom. He doesn't seem to understand why she doesn't come home. And he cries for his sister Lacie. He comes to me many times during the week and asks me, Grandmama, do you miss my Lacie. And I tell him yes. He says, I'm worried about my Lacie."[8]

In the second example, during closing arguments, the prosecutor revisited what legal scholar Jennifer Culbert has called Nicholas's "lonely suffering," as he lay conscious while his mother and sister died.[9] In arguing for the death penalty, the prosecutor extrapolated in his comments on the continuing effects of Nicholas's trauma and grief, stating:

> But we do know that Nicholas was alive. And Nicholas was in the same room. Nicholas was still conscious. His eyes were open. He responded to the paramedics. He was able to follow their directions. He was able to hold his intestines in as he was carried to the ambulance. So he knew what happened to his mother and baby sister.
>
> There is nothing you can do to ease the pain of any of the families involved in this case. There is nothing you can do to ease the pain of Bernice and Carl Payne, and that's a tragedy. There is nothing you can do basically to ease the pain of Mr. and Mrs. Zvolanek, and that's a tragedy. They will have to live with it the rest of their lives. There is obviously nothing you can do for Charisse and Lacie Jo. But there is something you can do for Nicholas.
>
> Somewhere down the road Nicholas is going to grow up, hopefully. He's going to want to know what happened. And he is going

to know what happened to his baby sister and his mother. He is going to want to know what type of justice was done. He is going to want to know what happened. With your verdict, you will provide the answer.[10]

As law and humanities scholar Peter Brooks writes, "After listening to this story, there is no turning back."[11] Legal scholar Susan Bandes writes, "How can one argue, in light of these attributes, that the victim impact statement is a story that should not be told, one that evokes emotions that ought to be suppressed?"[12] Such tragic narratives speak to the effort-full labor of creating cultural meaning. Against the imagery of Nicholas's bodily injury—his gaping wounds and his unbearable consciousness through it all, the state's attorney does a good deal of identification work, in particular, linking the void that separates jurors from Nicholas's suffering to the idea of what can and cannot be done for him and the central actors caught in this maelstrom of violence. *Payne*, then, is a case, as Austin Sarat, has argued in other work, about the horrors of inexplicable loss—about those who "live . . . in another space."[13] It is about the idea that there is "nothing" we can do, as the state's attorney puts it, in the face of such loss, except answer death with death. The case is also about the travesty of distant others, those I have referred to as penal spectators, imagining that space, about how we imagine how survivors live with inexplicable loss.[14] In this respect, I believe *Payne* gives us an unfortunate roadmap for the broad devaluation of suffering in criminal justice contexts specifically through the problem of empathy in legal imagining.

For better or worse, my reading of *Payne* is something of an exorcism. It has developed around needling and nagging tensions that have been present in my research and teaching for some time. The fall I began graduate school, the Sentencing Project released a study reporting that one out of three black men were under some form of criminal justice supervision, highlighting the central issue of our time in criminal justice: racial disparity—the kind of glaring disproportionality that *Payne* typifies, a capital case that highlights black on white violence and the worth of some victims (and perpetrators) over others.[15] I went on to spend ten years in the field working with perpetrators, prisoners, victims, and their families as well as correctional officers, wardens, and execution team members, wrestling with the ambiguities, ironies, and severing of social relations at the heart of criminal justice practice. In all of this, there is as well ten years of pedagogical reflections, based upon my classroom experiences teaching punishment and capital punishment, running endlessly up against the harsh two-sided, polarized ways in which young people in the United States imagine relationships between perpetrators and victims and the mind-bending work required on their parts to break out of those limits.

The work also reflects three recent shifts in my scholarship. The first is continuing work in an emergent literature on empathy—in particular, a dark empathy perspective that assumes, against the current popular grain of thought, that empathy is a modality that is not inevitably prosocial or benevolent in its efforts or effects.[16] The second is a critical carceral studies scholarship that is both interventionist and expansive in its reconceptualizing of the cultural practices of punishment, against the backdrop of mass incarceration in the United States. This is a new and marked commitment, as Caleb Smith outlines in this volume, to "a critical research program into cultural representations of the geographies of contemporary life," where crime is often imagined as a "disturbance in the landscape, especially the cityscape," spectacularly visible in popular culture and yet completely erased from national politics. Beneath all of this is a feminist interpretive approach that privileges subjectivity, affect, and questions, as Judith Butler's work foregrounds, of grievability—the life that can and cannot be mourned.[17]

Finally and more personally, this work is informed by my finding myself one short year ago in my newfound home of Tennessee in a classroom teaching this case. I had just completed a yearlong fellowship immersed in scholarship and rigorous dialogue on empathy.[18] Now, *Payne* was strangely disorienting. I was emotional, thinking of Charisse Christopher and her two-year-old daughter through my own circumstances—also a single mom with a two-year-old daughter—and its attendant vulnerabilities and complexities, layered through the violence of social structure. I also knew that my identification—my imaginings—were ridiculous. The abyss that separates me from Charisse Christopher and her life and death in Millington, Tennessee, is unfathomable. Her fate is simply my voyeuristic and horrible imagining. This kind of dark empathy is one that I believe shapes our ideas about punishment and justice in profound ways. The legacy of *Payne* is steeped in this kind of imagining—a way of making sense of the world that is inevitably deeply removed from the deaths of Charisse and Lacie, the suffering of Nicholas, the state killing of Pervis Payne, and the suffering of all of their loved ones.

Lies, Damned Lies, and *Payne*

In *Payne*, the U.S. Supreme Court reversed its prior holdings of only a few years before, a stark break with precedent, and allowed for the inclusion of victim impact evidence[19] in capital trials, foregrounding the new and central role of victims in the politicization of crime and criminal justice, a ruling in line with the punitive turn in the United States toward crime, prisoners, and capital defendants. Specifically, the court argued that the government could not be constitutionally barred from offering a "quick glimpse" of the life extinguished by capital murder—a perspective, the majority went on to argue, that is central in "balancing" the unfair weight of attention given to the capital defendant with then chief justice Rehnquist arguing that "virtually no limits are placed on the relevant mitigating evidence a capital defendant may introduce concerning his own circumstances."[20] Citing the Tennessee Supreme Court, the U.S. Supreme Court affirmed, "It is an affront to the civilized members of the human race to say that at sentencing in a capital case, a parade of witnesses may praise the background, character and good deeds of the Defendant (as was done in this case), without limitation as to relevancy, but nothing may be said that bears upon the character of, or harm imposed, upon the victims."[21] In fact, during the sentencing phase of the trial, the defense had called Payne's parents, his girlfriend, and a clinical psychologist to testify—a rather sad parade in size and impact. Nonetheless, as Justice Scalia had previously written, "Many citizens have found one-sided and hence unjust the criminal trial in which a parade of witnesses comes forth to testify to the pressures beyond normal human experience that drove the defendant to commit his crime, with no one to lay before the sentencing authority the full reality of human suffering the defendant has produced,"[22] weighted language, as Jennifer Culbert points out, where the social forces and conditions that culminate in violence are reduced to "pressures" faced by the defendant whereas the victim's experiences mark "the full reality of human suffering."[23]

Social science research post-*Payne* has consistently demonstrated how limited as well as how alienating this "quick" attention is to the lives and deaths of capital defendants. Some have gone on to show how this telescopic view of biography without attention to the social conditions of violence further demeans victims and their loved ones. For instance, social psychologist Craig Haney, whose work includes the production of social histories[24] for capital defendants, argues that they provide a "rare glimpse into the social and psychological organization of lethal aggression in our society."[25] Social histories are pivotal windows into the social forces that create the conditions for violence. They rarely materialize in capital cases, and, as Haney argues, "genuine narratives of life and death" are "difficult to find," with the majority of capital defendants going "to death row and even to the execution chamber without anyone having heard and considered the harsh facts of their brutal lives or meaningfully analyzed the sobering lessons that are contained in their social histories."[26] Consequently, "[t]he inevitable patterns of poverty, abuse and neglect, of institutional failure and the like—the undeniable fact that many capital defendants were victims long before they became victimizers—are brushed aside lest they complicate the moral certainty with which we proceed. To my mind, at least, we fail to pay fitting tribute to the victims of these crimes until we grapple honestly with the forces that drove their perpetrators."[27]

Perpetrators too, then, live in another, and inevitably related, space to that of victims—one of structural violence—to which the vast majority of citizens cannot easily relate.[28] The jarringness of this relationship is evident in the fact that the stories of sexual, substance, and physical abuse, normalized in childhood contexts of poverty and racism, rather than sites for identification are more often alienating in their sheer distance from the lives of ordinary middle-class actors. As sociolegal scholars Kerry Dunn and Paul Kaplan write, these actors may be understood as "executable subjects," "being[s] who [are] no longer deemed worthy or capable of nearly all of the rights usually attributed to human beings in Western society" by way of individuating discourses that materialize in capital mitigation.[29] Against these logics, and as Stephen Garvey argues elsewhere in this volume, we approach conditions of life in which questions are raised about the state's role in the production of crime, including a failure to provide the most basic of social needs—medical care, education, employment, and so on—in a manner that leaves one without the hope of a future, a context of "second-class" citizenship. In totalizing concepts such as the "full extent of the harm" caused by the murderer's actions and the "full range of foreseeable consequences," *Payne* nonetheless invokes the idea that in its troubled, half-hearted estimations of individual lives—those of both victims and perpetrators—some sort of bare reckoning is achieved. These concepts are startling in their limits—which, like the "quick glimpse" of life, undermine the very experience they seek to represent. With no totalizing way in which to capture the social effects of life and death—and no formal recognition of this as a problem in itself, the court instead must choose particular ways to address life and death in any judicial interpretation. In this way, particular attachments to capital lives and deaths are encouraged and achieve recognition in and after *Payne*, and, in that process, other more complex relationships to lives and deaths are submerged.

Among the many kinds of jurisprudence *Payne* engages and promotes (jurisprudence of victims, of pain, of rights, and other things), the most basic one is a jurisprudence of life and death, not simply about the worth of lives but about a marked determination to disregard life and death in all of its complexity. So why rehash *Payne*, one of the most written about landmark rulings? As Minow writes, there are lies we countenance, "knowing misrepresentations" to which we "extend approval or tolerate" and confronting the "choice of lies" raises the most basic issues of governance.[30] *Payne* allows us to confront the questions and lies, the foregroundings and foreclosures, the lives and deaths that undergird the broad practice of law and punishment in the United States at its visceral base level. If, as Austin Sarat argues, "the distinctive business of law in the late modern era" is "to understand and justify pain and death," and if we seek to alter the legal landscape of suffering, *Payne* has many lessons.[31]

The Exquisite Corpse

Payne begins unusually in comparison with most court opinions, at the limits of law and life, with a lengthy circumstantial story that vividly describes the bloody scene in Charisse Christopher's apartment. Justices are conscious stylists, attentive to the wording of their opinions and the dramatic openings and closings of their commentary, astute in how the framing of their questions communicates possibilities and (fore)closures. More significantly, as cultural anthropologist Veena Das writes, when entering "the scene of devastation," one inevitably raises questions about "how one should inhabit a world that has been made strange through the desolating experience of violence and loss," what might be imagined as "approaching the world . . . through a kind of mourning for it."[32] The politics of mourning sit center stage in *Payne*, as the Supreme Court dwells heavily and repetitively on the heinousness of the crime scene, the place of bodies, and the limbo between life and death, detailing the demand for acknowledgment such brutality inevitably raises. Here, chief justice William Rehnquist, delivering the opinion of the court, writes vividly of the crime scene: "Inside the apartment, the police encountered a horrifying scene. Blood covered the walls and floor throughout the unit. Charisse and her children were lying on the floor in the kitchen. Nicholas, despite several wounds inflicted by a butcher knife that completely penetrated through his body from front to back, was still breathing. Miraculously, he survived. . . . Charisse's body was found on the kitchen floor on her back, her legs fully extended. She had sustained 42 direct knife wounds and 42 defensive wounds on her arms and hands. The wounds were caused by 41 separate thrusts of a butcher knife. . . . Lacie's body was on the kitchen floor near her mother.[33]

Justice O'Connor, concurring and defending the prosecutor's closing arguments, writes: "Charisse Christopher was stabbed 41 times with a butcher knife and bled to death; her 2-year-old daughter Lacie was killed by repeated thrusts of that same knife; and 3-year-old Nicholas, despite stab wounds that penetrated completely through his body from front to back, survived—only to witness the brutal murders of his mother and baby sister. . . . [T]he prosecutor sought to remind the jury that Charisse and Lacie were more than just lifeless bodies on a videotape, that they were unique human beings."[34] She continues, "'Murder is the ultimate act of depersonalization.' . . . It transforms a living person with hopes, dreams, and fears into a corpse, thereby taking away all that is special and unique about the person. The Constitution does not preclude a State from deciding to give some of that back."[35]

Justice Thurgood Marshall, who dissented in the case, appears as a lone voice challenging the state's attorney, with regard to the gory visual evidence and the inclusion of victim impact evidence:

Justice Marshall: My other question was the record in this case shows that the jury was shown pictures of the dead bodies, the brutal . . . blood all over the place, and everything that could be photographed was shown to the jury, and practically no defense.
  What in the world did you need any more evidence for?
Mr. Burson: Well, I think the point is, it was relevant, it was probative, and the trial judge made that decision.
Justice Marshall: What more did you need?
Mr. Burson: Well, I think that—
Justice Marshall: Can you imagine any jury not convicting?
Mr. Burson: I think that they needed a . . . at least a characterization of the victim as a unique human being, other than just as a corpse.
  And that's all I think the . . . what was depicted in what you are speaking of.
Justice Marshall: You mean you needed more than a bloody body?
Mr. Burson: Your Honor, I would respectfully say that the State was entitled to put on more than a bloody body, yes, sir.[36]

Payne is preoccupied with the living dead, posing the problem for law of what it means to make decisions about life and death, to talk of justice, memory, and memorial. It assumes the task of rescuing the dead, of breathing him or her back to life as the state argues that in the victim the jury must see not a corpse but a unique, living human being, a pursuit conducted in a manner and with the knowledge that this may create yet another corpse, that of the defendant. In the discourse of bloody bodies, legal limits on pain ring hollow and ghostly presences proliferate. As Justice Souter writes, *Payne* recognizes that defendants must, on some level, know that victims are not "valueless fungibles" but "that death is always to a 'unique' individual, and harm to some groups of survivors is a consequence of a successful homicidal act so foreseeable as to be virtually inevitable," thereby deepening the defendant's responsibility.[37] This imagining of the living dead importantly extends to and builds upon the pain of the victim's family and loved ones. In the precedent case of *Booth v. Maryland* (1987), an elderly couple, Irvin and Rose Bronstein, had been stabbed to death in their home during a robbery. A three-and-a-half page single-spaced narrative based upon interviews with the Bronsteins' son, daughter, son-in-law, and granddaughter was read during the trial, concluding with the following:

> As described by their family members, the Bronsteins were loving parents and grandparents whose family was most important to them. Their funeral was the largest in the history of the Levinson Funeral Home and the family received over one thousand sympathy cards, some from total strangers. They attempted to answer each card personally. The family states that Mr. and Mrs. Bronstein were extremely good people who wouldn't hurt a fly. Because of their loss, a terrible void has been put into their lives and every day is still a strain just to get through. It became increasingly apparent to the writer as she talked to the family members that the murder of Mr. and Mrs. Bronstein is still such a shocking, painful, and devastating memory to them that permeates every aspect of their daily lives. It is doubtful that they will ever be able to fully recover from this tragedy and not be haunted by the memory of the brutal manner in which their loved ones were murdered and taken from them.[38]

Here, as with *Payne*, the state's construction of grief is one that is carefully linked to irrevocable trauma, permeating "every aspect of their daily lives." The bereaved are stuck and any possibility of an otherwise is muted as "[i]t is doubtful that they will ever be able to fully recover." Such a passive account of these actors positions them forever in limbo, "haunted by the memory of the brutal manner in which their loved ones were murdered and taken from them." The statement was read to the jury in full, over the objection of the defense counsel. The jury recommended death. In delivering the opinion in *Booth*, overturning the use of victim impact evidence, Justice Powell wrote:

> One can understand the grief and anger of the family caused by the brutal murders in this case, and there is no doubt that jurors generally are aware of these feelings. But the formal presentation of this information by the State can serve no other purpose than to inflame the jury and divert it from deciding the case on the relevant evidence concerning the crime and the defendant. As we have noted, any decision to impose the death sentence must 'be, and appear to be, based on reason rather than caprice or emotion.' The admission of these emotionally-charged opinions as to what conclusions the jury should draw from the evidence clearly is inconsistent with the reasoned decisionmaking we require in capital cases."[39]

Importantly, this statement focuses upon the conventional concern with victim impact evidence, its emotional and inflammatory possibilities, which are real enough. However, across these victim impact cases, little attention is given to the fact that the symbolic use of statements of grief and loss are attached to static actors in a manner that maintains them between life and death. As Austin Sarat describes in his citation of the *Booth* case, the Bronsteins' children are relegated to a living death that is immutably tied to revenge.

> The victim's daughter . . . states that she doesn't sleep through a single night and thinks a part of her died too when her parents were killed. She reports that she doesn't find much joy in anything and her powers of concentration aren't good. She feels as if her brain is on overload. . . . The victim's daughter states that wherever she goes she sees and hears her parents. . . .
>
> The victims' son states that he can only think of his parents in the context of how he found them that day, and he can feel their fear and horror. It was 4:00 P.M. when he discovered their bodies and

this stands out in his mind. He is always aware of when 4:00 P.M. comes each day, even when he is not near a clock. . . . He is unable to drive on the streets that pass near his parents' home. . . . He is constantly reminded of his parents. He sees his father coming out of synagogue, sees his parents' car, and feels very sad whenever he sees old people. . . .

This statement, presented in a public forum in the third-person, clinical narrative of a state official, nonetheless conveys the pain, grief and torment of the daughter left behind. It does the double labor of claiming for her both a secondary victim status and, at the same time, identifying her as a murder victim herself. She is a kind of corpse yet she is haunted by uncontrollable memories. It is as if her parents are not entirely dead; they live on in visions and voices known only to her. Such haunting visions and voices stir the vengeful desires of all survivors. . . .

From anonymity to embodiment, from absence to presence, victim-impact evidence becomes a vehicle for resurrecting the dead and allowing them to speak in the trials of their murderers.[40]

But such grave deference is temporary, invoking an image of loss and grief, not so as to problematize the structural place of violence *and* grief, but to claim law's power in dispensing death. Rehnquist and O'Connor, Sarat argues, playing the "theme of death and resurrection," insist that "giving back is actually pay back." This symbolic use plays out in depictions of the Bronsteins' son, when the state argues, "'[H]is parents were not killed, but were butchered like animals. He doesn't think anyone should be able to do something like that and get away with it. He is very angry. . . . He states that he is frightened by his own reaction to what he would do if someone hurt him or a family member.'"[41]

And on behalf of their daughter, "her parents were stabbed repeatedly with viciousness and she could never forgive anyone for killing them that way. She can't believe that anyone could do that to someone. The victims' daughter states that animals wouldn't do this. They didn't have to kill because there was no one to stop them from looting. . . . The murders show the viciousness of the killers' anger. She doesn't feel that the people who did this could ever be rehabilitated and she doesn't want them to be able to do this again or put another family through this."[42]

In these eerie visions of the dead, there is a structuring absence. Punishment—and punitive imaginations—are no real use in response to loss.

Punishment and, specifically, death are simply what we ought to do when there is "nothing" that can be done. It is not simply, as *Payne*'s critics have insisted, that vengeance and bloodletting are the only answer for the state and the bereaved. It is that first, there is no complex connection made between the blood cry and grief (what else can I do, the bereaved might ask), and, second, there is no alternative discourse for the problem of pain and suffering in the law—or more broadly in the cultural imaginary. There is no recognition of a grief that can be and is lived otherwise.

The problem the court encounters with the raising of the dead then is threefold. First and formidably, it marks a trajectory toward death—specifically, the death of the defendant—as such irrecoverable loss is framed in vengeful tones as only answerable with death. Second, this penalty is arrived at in a manner that depends upon maintaining the grieving and the condemned, politically and symbolically, somewhere between life and death (Pervis Payne awaits death still on Tennessee's death row, twenty-five years after the murders). Finally, it does all of this with a working knowledge of the inevitable worth of victims. Only certain members of the dead will be raised in the eyes of the law. Legal scholar Vivian Berger voices the outrage and concerns of *Payne*'s many critics when she writes, "Much worse, however, from the vantage point of particular survivors than sentencing trials revolving about the deceased's virtues are ones that, in the post-*Payne* world, will either ignore devalued victims or, worst of all, provide a forum for airing their defects."[43]

In this way, it is not simply that *Payne* overlooks the inadequate courtroom representations of most defendant's lives as it steps steadily toward death, necessarily countering legal and political efforts to arouse sympathy for the devil, nor that it foregrounds the irrational pain and needs of victims. Rather there is another well-documented sleight of hand with regard to the worth of victims. The justices are acutely aware of this problem as, in the course of oral argument, they engage in strange empathic exercises, imagining a number of hypothetical cases built upon victim identification and intersubjective processes as they worry about possible unequal outcomes: the murder of the president versus that of a homeless person, the church-going father of four versus the single parent, two hijackers, whose crimes each cause a death—one victim is "beloved by society and leaves behind aggrieved survivors," the other a "reprobate" with no survivors. Here, the justices wrangle with their recognition of one of the hidden principles of criminal justice about which everyone knows, that justice is far from blind, that perpetrators and victims have different worth, marked by a series of social vectors. In their hypothesizing, they nonetheless ignore the most egregious factor in capital cases: race.

The devaluation of victims on the basis of race, a finding that is central to the major social science projects on modern capital punishment, poses a taxing problem for *Payne*'s ultimate claims to concern and compassion for all victims,[44] particularly as the evidence of racial disproportionality in capital punishment is something that the Supreme Court not only ignored but gave up on in a sweeping gesture of futility in *McCleskey v. Kemp* (1987). *Payne* ultimately recognizes the problem of devaluation full on and argues, nonetheless, with the inclusion of victim impact evidence, decision making may be steered away from the fundamental principle of law—its rational moorings—toward emotionally charged opinions. That these opinions are remarkably removed from the complex lives and experiences of grieving victims, that when these opinions materialize at all it is in ways that are inevitably classed, raced, and potentially fatal in their inflammatory nature is viewed as necessary in any effort to recognize, with noted irony, that the victim, more than a "bloody corpse," is "a unique, living human being."

Empathy

In this legal world built upon imagining, the court recognizes then that identification is precarious and unpredictable—and yet entirely central to the power of law. They know, as do we, that law is selective in its attention to pain and death and that suffering is, to some degree, the loss of justice. As feminist scholar Lauren Berlant writes, "Justice . . . seeks out the cold, hard facts against the incoherent mess of feeling," but "when we raise questions about the scale of suffering, the measures of justice, or the fault of the sufferers," we run ashore as "the modern social logic of compassion can as easily provide an alibi for an ethical or political betrayal as it can initiate a circuit of practical relief."[45] *Payne* presents itself first and foremost as an effort to assess the urgency, salience, and relevance of another's pain—a position that, in light of the above and in every way, provokes righteous outrage from all directions. In contexts of injury and as we see in *Payne*, legal scholar Alan Hyde argues, the lawyer's obligation is to "create empathy and identification with the victim through the rhetorical worlds of testimony and summation," central to the construction of legal narratives."[46] Furthermore, he argues that empathy is "literally the only tool the jury can employ to fix a measure of damages."[47]

Within this framework there is a logic to law that encourages a particular form of empathic judgment—a particular way to ask the most fundamental social justice questions: "Does a scene involve one person's suffering, or a population's? What kinds of exemplification are involved when a scene of compassion circulates in order to organize a public response, whether aesthetic, economic, or political? When we want to rescue X, are we thinking of rescuing everyone like X, or is it a singular case that we see? When a multitude is symbolized by an individual case, how can we keep from being overwhelmed by the necessary scale that an ethical response would take?"[48]

Empathic judgment and the compassion it inspires, Berlant argues, generally is seen as depending upon "the demonstrated capacity not to turn one's head away but to embrace a sense of obligation to remember what one has seen and, in response to that haunting, to become involved in a story of rescue or amelioration: to take a sad song and make it better."[49] But this approach, as Berlant points out, is inevitably both superficial and suspect. The question of what to do with the "weight of the world" is also a question of how to engage meaningfully with a vast archive of subjective experiences of inequality so powerful and intricate that intersubjective identification, social response, and certainly law shudder—and often fail.[50] In this way, the aesthetics of compassion and the performance of empathy always reveal a hornet's nest of problems about the nature of social and legal response and their dark undertow: that scenes of vulnerability produce desires to withhold attachment—that we are irritated by the scene of suffering always in some way—that ultimately this is something about which there is nothing we can do.

In this way, as contemporary research has begun to explore, empathy has perilous foundations.[51] *Payne* points to the problem of trodding too lightly over the complexity of acknowledgment, including that certain forms of recognition, pathologies of recognition, as Patrice Canivez writes, "turn out to be forms of alienation *in* or *from* the world," where "the desire for recognition may express itself and be used in such a way that individuals become entirely manipulated."[52] Berlant develops this kind of reflexivity further, pointing to its elements of denial, shallowness, and self-orientation.

> Repeatedly, we witness someone's desire to not connect, sympathize, or recognize an obligation to the sufferer; to refuse engagement with the scene or to minimize its effects; to misread it conveniently; to snuff or drown it out with pedantically shaped phrases or carefully

designed apartheids; not to rescue or help; to go on blithely without conscience; to feel bad for sufferers, but only so that they will go away quickly. In this books' archive, the aesthetic and political spectacle of suffering vulnerability seems to bring out something terrible, a drive not to feel compassion or sympathy, an aversion to a moral claim on the spectator to engage, when all the spectator wants to do is to turn away quickly and harshly.[53]

It is at the limits of law and the social then that empathy and compassion risk taking on the most artificial of constructions and may result in the creation of a pure fiction largely centered upon the needs of self, not others. Empathy all too often simply implies choosing a side, a favoring of one who is more closely like one's self or whose feelings seem more urgent and immediate than others. It may culminate in a narrow perspective that is partisan and inconsistent with the equality of law. Empathy may align with violence and vengeance and thus requires judgments about the proper place of emotion and identification in social life and jurisprudence. It may occur in excess—one might empathize too much with another and, in the process, either withdraw or lose a sense of self, prompting a return to self-concern and the neglect of another. In capital cases, such alignments are acutely problematic, often the foundation for a dangerous form of aggressive solidarity and excessive rage in response to perpetrators that does little to support the kind of clear-headed deliberation needed for recovery of victims and offenders alike. In the midst of the projection or loss of self, empathy may easily cross into an inflammatory and emotional irrationality, emblematic of law's madness, that is naturalized and justified in the name of victims and the outrage at perpetrators, even as it profoundly devalues real experiences of victimization and (often, on the part of the empath, unexperienced) vulnerability. Finally, empathy can arise from unworthy motives. Empathy does not prevent one from taking pleasure in another's pain—or pursuing self-interest, manipulation, deception, and patronizing, even colonizing, benevolence, all through the language of the best of intentions. This dark side of empathy is irrevocably bound up with punitive imaginaries and their privileging of retribution and revenge over complex forms of solace and long-term attention to loss and grief. Consequently, there are deep obstacles to the kind of identification required for a virtuous empathy, especially as social encounters are at their base experientially incomplete and partial, fraught with mistakes, misfires, and uncaring, undeserving, and impossible reads.

The zero-sum empathy game of the victim or the perpetrator has served to distract us from the fact that in the complex world of empathy, suffering, and violence, concrete relationships are constantly being achieved, and also failing. The separateness at the heart of *Payne*—this "other space" to which all the main actors are relegated—the ethical loneliness of victims and perpetrators—does not mean that the possibility of relatedness disintegrates, rather that acknowledgment and understanding of others are processual, always being deconstructed and reconstructed, destroyed and reborn. Because empathy most often materializes in these contexts as a possibility in the aftermath of harm done, then whatever form empathic knowledge takes, it often develops in contexts of pain, confusion, and humiliation as victims and perpetrators attempt to make sense of their now different lives. In the aftermath of crime and punishment, victims, perpetrators, and their loved ones will have numerous reasons to promote and hinder understandings of themselves, often fearing how others, particularly those in power, will use intimate knowledge against them and their already maligned subject positions. *Payne* exemplifies this project—an account that privileges its own righteous anger even as it denies a reflexive and constitutive account of empathy's relationship to vulnerability and suffering.

In this regard, *Payne* is profoundly indicative of a problem with Western empathy in that it is not about the suffering of others but the discomfort of "us"—a universalized we that is safely removed from the spaces and contexts within which perpetrators and victims endure.[54] In this discursive formation, feeling bad for others may simply be a way to feel good about ourselves and a redemptive way in which to salvage law as public protector and eradicator of social ills. Here, as Patricia Williams argues, "So much of what is spoken in so-called objective, unmediated voices is in fact mired in hidden subjectivities and unexamined claims that make property of others while denying such connections."[55] Such dispossession mitigates any kind of radical or collective responsibility in our approach to social problems, in particular the social conditions of violence. It allows for further distancing from those who are caught in contexts of social suffering and social death. And finally, because the basis of these claims is framed as normative and universal—who cannot sympathize with Nicholas's pain?—all pain has been spoken for. There is no thing or one capable of care or repair, no trauma that remains accessible, "nothing" about which "we can do." This is an especially seductive framework for privileged social actors who would seek to maintain a comfortable distance between themselves and the troubling pain and suffering of others. Even as victims have come to sit center stage in our contemporary understanding of the world, in the claim to rights and the discourse of "wounded attachments,"[56] rarely have we heard explicitly from or about them. As Didier Fassin and Richard Rechtman write, in that process, we have learned "nothing, or almost nothing, of their subjectivity—or interiority—as victims. Survivors of disasters, oppression, and persecution adopt the only persona that allows them to be heard—that of victim. In doing so, they tell us less of what they are than of the moral economies of our era in which they find their place."[57] For Fassin and Rechtman, the inevitable legitimation of some victims and not others under the category of trauma is not simply about the historical record of who counts and who does not but, like *Payne*, "defines the empirical way in which contemporary societies problematize the meaning of their moral responsibility in relation to the distress of the world."[58]

Payne's declarations then come with a number of niggling contingencies that ultimately undermine its commitment and foregrounding of victims. The only violence and justice that *Payne* allows us to see is a single event, the one-off instance of murder and, in the backdrop, an anticipated execution. We are provided only snapshots of lives lived in pain, models of suffering that depend upon a toxic taxonomy in law by way of a single scene of violence. The only measure of "impact" about what it means to love someone who is murdered is a grandmother's short statement about the grief of a child and the statements of loved ones about a man whom they would not wish to see killed, a girlfriend's and parents' descriptions of the hardness of life. The rest is all spoken for and by state actors. A contemporary wave of research on victims (of all types) poses the central problem of these static depictions, frozen in time and space: "Neither representation provides room for the agency, political subjectivities, intentions, dilemmas, ambivalence, thoughts, resilience, creativity and strategies" of victims and perpetrators.[59] The antipathy toward these monolithic portrayals is central to the first wave of research to follow the families of capital victims and perpetrators. As literature on the condemned now maps, the voicelessness, invisibility, isolation, trauma, grief, and powerlessness of victims' families bear an uncanny resemblance to the experiences of the families of the condemned.[60]

Much of this paradox is captured in Werner Herzog's documentary, *Into the Abyss* (2011), a film that explores the lives of actors caught in capital contexts and their various perspectives—chaplains, execution team members, the condemned, their families, the loved ones of victims, and the surrounding community. The case involves a triple murder committed by two young men in a small town in Texas, one of whom is eventually executed, the other given a life sentence due to his father's testimony on his behalf in the sentencing phase. The victims' family members underline much of *Payne*'s complexity in their interviews with Herzog, scenes that look very much like victim impact statements. We learn from accounts by Charles Richardson (who lost his brother) and Lisa Stolter-Baloun (who lost her mother and brother) that the victims and perpetrators and their families knew one another, all living together in the same community (although separated by gated neighborhoods and socioeconomic markers like sports cars). Their accounts of their broader lives are remarkably similar as they speak to a political economy of poverty, stratification, violence, and frequent intersections with criminal justice. These are families whose grief is interrupted (by law enforcement at a funeral and incarceration across generations) and whose life stories are defined by "accidental" and intentional violent deaths—cascades of lost loved ones (so much so that Lisa removes her phone from her home in order to receive no more bad news). The community exists in the cultural shadow of an expectation for a loss of life. Small and singular lives are lived against staggering social forces, where actors nonetheless cling to stories of rugged individualism and responsibilization, where a loved one is "all you have" (as Charles states of his brother, it was "me and him" against the world), where you are somehow responsible for the world of violence around you. Here, unlike in carefully choreographed capital narratives, biographies bleed out of social configurations, where aggravators and mitigators, victims and perpetrators, come together.

The experience of loss that *Payne* chooses to recognize, rather than reflecting this kind of complex landscape of loss, is emblematic of popular myths and discourses on grief—evidence that logics of retribution are not far removed from distancing discourses on death and dying in the United States. Legal scholar Jodi Madeira argues in her recent volume *Killing McVeigh*—a thoughtful map of the experiences of survivors and victims' families in the aftermath of the Oklahoma City bombing—that complex forms of memory work and closure have been systematically denied by culture, particularly by way of the institutions of law and media.

> First, closure is most affirmatively *not* what contemporary culture says it is—absolute finality, in the sense of such colloquial phrases as "over and done with," "dealt with," "put behind one's self," "let by-

gones be bygones," "forgive and forget." Closure is not a state of being, a quality, or even a realization. If closure exists at all, it must be as a process, a recursive series of adjustments that a self makes in response to external, often institutional, developments. It involves struggles between self and other, embodiment and disembodiment, agency and passivity, speech and silence. This view of closure as a strategic, sense-making process suggests that it not only cannot but *should not* be exorcised from contemporary culture.[61]

Judith Butler writes similarly on the manner in which grief and mourning are fundamentally social and transformative.

There is losing, as we know, but there is also the transformative effect of loss, and this latter cannot be charted or planned. One can try to choose it, but it may be that this experience of transformation deconstitutes choice at some level. I do not think, for instance, that one can invoke the Protestant ethic when it comes to loss. One cannot say, "Oh, I'll go through loss this way, and that will be the result, and I'll apply myself to the task, and I'll endeavor to achieve the resolution of grief that is before me." I think one is hit by waves, and that one starts out the day with an aim, a project, a plan, and finds oneself foiled. One finds oneself fallen. One is exhausted but does not know why. Something is larger than one's own deliberate plan, one's own project, one's own knowing and choosing.[62]

Finally, Susan Hirsch, legal anthropologist and survivor of the 1998 East Africa Embassy bombings, where her husband died, writes that victim impact statements are always double-edged opportunities for the grieving: "Recounting a story in public may allow it to veer out of the teller's control. Victims may break down while testifying—crying, shaking, unable to complete the story," invoking feelings of having failed at the *one* duty that could be performed for a loved one.[63] "Less obviously," Hirsch adds, "the state's goals shape victims' stories; the prosecution routinely focuses not on what had the most impact on a victim but what will have the most impact in convincing a jury to impose the harshest penalty."[64] Across her narrative, she imagines, against the symbolic and political uses of victim statements for conviction and death, what it might be to sustain "an intimate and heartfelt expression of reverence for dead and living victims" within the law,⁶⁵ where we might be able "to recognize the importance of the inter-relationships between the inherent, experiential and structural qualities of both vulnerability and victimization."⁶⁶ Perhaps this is not a space for the law directly, but it raises the question of what kinds of experiences and performances of loss the law might aspire to recognize. Instead, in *Payne*, when the prosecutor argues that "*[t]here is nothing you can do*" repeatedly, with the force of law behind him, relationships, possibilities, and people disappear on both sides of the table.

Bare Life and Mourning

> Law is not like literature, but people are not rattlesnakes. The Court's recent death penalty jurisprudence has a decidedly political agenda—it dehumanizes the defendant in order to more easily cast him out of the human community. We ought not to pretend that storytelling and empathy are value neutral, when in fact they are potent weapons in the battle over a basic question of values: whether every human being is entitled to some dignity.
>
> —Susan Bandes, "Empathy, Narrative, and Victim Impact Statements"

The "quick glimpse of life" at the heart of *Payne* is not so far removed from "bare life" considerations. Political philosopher Giorgio Agamben argues, "If there is a line in every modern state marking the point at which the decision on life becomes a decision on death, and biopolitics can turn into thanatopolitics, this line no longer appears today as a stable border dividing two clearly distinct zones."⁶⁷ The force of law, then, focuses upon the instability of this boundary, anxiously apparent in law's capacity to generate and maintain exceptions. In this zone of indeterminacy, the victim, as yet another category of inclusive exclusion, is symptomatic of law's double-sided essence where rights won may offer new and more insidious foundations for power against those very actors. The question of how the rights-bearing actor might be related to the life stripped of political identity and meaningful recognition is one that allows for more candid reflections upon the worth of people, including the relative absence of dignity⁶⁸ and alternatives to punitiveness in the cultural imagination. It also exposes us to law's bafflement with and denial of the multiplicity of ways in which violence, grief, and loss may materialize. In this way, *Payne* poses the kinds of problems that disrupt the ability of the state to adjudicate membership in the political community of its most pain-filled members. Here, victims and perpetrators are treated as legal monsters: living corpses, grief stricken, and volatile hybrids, irreconcilable bodies of threat and bearers of rights, caught between a politics of pity and a politics of risk, moving from suffering beings to dangerous beings to half-dead beings, with perpetrators on death row and survivors in the grief-filled afterlife of a capital case. The life that may be killed by abandonment is not so far removed from that of the victim or the perpetrator in *Payne* because in many respects, the life devoid of value is the life whose pain we imagine there is nothing about which we can do.

The questions and hauntings at the heart of *Payne* are similarly not unrelated to the cultural assumptions and intersubjective relations at the heart of the contemporary practice of mass incarceration in the United States and a rapidly developing international criminal justice. As anthropologist Kamari Maxine Clarke writes, the question of "what is actually in the interest of victims" is a question that is "central to the reconfiguration of sovereignty today."[69] She writes, "By working on behalf of victims—'bare life' survivors whose existence is maintained by virtue of their exclusion as political agents—it is important to recognize that the power of the decision over what constitutes the life that is thereby taken outside of the political sphere (the polis) is actually the site of sovereignty . . . the force of law—its techniques of coercion and the disciplinary mechanisms—that makes possible the new world order of justice and politics."[70] In this way, the punitive imagination, with its individualistic and retributive lens, is only one possible vision and performance of law and sovereignty, one that is quickly being interwoven across local, global, and transnational space by way of the rule of law and the symbolic political value of the victim. I am interested in a deeper and more rarely articulated or theorized global carceral imagination, one that follows the most vulnerable, those subjectivities that are linked across sites of structural violence, disaster and conflict dislocation, "open-air" prisons, concentration and refugee camps through a wide swathe of potential performances and recognitions within and beyond the law. In Vivian Berger's personal response to *Payne*, she writes of her clinical work as a child of Jewish refugees who escaped the death camps: "I had also learned that survivors of ordinary homicides undergo forms of rage, grief, fear, guilt, fatigue, numbing, and other symptoms of post-traumatic stress disorder remarkably similar to those of victims of mammoth catastrophes such as the Holocaust and Hiroshima."[71] A life, as she puts it, that is inevitably "sensitized . . . from the beginning to the social divisiveness, not to speak of immorality, of valuing some lives over others."[72] She hopes that victims will recognize "*Payne*'s approach as a fraud on themselves and on those whose shoes they have donned" and that *Payne* "denigrates victims while falsely promising help to their mourners."[73] In the politics and performance of mourning, one worry then is that unacknowledged or disacknowledged grief, the kind that is subject solely to symbolic and political use as opposed to the life lived with loss, perpetuates a certain construction of rage—the use of a deeply personal and irrational grief—as a static call for revenge and a denial of structural violence, hopelessly mired in various levels of social and biological death.

Payne furthermore ultimately depicts the pain of loss as unshareable[74] and demands a punitive response. In that effort, I believe it nonetheless discloses that in the making and unmaking of the world, there is a transaction at the heart of pain—where one person's "statement 'I am in pain' becomes the conduit through which [she] may move out of an inexpressible privacy and suffocation of [her] pain."[75] As Das argues, this does not mean one is understood but neither does it mean that pain is "that inexpressible something that destroys communication or marks an exit from one's existence in language. . . . Instead," and this is most critical, "it makes a claim asking for acknowledgment, which may be given or denied."[76] Judith Butler writes,

> When we lose certain people, or when we are dispossessed from a place, or a community, we may simply feel that we are undergoing something temporary, that mourning will be over and some restoration of prior order will be achieved. But maybe when we undergo what we do, something about who we are is revealed, something that delineates the ties we have to others, that shows us that these ties constitute what we are, ties or bonds that compose us. It is not as if an "I" exists independently over here and then simply loses a "you" over there, especially if the attachment to "you" is part of what composes who "I" am. If I lose you, under these conditions then I not only mourn the loss, but I become inscrutable to myself. Who "am" I, without you? When we lose some of these ties by which we are constituted, we do not know who we are or what to do. On one level, I think I have lost "you" only to discover that "I" have gone missing as well. At another level, perhaps what I have lost "in" you, that for

which I have no ready vocabulary, is a relationality that is composed neither exclusively of myself nor you, but is to be conceived as *the tie* by which those terms are differentiated and related.[77]

In this manner, law could be more like a kind of mourning. It might remember, as penologist Nils Christie writes, that "[l]oss might lead to sorrow, and mourning. It might also lead to anger, and punishment," but "[i]f pain is to be given away, it is only acceptable in a form with structured similarities to mourning."[78] Here, the "strangeness of the world revealed by death, by its non-inhabitability," Veena Das adds, "can be transformed into a world in which one can dwell again, in full awareness of life that has to be lived in loss."[79] The force of relations at this intersection of lived experience might help us, according to anthropologist Clara Han, "give up our capacity to quickly judge others" and instead "become receptive to both the hurts *and* the possibilities in this world."[80] The relationships between perpetrators and society, victims and society, perpetrators and victims are undeniable. Those relationships may be lived in deep disconnection and may also someday be recovered in mysterious and unanticipated ways—with varying degrees of intensity across time and space. In the unwished for shattering of space and lives, possibilities for social change nonetheless open up. As so many victims and their loved ones have argued, the embodied experience of having journeyed on this difficult and painful path, somehow and sometimes gives them a different kind of visionary insight, a plurality of visions that is fluid, flexible, and open ended. Putting one foot in front of the other, they carve pathways to better and worse lives.

As it stands, law's efforts to recognize victims in *Payne* follow a continuum that marks, as Wendy Brown argues, a "strikingly unemancipatory political project."[81] This trajectory emerges ironically from the kinds of claims that would seek to imagine an otherwise—but nevertheless culminate in a "foreclosure" of freedom by way of politicized identity's "impulse to inscribe in the law and in other political registers its historical and present pain rather than conjure an imagined future of power to make itself," the kind of future Nicholas might have needed.[82] Such absences are not just a failure of imagination but a failure to understand how desire—our desires—for recognition are undergirded by configurations (neoliberalism, capitalism, disciplinary structures that drive law) that obscure deeper needs, structure violence, and drive our failed imagination and political projects. In the discourse of wounded attachments, hierarchies of pain and human worth are inevitable, with some claims achieving expression and others submerged forever. But the problem with a "pain-filled identity politics" or the victims' rights movement was never people's pain but rather a distant, superficial, symbolic response by others to pain that was not theirs—an inattention that culminated in a clamoring and proliferation of the language of rights—that had the fatal irony of allowing distant others never truly to be concerned with the conditions, experiences, and realities that structure suffering. It may very well have distanced victims from their own pain and certainly exacerbated it. As Brown goes on to argue, one possibility in all of this is that "the problematic of pain installed at the heart of many contemporary contradictory demands for political recognition" may long for something "more than revenge," more than death, and that may simply be "the chance to be heard into a certain release, recognized into self-overcoming, incited into possibilities for triumphing over, and hence, losing, itself," requiring "a radically democratic political culture that can sustain such a project in its midst without being overtaken by it . . . even as we acknowledge the elements of suffering and healing we might be negotiating."[83] *Payne* reveals the necessity of a reckoning and recognition with the nature of our cultural capacity to discern and make a future at all . . . for all. All of which brings me back to Nicholas, who, I (precariously) imagine, still worries for his mom and his sister as a young man today. What might it have meant for the law truly to concern itself with Nicholas's life, the "down the road" that the state's attorney imagines for us?

Let me answer with an equally unacceptable imagining—the kind that follows *Payne* with all of its vectors of outrage, mad hypotheticals, bipolar oppositions. In the face of the unfathomable, in the event of my own violent death, I would want my daughter to be surrounded by a community of actors, near and far, private and public, who exist daily in the knowledge that terrible tragedy can happen and that violence and death are the province of distinctly human domains as is life. I would want actors who could live with her through the onslaught of irreconcilables, the repetitious immersion in details, returns, and revisions, necessary to arrive elsewhere. Amid the inevitable fleeting, pithy symbolic responses that might aggravate her pain, I would hope that these actors would be there for the *longue durée*, for the protracted process, as she moves through space and time in search of a hard-earned solace that carries with it futurity. In the event that nothing can be known of the uniqueness of my death and the place of pain in her lived life after, or that of millions of others, I would hope simply for the wish—for the imagining of a discourse like this within the law—a usable antidote to the punitive imagination that devalues us all, the kind of hope that we might extend to Nicholas. We might think of this as a law of the living—law that is immanent in all of life's many forms—including its senseless tragedies.

Acknowledgments

This paper benefitted from discussions and engagements 1) as a visiting fellow and participant in the 2010-2011 "Virtuous Empathy: Scientific and Humanistic Investigations" project funded by the John Templeton Foundation and hosted by Indiana University's Poynter Center for the Study of Ethics and American Institutions; 2) as a participant in "The Punitive Imagination" Symposium hosted by the University of Alabama Law School in 2012; and 3) as a guest speaker at the Center for the Study of Social Justice at the University of Tennessee. I would like to thank Austin Sarat, Patricia Ewick, and anonymous reviewers for their helpful comments.

Cases

Booth v. Maryland, 482 U.S. 496 (1987)
McCleskey v. Kemp, 81 U.S. 279 (1987)
Payne v. Tennessee, 501 U.S. 808 (1991)
South Carolina v. Gathers, 490 U.S. 805 (1989)
State of Tennessee v. Payne, 791 S.W.2d 10 (Tenn. 1990)

Notes

1. Martha Minow, "Which Question? Which Lie? Reflections on the Physician-Assisted Suicide Cases," *Supreme Court Review* 1997 (1997): 2.

2. Id. at 25.

3. Id. at 20.

4. Id. at 26.

5. Giorgio Agamben, *Homo Sacer: Sovereign Power and Bare Life* (Meridian: Crossing Aesthetics), Kindle edition, 1559–66.

6. Id. at 1355–63.

7. Austin Sarat, "Introduction: On Pain and Death as Facts of Legal Life," in *Pain, Death, and the Law*, ed. Austin Sarat (Ann Arbor: University of Michigan Press, 2001), 5.

8. *Payne v. Tennessee*, 501 U.S. 808 (1991) at 814.

9. Jennifer Culbert, "The Sacred Name of Pain: The Role of Victim Impact Evidence in Death Penalty Sentencing Decisions," in *Pain, Death and*

the Law, ed. Austin Sarat (Ann Arbor: University of Michigan Press, 2004), 103–35.

10. *Payne v. Tennessee*, 815.

11. Peter Brooks, "Illicit Stories," *Diacritics* 25 (1995): 42 (40–51).

12. Susan Bandes, "Empathy, Narrative, and Victim Impact Statements," *University of Chicago Law Review* 63 (1996): 362 (361–412).

13. Austin Sarat, "Imagining the Law of the Father: Loss, Dread, and Mourning in the Sweet Hereafter," *Law and Society Review* 34 (2000): 4 (3–48).

14. Michelle Brown, *The Culture of Punishment* (New York: New York University Press, 2009).

15. Marc Mauer and Tracy Huling, "Young Black Americans and the Criminal Justice System: Five Years Later" (Washington, D.C.: Sentencing Project, 1995).

16. See Carolyn J. Dean, *The Fragility of Empathy after the Holocaust* (Ithaca, NY: Cornell University Press, 2004); Jodi Halpern and Harvey M. Weinstein, "Rehumanizing the Other: Empathy and Reconciliation," *Human Rights Quarterly* 26 (2004): 561–83; Douglas Hollan, "Being There: On the Imaginative Aspects of Understanding Others and Being Understood," *Ethos* 36, no. 4 (2004): 475–89; Mona Lynch and Craig Haney, "Mapping the Racial Bias of the White Male Capital Juror: Jury Composition and the 'Empathic Divide,'" *Law and Society Review* 45, no. 1 (2011): 69–102.

17. Judith Butler, *Precarious Life: The Powers of Mourning and Violence* (New York: Verso, 2004).

18. The fellowship was supported by a grant from the Templeton Foundation, "Virtuous Empathy: Scientific and Humanistic Investigations," directed by Richard Miller and housed at Indiana University's Poynter Center for the Study of Ethics and American Institutions.

19. The victim impact statement is a written statement that describes the impact of the crime on the victim and/or the victim's family. It is often attached to a presentence report and given orally by an officer of the court. It may include information on the seriousness of the victim's physical, emotional, and psychological injuries. It may include such matters as the victim's opinion of the offender, her fear of revictimization, her opinion on the recommended sentence, and even her own sentence recommendation. Over the years, victim impact evidence has assumed complex forms without a standard for scope, quantity, or type. This kind of evidence now includes the victim's good character, talents, intelligence, spirituality, work ethic, education, and community standing with few limits on the number of witnesses who can give victim impact evidence. It also allows for a wide range of evidence concerning the mur-

der's effects on the victim's family. Various kinds of media may be included as well: poems, videos, predeath photos, or items made by the victim.

20. *Payne v. Tennessee*, 822.

21. Id. at 826.

22. *Booth v. Maryland*, 482 U.S. 496 (1987) at 2542.

23. Culbert, "The Sacred Name of Pain," 128.

24. Social histories are inquiries based upon repeated in-depth interviews, the review of any and all official institutional documents pertaining to the defendant's life, and extensive interviews with family members and those who knew the defendant at various life stages.

25. Craig Haney, "Psychological Secrecy and the Death Penalty: Observations on 'the Mere Extinguishment of Life,'" *Studies in Law, Politics and Society* 16 (1997): 6 (3–69).

26. Id. at 11, 22.

27. Id, 22.

28. See Diana Minot, "Silenced Stories: How Victim Impact Evidence in Capital Trials Prevents the Jury from Hearing the Constitutionally Required Story." Here is an excerpt from her reading of the sentencing phase of *People v. Foster*, 242 P.3d 105, 124–25 (Cal. 2010):

> Four of defendant's siblings testified concerning their childhood. Larry testified that Pearl and Art beat the children, sometimes while the children were tied up, and forced them to steal. . . . Art killed Larry's sister Helen . . . by smothering her. In 1957, the children were taken by the State of Nebraska and placed in Whitehall Home for Children. Larry stated that a housemother at Whitehall taught both the defendant and him about sex, instructing them that "you got to hit them in the mouth before you do anything or they don't like it." He testified that he and defendant were transferred to a state mental institution, where they were beaten and sexually abused and drugs were administered. . . . Another sibling, Steven, corroborated the foregoing testimony and also recounted that "the first sexual experiences were the girls with Art and the boys with mom." The eldest daughter, who ran away before Art joined the family, testified that her father molested her, with Pearl's knowledge, and that Pearl blamed the daughter for the molestation.

There is little way in which to relate to the ordinariness of violence and trauma in this kind of mitigating evidence.

29. Kerry Dunn and Paul J. Kaplan. "The Ironies of Helping: Social Interventions and Executable Subjects," *Law & Society Review* 43, no. 2 (2009): 337.

30. Minow, "Which Question? Which Lie?," 20, 28.

31. Austin Sarat, "Introduction: On Pain and Death as Facts of Legal Life," 14.

32. Veena Das, "Language and Body: Transactions in the Construction of Pain," in *Social Suffering*, ed. Arthur Kleinman, Veena Das, and Margaret Lock (Berkeley: University of California Press, 1997), 68–69.

33. *Payne v. Tennessee*, 812–13.

34. Id. at 832.

35. Id.

36. Oral argument transcripts found at http://www.oyez.org/cases/1990-1999/1990/1990_90_5721, accessed July 21, 2012.

37. *Payne v. Tennessee*, 838.

38. *Booth v. Maryland*, 42.

39. Id. at 26.

40. Sarat, "Vengeance, Victims and the Identities of Law," *Social & Legal Studies* 6, no. 2 (1997): 172, 177.

41. Id. at 173, citing *Booth v. Maryland*, 512.

42. Id. at 173, citing *Booth v. Maryland*, 512.

43. Vivian Berger, "*Payne* and Suffering: A Personal Reflection and a Victim-Centered Critique," 20 Fla. St. U. L. Rev. 21 (1992), 49 (21–65).

44. David Baldus, C. Pulaski, and G. Woodworth, *Equal Justice and the Death Penalty* (Boston: Northeastern University Press, 1990).

45. Lauren Berlant, "The Subject of True Feeling: Pain, Privacy and Politics," in *Cultural Pluralism, Identity Politics, and the Law*, ed. Austin Sarat and Thomas R. Kearns (Ann Arbor: University of Michigan Press, 1999), 11 (49–84).

46. Alan Hyde, *Bodies of Law* (Princeton: Princeton University Press, 1997), 32.

47. Id. at 32.

48. Lauren Berlant, "Introduction: Compassion (and Withholding)," in *Compassion: The Culture and Politics of an Emotion*, ed. Lauren Berlant (New York: Routledge, 2004), 6 (1–13).

49. Id, 7.

50. Pierre Bourdieu, *The Weight of the World: Social Suffering in Contemporary Society* (Stanford: Stanford University Press, 1999).

51. See Amy Coplan and Peter Goldie, *Empathy: Philosophical and Psychological Perspectives* (New York: Oxford University Press, 2011); Suzanne

Keen, *Empathy and the Novel* (New York: Oxford University Press, 2007); Nancy Sherman, "Empathy and Imagination," *Midwest Studies in Philosophy* 22 (1998): 82–119; Lauren Wispé, "History of the Concept of Empathy," in *Empathy and Its Development*, ed. Nancy Eisenberg and Janet Strayer (New York: Cambridge University Press, 1987).

52. Patrice Canivez, "Pathologies of Recognition," *Philosophy and Social Criticism* 37 (2011): 851 (851–77).

53. Lauren Berlant, "Introduction: Compassion (and Withholding)," 10.

54. Many of the claims about empathy in this chapter are critiques of Western notions of the term. A good deal of empathy scholarship has pointed to the term's cultural underpinnings. Important sources include Wispé, "History of the Concept of Empathy"; Carolyn Dean, *The Fragility of Empathy after the Holocaust* (Ithaca, NY: Cornell University Press, 2004); Keen, *Empathy and the Novel*; and C. Jason Throop, "On the Problem of Empathy: The Case of Yap, Federated States of Micronesia" *Ethos* 36 no. 4 (2008): 402–26.

55. Patricia Williams, *The Alchemy of Race and Rights: Diary of a Law Professor* (Cambridge, MA: Harvard University Press, 1992), 11.

56. Here, we might measure the tension between the necessary claim for rights against their inherently problematic place in law, as outlined by Patricia Williams (*The Alchemy of Race and Rights*), against the critique of rights claims as fundamentally exclusionary (Wendy Brown, "Wounded Attachments," *States of Injury: Power and Freedom in Late Modernity* (Princeton, NJ: Princeton University Press, 1995).

57. Didier Fassin and Richard Rechtman, *The Empire of Trauma: An Inquiry into the Condition of Victimhood* (Princeton, NJ: Princeton University Press, 2009), 279.

58. Id. at 284.

59. Jacqueline Aquino Siapno, "Living through Terror: Everyday Resilience in East Timor and Aceh," *Social Identities* 15 (2009): 50.

60. Elizabeth Beck, Sarah Britto, and Arlene Andrews, *In the Shadow of Death: Restorative Justice and Death Row Families* (New York: Oxford University Press, 2007); Susan F. Hirsch, *Terrorism, Grief, and a Victim's Quest for Justice* (Princeton, NJ: Princeton University Press, 2006); Jody Madeira, *Killing McVeigh: The Death Penalty and the Myth of Closure* (New York: New York University Press, 2012); Susan Miller, *After the Crime: The Power of Restorative Justice Dialogues Between Victims and Violent Offenders* (New York: New York University Press, 2006); Susan Sharp, *Hidden Victims: The Effects of the Death Penalty on Families of the Accused* (Brunswick, NJ: Rutgers University Press, 2005).

61. Madeira, *Killing McVeigh*, xxiii.
62. Butler, *Precarious Life*.
63. Susan Hirsch, "Victims for the Prosecution," *Boston Review*, found at http://bostonreview.net/BR27.5/hirsch.html, accessed June 21, 2012. See also: Susan F. Hirsch, *Terrorism, Grief, and a Victim's Quest for Justice* (Princeton, NJ: Princeton University Press, 2006).
64. Id.
65. Id.
66. Sandra Walklate, "Reframing Criminal Victimization: Finding a Place for Vulnerability and Resilience," *Theoretical Criminology* 15 (2011): 179–84; 183.
67. Agamben, *Homo Sacer*, 122.
68. See Carol Steiker's elaboration of dignity in this volume.
69. Kamari Maxine Clarke, "Global Justice, Local Controversies," in *Paths to International Justice: Social and Legal Perspectives*, ed. Marie-Benedicte Dembour and Tobias Kelly (Cambridge: Cambridge University Press, 2007), 151; see also Kamari Maxine Clarke, *Fictions of Justice: The International Criminal Court and the Challenge of Legal Pluralism in Sub-Saharan Africa* (New Haven, CT: Yale University Press, 2009).
70. Id. at 158.
71. Berger, "*Payne* and Suffering," 62–63.
72. Id. at 63.
73. Id. at 65.
74. Elaine Scarry, *The Body in Pain: The Making and Unmaking of the World* (New York: Oxford University Press, 1985).
75. Das, "Language and Body," 70.
76. Id.
77. Butler, *Precarious Life*.
78. Nils Christie, *Limits to Pain* (Oslo: Universitetsforlaget, 1981), 100.
79. Das, "Language and Body," 69.
80. Clara Han, *Life in Debt: Times of Care and Violence in Neoliberal Chile* (Berkeley: University of California Press, 2012), 234–35.
81. Wendy Brown, "Wounded Attachments," in *States of Injury: Power and Freedom in Late Modernity* (Princeton, NJ: Princeton University Press, 1995), 5.
82. Id. at 66.
83. Id. at 74–75.

Afterword

Time, Imagination, and Punishment

Patricia Ewick

Beginning in February 2013, over one hundred of the detainees at Guantanamo Bay Naval Base began a hunger strike to protest their indefinite detention without trial. The Guantanamo hunger strike catapulted the legal plight of the prisoners back into the news and has generated concern, if not sympathy, for the internees. Headlines in the *New York Times* have referred to the Guantanamo "stain," declaring that "Despair Drives Guantanamo Detainees to Revolt."[1] An op-ed recounted the story of one prisoner, Samir Naji al Hasan Moqbel, including graphic details of the forced feeding he endures twice a day. It also included an account of his innocence, his family, and his resolve to die so that "the eyes of the world will once again look to Guantanamo before it is too late."[2]

The forced feeding so vividly described in the op-ed has been condemned by human rights activists around the world. The American Red Cross and the American Medical Association have described it as a form of torture. Jeremy Lazarus, president of the American Medical Association, in a letter addressed to Chuck Hagel, secretary of defense, said that the forced feeding of detainees violates "core ethical values of the medical profession." He went on to state, "Every competent patient has the right to refuse medical intervention, including life-sustaining interventions." A group of United Nations human rights officials stated: "Hunger strikers should be protected from all forms of coercion, even more so when this is done through force and in some cases through physical violence."[3] Even President Obama has decried the situation, "It is not sustainable. The notion that we are going to keep 100 individuals in no man's land in perpetuity." He added, "All of us should reflect on why exactly we are doing this?

Why are we doing this?"[4] What is most remarkable about Obama's question is that he is asking it at all. His invitation for reflection is an indication of the relative success of the hunger-striking prisoners. The eyes of the world are not just on the prisoners at Guantanamo; they are focused on their captors as well.

The most famous hunger strikes in recent history were those staged by the Irish Republican Army (IRA) detainees in 1981 in which ten prisoners eventually died.[5] The IRA detainees were striking for political prisoner status, which had been revoked in the mid-1970s when the British government refused to acknowledge their nationalist cause, calling them "ordinary" (not political) criminals and terrorists. According to Mulcahy, the strike—or more precisely the willingness of the prisoners to strike until death—was less a means to secure some end, such as the right not to wear a uniform than it was an enactment of the very status they were claiming.[6] Their willingness to die for their commitment to a principle was a powerful rejoinder to the government's argument that they were nothing more than common criminals.

The hunger strike is thus a dramatic performance that is less instrumental than it is ontological. In Kafka's "The Hunger Artist," the protagonist locks himself in a cage and starves for the amusement of onlookers. "It is the public gaze that keeps him [the hunger artist] visible, however ruthlessly he wills his flesh to disappear, and it is only when he is deprived of this surveillance that he dies. The moral seems to be that it is not by food that we survive but by the gaze of others; and it is impossible to live by hunger unless we can be seen or represented doing so."[7]

The spectacle of hunger exposes not only the abjection and principled commitment of its practitioners but, as importantly, it displays the power of its target. In essence, as a tactic of protest, the hunger strike activates and then uses the power of the target against itself. For this reason Gene Sharp has referred to such tactics as political jujitsu.[8] Those targeted by the strike can either allow the strikers to die (as Margaret Thatcher did in 1981) or intervene through forced feeding (as the United States is currently doing in Guantanamo). In choosing either of these responses, the target cannot refrain from publically exercising and displaying a power that lies at the heart of the protest.

There are countermoves that the target of hunger strikes can make. In 1911, in the midst of strikes by imprisoned suffragists, the British Parliament passed the Cat and Mouse Act which allowed authorities to release prisoners who were striking and reincarcerate them at a later date.⁹ The Cat and Mouse Act interrupted the spectacle of starving and—deprived of the gaze of others—presumably the act of starving itself.

Of course, there are also counter-countermoves that strikers can make to ensure that even death will not disrupt the spectacle of hunger. In the 1981 IRA strike, ten men initially began the strike; as one died, another prisoner would take his place so that there were always ten men starving. This macabre relay race also worked to maintain the resolve of the strikers themselves. After the initial deaths, the pressure to continue was immense. To have given up would have rendered the sacrifices of their comrades meaningless.

Whether we conceive of the hunger strike as a game of cat and mouse, a jujitsu match, or a relay race, its dynamic possibilities lay bare the inescapable relationality of punishment. Hunger strikes stand as an extreme case of power collapsing under the weight of its own intensity. They also illustrate the ontological traps that penal power can trigger in its efforts to incapacitate its objects. In this afterword, I will argue that the excesses of our system of mass incarceration—not simply our extrajudicial prison in Cuba—have undermined its moral warrant to punish. More specifically, I will make the case that we have created a landscape of abjection that has many asking, like President Obama, "Why are we doing this?"

The After War on Crime

We are at a critical juncture in the history of contemporary punishment in the United States. After almost four decades of an unrelenting buildup of the penal state, there are some indications—nascent and ambiguous—that we may be approaching if not the end of the war on crime at least a period in which we are drifting toward greater restraint in our punishment practices.¹⁰ The prospect of the de facto abolition of capital punishment—as more and more states eliminate or declare a moratorium on executions—represents the most conspicuous abatement of the severity of punishment, yet there are other less dramatic reforms, proposals, and protests that signal a crisis in the penal state. The Fair Sentencing Act of 2010 has reduced the weight ratio of crack cocaine to powder cocaine and eliminated the mandatory minimum five-year sentence for possession of crack cocaine, a major driver of skyrocketing prison populations. Consequently, in 2010 prison releases exceeded admissions for the first time since the Bureau of Justice Statistics began collecting data in 1977.¹¹ In a time of fiscal crisis and global insecurity, we are beginning to confront the unsustainability of the punishing state.

Reflecting on these changes, Mary Louise Frampton, Ian Haney Lopez, and Jonathan Simon have declared, "This war on crime although currently at or near its peak in terms of imprisonment rates and law enforcement power is in some important sense over."[12] While such a conclusion may be premature and perhaps even naive, one thing is clear: the unabated and largely uncontested intensification and expansion of the carceral system has moderated and there is some compelling evidence that there is a cultural and political turning away—or at least questioning—of the politics of revenge that has fueled it.

If we are standing at this threshold of a new culture of punishment—then it is all the more important to consider the deep and durable effects decades of mass incarceration has had on whom, what we are, and where we might be headed. We need to take stock of the damage that has been done to generations of men and women whose lives have been destroyed, as well as to communities hollowed out by the loss of so many to our democracy and to our culture. We need to envision possibilities of punishing justly and humanely.

I must admit when I first heard the title of this symposium, "The Punitive Imagination," I was not thinking of justice, reform, or the possibility of punishing humanely. It was against the historical backdrop of penal populism and the politics of revenge that I, instead, inflected the word *punitive* and glossed over the word *imagination*. I assumed that the title's referent was to a punishing and harsh imagination—an imagination inflamed by fear and anxiety, creatively finding new and extreme ways of inflicting punishment. I thought of the ways in which this punitive imagination feeds fantasies of living in a risk-free world, purged of dangerous others. It was an imagination manifest in a politics and a culture that is stalked by the specter of vulnerable victims and predatory criminals. It was with all of these entailments in mind that I sat down to read the essays in this volume. It is a measure of their power that they led me finally to inflect the word *imagination* instead of *punitive*. In various ways each of the essays suggest to me the degree to which the punishing state has been as much a result of the *suppression* of imagination as it has been a *product* of imagination. They led me to appreciate how a reactivation of imagination is crucial if we are to move through this threshold.

When I say that the carceral state has been predicated on the suppression of imagination I refer more precisely to the ways in which time—or temporality—is implicated in our contemporary practice of mass incarceration. Imagination necessarily involves projecting a future or invoking a past, since that too involves an act of creative reconstruction. At the heart of imagination, in other words, is a counterfactual—what might have been; what might be. But whether it is retrospective or prospective, *to imagine* is always and necessarily to transcend the present. A theme running through the essays in this volume is the degree to which the carceral state has been constructed on a perversion of the temporality inherent in imagination. They have underscored how much of the punishing state is based on the annihilation of past and future and, consequently, the foreclosure of any possibility of change, alteration, or becoming. It is my argument in this afterword that a penal system that denies its captives a past or a future denies itself one as well. Even more than the crushing cost of mass incarceration, it is this realization that is contributing to the overwhelming sense of futility and waste that is beginning to enter our public discourse about punishment.

Caleb Smith considers time in the context of a penal system that has abandoned any recognizable discourses of justice and whose only objective is to incapacitate. He notes that unlike other justifications of punishment–retribution, rehabilitation, or deterrence—incapacitation is severed from the crime; in this sense it floats free from the past. "[I]ncapacitation is putatively about preventing the inmate from committing some unspecified *future* transgression. . . . Incapacitation needs no reference to a past event; it is anxiously prospective. From one point of view, then, incapacitation is not really a theory of punishment at all. It is a policy for the management of social instability and social space. It does not require a vengeful memory. Its signature effects are insecurity and fear."[13]

I would amend this characterization of incapacitation as anxiously prospective or perhaps interpret it somewhat differently. Incapacitation may be premised on a possible future crime, but in avoiding that eventuality, it consigns inmates to a ceaseless present. Incapacitation constructs a never-ending present, freezing one in time and suspending one in space. By contrast, other justifications for punishment define by virtue of their own internal logic a point at which they might conceivably achieve their ends. We can imagine declaring for instance: "He is reformed," or "We are avenged." But no such declaration can be made in the case of incapacitation. It can never once and for all fulfill its own objectives. There is no conceivable point in time at which we would say, "He is, finally, incapacitated enough." That future about which we are so anxiously oriented, in which some hypothetical crime might occur, is not something we are moving toward nor is it something we are trying to change or avert. Rather, it is something we are running from, endlessly and in place.

Stephen Garvey's essay is also about the erasure of time. By treating all citizens the same in the course of punishment, the state fails to perceive that particular temporality known as a life: that our humanity inheres in the fact that we are born, live, and die—the so-called beginning, middle, and end that are the sine qua non of narrative. Stories, of course, are based on the unfolding of chained events in relational settings that culminate in such a way as to make those events, actors, and relationships meaningful. Yet when we fail to perceive those whom we punish to be psychologically, historically, and sociologically complex beings, we flatten them—focusing only on the moment of the crime or of the punishment.[14] We deprive them of a story, which, as David Luban argues, is to deny them their dignity.[15] According to Kaufman-Osborn, rather than a story, we endow the penal subject with a will, which in turn becomes the justification for punishment. "[I]f it is to justify the pain it inflicts, the legal order must abstract the individual subject from the constitutive relational contexts it inhabits and then, retrospectively, identify the autonomous will of that deracinated being as the first cause of the harm for which it is blamed and then punished."[16]

Furthermore, in ignoring that narrative we call a life, the state is free to ignore its own complicity in creating what Garvey refers to as "second-class citizens." Garvey argues that the state's authority to punish (as opposed to merely coerce compliance) is undermined when it is complicit in producing the conditions that consign some of its subjects to lives of deprivation, violence, living outside of the polity, to "a life without hope." Since hope is a debt we pay to the future, to deprive someone of hope is to also suspend them in time, to an unchanging present. Recognizing the distinctive pain of such a state, the Supreme Court ruled in *Graham v. Florida* (2010) that life without parole for juveniles involved in nonhomicide crimes violated the proportionality principle of the Eighth Amendment. Justice Kennedy's majority opinion stated that it was the particular deprivation of hope that made such a sentence cruel. "It deprives the convict of the most basic liberties without giving hope of restoration, except perhaps by executive clemency—the remote possibility of which does not mitigate the harshness of the sentence."[17]

Indeed it is possible to extend Garvey's argument and the force of his critique by recognizing that the chief mechanism for producing what he calls "second-class citizens" during the past forty years has been the criminal justice system itself. The state does not merely fail to protect or preserve a subject's first-class citizenship, through the act of punishing it produces second-class citizens. In a regime of mass incarceration the state also becomes a principle, not merely an accomplice in ensuring that legally innocent citizens—the families and communities devastated by systematically racist criminal justice policies—are also doomed to a life of exclusion, deprivation, and second-class citizenship. "'Incarceration,' Wacquant writes, 'has de facto become America's largest government program for the poor.' As the ascendant neoliberals (Republicans and Democrats alike) took apart the midcentury's institutions of welfare and public health, and as the industrial economy gave way to a postindustrial order, characterized by a heightened instability and the erosion of workers' rights, governments began using prisons to manage a whole range of social problems—mental illness, drug addiction, vagrancy, and above all poverty itself—which had previously been addressed by other means."[18]

Garvey's argument is that the state should moderate its punitive response to the crimes of second-class citizens due to the fact that it failed to protect their positive rights to be free from deprivation, indignity, and violence. We could go even further, however: for the past forty years second-class citizenship has actually become the basis for enhancing, rather than mitigating, the severity of punishments. In other words, punishment as a mechanism for racial exclusion has been accomplished not merely by holding second-class citizens equally responsible as first-class citizens but by systematically exposing them to harsher punishments than so-called first-class citizens. Racially motivated stop-and-frisk policies, racially keyed drug laws, and the disproportionate use of the death sentence for African American defendants ratchet up the vulnerability of poor and nonwhite citizens to the punitive state and further undermine the state's right to punish.

At the heart of Garvey's critique is the claim that punishment is inescapably relational and that the morality of responsibility (under what conditions do we hold an actor responsible for his transgression?) and the morality of holding others responsible (under what conditions does the state have standing to hold citizens responsible for committing a crime?) are internally linked. When the state treats you like a second-class citizen it fundamentally changes the nature of that relationship. The state no longer stands in a moral relationship predicated on a set of mutual responsibilities and obligation with its citizens. "It is instead more akin to the relationship between an occupying power and those within the territory it occupies. Those subject to its demands give their obedience based on nothing more than fear. In this connection it should come as no surprise that when second-class citizens describe their relationship with the state, the language they sometimes use is the language of one subject to the supervision of an occupying power: remote, threatening, alienated, alienating."[19]

Of course, occupation, like incapacitation, is never ending; it never leads to anything other than itself or its own downfall. Because occupier and the occupied are defined in relation to one another, they share a fate. In some ways, in consigning its incarcerated to a ceaseless present without hope, the state is likewise incapacitated.

Michelle Brown's essay enlarges the frame of analysis to include not only the one who punishes and the one who is punished. It also includes the penal spectators, who are not directly involved in the practice of punishment but who are nonetheless implicated by virtue of witnessing punishment from a secure place within the sovereignty and by the fact that they "exercise exclusionary judgment from afar."[20]

In a magnificent and moving discussion of *Payne v. Tennessee* and the role of victim impact statements Brown depicts how victims, their families, and defendants are frozen in time and how we as penal spectators are implicated in the act of punishment. The "quick glimpse" that we catch of them at trial is remarkable, not primarily because it is so brief and sparse but because it is so unchanging, so irrevocable. They are all consigned to that state of the "living dead" exquisite corpses—dreadful because they are suspended in a permanent condition of neither being nor becoming "The bereaved are stuck," she writes, "and any possibility of an otherwise is muted." The defendants share a similar fate: "Social histories are pivotal windows into the social forces that create the conditions for violence. They rarely materialize in capital cases, and, as Haney argues, 'genuine narratives of life and death' are 'difficult to find,' with the majority of capital defendants going 'to death row and even to the execution chamber without anyone having heard and considered the harsh facts of their brutal lives or meaningfully analyzed the sobering lessons that are contained in their social histories.'"[21]

The distance that separates the penal spectator occludes the pain that lies at the heart of punishment. In the face of this occlusion, Brown considers the restorative potential of empathy to bridge the distance between the pain of spectator, victim, their loved ones, and the perpetrator. Her conclusion is cautionary. Empathy is a volatile and disturbing emotion. In the context of a criminal trial it can easily become a zero-sum choice over whose pain and suffering to recognize; it can ignite outrage and hatred rather than compassion and understanding; it can disguise a self-centeredness that it seems to belie ("*I look at your pain, and see mine*"), thereby displacing the unique pain of victims and perpetrators with our universal suffering (disguised as empathy). Finally, as Brown reminds us, empathy with the suffering of others cannot only occlude their pain but our collective responsibility for producing it, as well. "This dark side of empathy is irrevocably bound up with punitive imaginaries and their privileging of retribution and revenge over complex forms of solace and long-term attention to loss and grief." In her imaginative conclusion Brown presents an alternative, one in which the glimpse is unfrozen, one in which victims (and presumably others linked by the "chain of pain" that constitutes punishment) could "move[] through space and time in search of a hard-earned solace that carries with it futurity."[22]

Recognition of the inescapable and problematic relationship between those who punish and those who are punished lies at the heart of Austin Sarat's call for a new abolitionism. In *When the State Kills* he argues that capital punishment, carried out in our name, diminishes and deforms us all, and he insists that we "ask what the death penalty does to us, not just what it does for us."[23] This insight also serves as the basis for what Carol Steiker calls our collective dignity. In punishing, at least in ways that humiliate, cause excessive pain, or deny the ontological uniqueness of the punished, we all bear the indignity and degradation that are directed toward prisoners and all those we punish. Steiker argues that despite the apparent distance that separates spectators and punished, we are not secure from the damaging consequences of punishment. Steiker refers to the dignitary losses we suffer as a result of degrading punishment practiced in our collective name. In other words, punishment that is indifferent to dignity pollutes our culture, hardens our hearts, blunts our sensibility, and violates our ontological sanctity. By fixing our frame of reference only on victims and offenders, we—the collective spectators—are eclipsed. We drop out of the scene and, thus, become blind to the consequences of excessive and degrading punishment for those who practice it or for those in whose name it is practiced.

In *Punishment and Culture*, sociologist Philip Smith argues, following Durkheim, that punishment is never simply about regulation, security, or economy.[24] It is inevitably about meaning: the meaning of the moral life of the collective, who we are, and what we value. Controlling these meanings is paramount. In punishing we are engaging in a morally perilous enterprise insofar as punishment necessarily entails doing things that would normally be subject to sanction: taking lives, liberties, or property, for instance.[25] Thus in punishing we are not simply expressing our disgust regarding the transgression or our condemnation of the criminal, we are also asserting the legitimacy and standing of the punishing agent. Accordingly, the rituals and practices of punishment must be designed to simultaneously express all three sentiments—disgust, condemnation, and legitimacy. In doing so, however, there is an ever-present danger that the boundaries between disgust, condemnation, and legitimacy will be blurred and the intended meaning will be subverted, rejected, or misread. Without sufficient care, a penal system that seeks to degrade and dehumanize makes itself vulnerable to humiliation and pollution.

The polluting capacity of punishment is most vividly displayed in forms of resistance in which prisoners deliberately engage in acts of self-abasement and degradation such as the hunger strikes discussed in the introduction. Such acts unleash what Robert Hertz has called the left sacred—that which is both profane and yet dreaded—that lies at the heart of punishment. By activating the dormant potential of punishment, typically so carefully contained, they seek to direct it to their captors.[26] In W. B. Yeats's play "The King's Threshold"[27] the King recognizes the threat of such self-abasements to his own legitimacy.

> He has chosen death, refusing to eat or drink,
> That he may bring disgrace upon me,
> for there is a custom, an old and foolish custom,
> that if a man be wronged, or think that he is wronged,
> and starve upon another's threshold till he dies, the Common people, for all time to come,
> will raise a heavy cry against that threshold,
> Even though it be the King's.

Hunger strikes—and perhaps the less public self-mutilations and abasements performed in solitary confinement—thus represent a usurpation of the role of punisher by the punished so that "he may bring disgrace upon [the King]." What so often goes unseen, or in the case of capital punishment, what is sanitized and medicalized, becomes graphically and dramatically available for viewing,[28] which forces us to confront what is done in our collective name. To recognize that it is on our threshold, not just the king's.

So with this recognition in mind, let me end this essay with reference to the Doomsday Machine envisioned by Leo Katz. In his challenging paper, Leo Katz explains why a Doomsday Machine approach to punishment—absolute, immediate, and lethal—could be justified—that it could be immune to charges of being excessive and disproportionate—if those who employ it understand what they are doing to be preventative rather than punitive. What is called the Alexander phenomenon—after Lawrence Alexander's original formulations of this argument—occurs when an actor's understanding of what he or she is doing changes the moral character of the act thus rendering what might be unjust, excessive, or cruel into something justifiable.

To illustrate this phenomenon Leo Katz includes an account from George Orwell's experience in the Spanish Civil War in which he failed to shoot an enemy soldier, despite his expressed intention to go to the front "shoot a Fascist." But when the opportunity presents itself, the enemy solider appears half dressed, holding his trousers up and hobbling along. Orwell did not shoot because at that moment he did not perceive the soldier to be a Fascist, just a fellow human creature. Leo Katz claims that none of Orwell's beliefs or desires changed, the only thing that changed was his understanding of what he was doing: shooting a fellow creature, not a Fascist.

I would like to offer a different interpretation of George Orwell's experience and draw a very different conclusion for understanding our punitive imaginations. I propose that when Orwell saw the man running with his pants down, he certainly did catch a quick glimpse of this man as a fellow human creature. But I would also argue that he saw more than simply a fellow creature running with his pants down. At that moment, Orwell also saw himself about to shoot a fellow creature running with his pants down. Even more precisely, Orwell saw the man and himself in relation to one another. And seeing and understanding that they were united in their humanity—inescapably linked in the very act of shooting and being shot—did much more than change the moral character of what he was doing. It, in fact, prevented him from doing it altogether. The message seems clear, recognizing our willingness and capacity to *be* Doomsday Machines—something a machine, by the way, cannot do—might just change our willingness to *act* like a Doomsday Machine. Orwell's story reminds us that imagination, particularly moral imagination, is ultimately a reflexive capacity. It entails seeing the present in terms of the past and future and seeing ourselves and what we do in terms of others with whom we navigate this temporality.

Notes

1. "The Guantanamo Stain," *New York Times*, April 26, 2013, found at http://www.nyttimes.com/2013/04/26/opinion/the-guantanamo-stain.html.

2. Samir Naji al Hasan Moqbel, "Gitmo Is Killing Me," *New York Times*, April 15, 2013, found at http://www.nytimes.com/2013/04/15/opinion/hunger-striking-at-guantanamo-bay.html.

3. Paul Harris, Tracy McVeigh, and Mark Townsend, "How Guantanamo's Horror Forced Inmates to Hunger Strike," *Guardian*, May 4, 2013, found at www.guardian.co.uk/world/2013/may.04.guarntanamo-hunger-strike.

4. Charles Savage, "Amid Hunger Strike, Obama Renews Push to Close Cuba Prison," *New York Times*, April 30, 2013, found at http://www.nytimes.com/2013/05/01/us/guantanamo-adds-medical-staff-amid-hunger-strike.

5. David Beresford, *Ten Men Dean: The Story of the 1981 Irish Hunger Strike* (New York: Atlantic Monthly Press, 1987); Padraig O'Malley, *Biting at the Grave: The Irish Hunger Strkies and the Politics of Despair* (Boston: Beacon Press 1990).

6. Aogan Mulcahy, "Claims-Making and the Construction of Legitimacy: Press Coverage of the 1981 Northern Irish Hunger Strike," *Social Problems* 42 (1995): 449.

7. Maud Ellman, *The Hunger Artists: Starving, Writing and Imprisonment* (Cambridge, MA: Harvard University Press, 2003), 17.

8. Gene Sharp, *The Politics of Non-violent Action* (Boston: Porter Sargent, 1973).

9. Sharman Apt Russell, *Hunger: An Unnatural History* (New York: Basic Books, 2005).

10. Patricia Ewick, "The Return of Restraint: Limits to the Punishing State," *Quinnipiac Law Review*, 31 (2013): 577.

11. Paul Guerino, Paige M. Harrison, and William J. Sobol, "Prisoners in 2010," Bureau of Justice Statistics, December 2011, http://bjs.ojp.usdoj.gov/index.cfm?ty=pbdetail&iid=2230.

12. Mary Louise Frampton, Ian Haney Lopez, and Jonathan Simon, introduction to *After the War on Crime: Race, Democracy, and a New Reconstruction*, ed. Frampton, Lopez, and Simon (New York: New York University Press, 2011), 3.

13. Caleb Smith, "Imprisonment without Justice," in this volume at 90.

14. See Mona Lynch, "The Contemporary Penal Subject(s)," in *After the War on Crime*, 89

15. David Luban, *Legal Ethics and Human Dignity* (Cambridge: Cambridge University Press, 2007), 71.

16. Timothy V. Kaufman-Osborn, "The Metaphysics of the Hangman," in *Studies in Law, Politics, and Society*, ed. Austin Sarat and Patricia Ewick, 20 (2000): 39. Daniel LaChance, "Last Words, Last Meals, and Last Stands: Agency and Individuality in the Modern Execution Process," *Law and Society Inquiry* 32 (2007): 701.

17. *Graham v Florida*, No. 08–7412, slip op. at 19 (May 17, 2010). See also Jonathan Simon, "Dignity and Risk: The Long Road from *Graham v. Florida* to Abolition of Life without Parole" in *Life without Parole: America's New Death Penalty?*, ed. Charles J. Ogletree Jr. and Austin Sarat (New York: New York University Press, 2012), 89.

18. Caleb Smith, herein, 91.

19. Stephen Garvey, "Injustice, Authority, and the Criminal Law" in this volume at 62.

20. Michelle Brown, *The Culture of Punishment: Prison Society, and Spectacle* (New York: New York University Press 2009), 8.

21. Michelle Brown, "'Which Question? Which Lie,'" in this volume at 133.

22. Id. at 151.

23. Austin Sarat, *When the State Kills: Capital Punishment and the American Condition* (Princeton NJ: Princeton University Press, 2001) 14.

24. Philip Smith, *Punishment and Culture* (Chicago: University of Chicago Press, 2008).

25. R. A. Duff and David Garland, "Introduction: Thinking About Punishment," in *A Reader on Punishment*, ed. Anthony Duff and David Garland (Oxford: Oxford University Press, 1994), 2.

26. Robert Hertz, *Death and the Right Hand* (Glencoe, IL: Free Press, 1960). "[The right] is the idea of sacred power, regular and beneficent, the principle of all effective activity, the source of everything that is good, favourable and legitimate; for the left, this ambiguous conception of the profane and the impure, the feeble and incapable which is also maleficent and dreaded" (100).

27. William Butler Yeats, "The King's Threshold," in *The Collected Plays of W. B. Yeats* (New York: Macmillan Company, 1953), 70.

28. Sarat, *When the State Kills*. Yet even the search for painless, sanitized death may ironically undermine the practice. Mona Lynch observes that as executions become more bureaucratized and routinized, they lose their po-

tency as cultural markers and become meaningless. "Transforming the institution of state punishment into a rationalized managerial model . . . denies the affective underside of punishing, thus may render it vulnerable and even unsustainable if and when such practices are scrutinized in the political and populist realms." "The Disposal of Inmate #85271," in *Studies in Law, Politics and Society*, ed. Austin Sarat and Patricia Ewick, 20 (2000): 25.

Contributors

Michelle Brown is an associate professor of sociology at the University of Tennessee.

Patricia Ewick is a professor of sociology at Clark University.

Stephen P. Garvey is a professor of law at Cornell University's School of Law.

Leo Katz is the Frank Carano professor at University of Pennsylvania's School of Law.

Austin Sarat is the William Nelson Cromwell professor of jurisprudence and political science, an associate dean of the faculty at Amherst College, and the Hugo L. Black visiting senior faculty scholar at the University of Alabama's the School of Law.

Caleb Smith is a professor of English and American studies at Yale University.

Carol S. Steiker is the Henry J. Friendly professor of law at Harvard Law School.

Index

Fictional characters alphabetized by first name.

abnormal mental condition, 43
abortion, 21, 36, 128
  premature, 109
abstraction of dignity, 28
  arbitrariness, 28
  excessiveness, 28
  severity, 28
  societal unacceptability, 28
accomplice, 53, 54, 77, 122, 123
actus reus, 77, 112
adverse consequences, 121
a fortiori, 53
Agamben, Giorgio, 128, 147
Alabama, 8, 27, 28, 29, 31, 32
  "hitching post" punishment, 8, 27, 28, 29, 31–32
Alexander, Gordon, 42, 63n4
Alexander, Larry, 113–116, 118, 119, 124, 168
Alexander phenomenon, 122, 168
Allen, Francis, 87, 90
American colonial era, 22
American Medical Association, 158
American Red Cross, 158
Anderson, Martin: *The Federal Bulldozer*, 97
Anglo-American law, 112
antebellum plantations, 87, 91
antiwar movements, 86
Aristotelian or "aretaic" conception of dignity, 21, 35

atonement, through punishment, 6
Attica, 86
attributionism, 69n23
attribution theory, 118
authenticity or authorship, ownership, 48
authority, 12, 47, 54–62, 75n50; as administer of pain, 1; having authority, 55–58; losing authority, 10, 58–62, 80n78; morality as, 63; state's, to coerce, 78n66; state's, to punish, 9, 10, 44, 59–60, 61, 62, 67n18, 77n66, 79n74, 81n84, 163
authority *ex hypothesi*, 60

Baca, Jimmy Santiago, 82, 99; "How We Carry Ourselves," 82–83, 85
Bandes, Susan, 130
barbarous prison conditions, 23
basic human needs, 29
Bazelon, David L., 64n9, 65n13, 74n49
Beaumont, 5
behavior controls, 43
belief-desire theory, 117–118
"bending the law," 13
benevolent dictator, 57
benevolent dictatorship, 58
Berger, Vivian, 139, 148
Berlant, Lauren, 140, 141
Bill of Rights, 20
bioethics, 21, 37

Birmingham Jail, 82
Blake, William, 8, 37; *Auguries of Innocence*, 37
blame, 1, 51
bodily functions, 24
body-cavity searches, 24
Booth v. Maryland, 129, 136–137
Bourdieu, Pierre, 91, 92
brainwasher, 49
brainwashing, 50, 73n43
Bratton, William, 92, 98
Brennan, William, 1, 8, 28
Breyer, Stephen, 25
British government, 159
British Parliament, 159
"broken windows" policies, 84, 92
Bronstein, Irvin and Rose, 136
Bronsteins' children, 137–138
Brooks, Peter, 130
Brown, Michelle, 13–14, 30, 99, 165–166; "'Which Question? Which Lie?': Reflections on *Payne v. Tennessee* and the 'Quick Glimpse' of Life," 127–157
Brown, Wendy, 150–151
brutality, 25, 26, 30, 31, 32
Buck v. Bell, 25
bumper stickers, 60
Bureau of Justice Statistics, 160
Burnham, Daniel, 96
Burson, Charles W., Jr., 135
Bush, George W., 5
Butler, Judith, 131, 146, 149

California, 11, 29, 88, 89, 92; overcrowded prisons in, 8, 28, 32; Stanford Prison Experiment, 26–27
cancer treatment, 123
Canivez, Patrice, 141
capacity to respond to reasons, 46–48, 50
capital defendants, 14, 132–133, 165
capital offenses, 33
capital punishment, 6, 7, 8, 28, 31, 127–128, 131, 140, 166, 167; abolition of, 160
capital sentencing, mandatory, 33
capital sentencing, standardless, 33
capital trials, 14
capital victims, 14
carceral state, 162
carceral system, 6, 161
Casey and Carhart decisions, 36
Cat and Mouse Act, 159–160
causal determinism, 48–50
causation, 50, 53
causation doctrine, 120
censure, 51, 55, 56
Chicago, 26
Chicago Tribune, 25
choice of lies, 127, 134
Christie, Nils, 150
Christopher, Charisse, 129–131, 134–135; Lacie, 131, 135; Nicholas, 129–131, 134, 143, 150–152; Zvolanek, Mr. and Mrs., 129
citizenship, 128
civilized society, 31
civil rights, 86
Civil War amendments, 87
Clarke, Kamari Maxine, 148
Clinton, Bill, 4, 5
closure, 145–146
coercion, using to punish for disobedience, 44, 45, 55, 61–63, 78n66, 80n78, 81n84
"collective" aspect of dignity, 23
collective conscience, 6
collective dignity, 7– 8, 10, 12, 22, 24–27, 30, 32, 34–37, 86
Collective Dignity and Criminal Punishment, 34–37
collective disagreements, 58
collective engagement with the suffering during an execution, 32
collective moral agency, 35
common criminals, 159
Communism, 106
Communist Party, 12, 104
compassion, 15
compatibilism, contemporary or new, 69n25
compatibilist, 71n29
complicity, 10, 52, 53, 54, 75n54, 76n56
concentration camps, 26
conscientious objectors, 103, 110
consciousness of wrongdoing, 112–113

conscription, 121
Constitution, 20, 135
constitutional imperative, 33
constitutional law, 19, 32
consumers of urban space, 92, 93
containment, prisons as, 11, 83, 89
contracts, 120–121, 123, 124
convict leasing, 87
core values, 10
correction, prison system, 87, 100n8
Cover, Robert, 127
crackdown, reactionary, in the prison system, 86
crime and punishment, 87
Crime Scene Investigation: Miami, 94
criminal actions, 13
criminal defendant, 43
criminalization of immigration policy, 19
criminal justice, 19, 22, 37, 88, 94, 130, 132
criminal law, 46–50, 53–54, 58, 69n25, 81n84, 109
criminal offenders, 104
criminal punishment, 20–37, 115
criminal sentences, 5
criticism, 118
cross-sex surveillance, 25
cruel and unusual punishments, 20, 25, 27, 33
cruelty, forbidden by the Eighth Amendment, 30
Cuba, 160
Culbert, Jennifer, 129, 132
culpability, 65n16
culpable breach, 56
culpable violation, 61
cultural violence, 127
culture of punishment, 161

Das, Veena, 134, 149–150
Davis, Mike, 92, 98; *Dead Cities*, 98
D.C. Circuit, 64n8
death camps, 148
death penalty, 28, 29, 31, 32, 127–129, 166; mandatory, 33
death row, 133
"death row syndrome," 29
Decatur, Illinois, 4

decency, 31
"decline of the rehabilitative ideal," 87
deconstruction of most welfare programs, 93
Deep South, 88
dehumanization, 8, 25, 30, 34, 82, 87
deindustrialization, 86
Delgado, Richard, 71n30
depersonalization, 135
deprivations of life or liberty, 20
desert judgments, 13, 112
detain, 90
determinism, 45–46, 69n25; and alternative possibilities, 45
deterrence, 3, 11, 28, 84, 89–90, 162
devaluation of victims, 140
dignitary, 166
dignity. *See* collective dignity; human dignity; individual dignity.
dignity-based arguments, 8, 24, 27, 29
dignity of life, 36
dignity of man, 28
diminished capacity to respond to reasons, 9, 46–47, 60
diminished responsibility, 64n8
dislocation, 128
disobedience, and coercion to punish, 44, 45, 55, 61–63, 78n66, 80n78, 81n84
dispossession, 82, 128
disproportionality of the sanction, 116
disproportionate penalties, 121
disproportionate punishment, 13, 110
dissociation theories, 72n37
District of Columbia, 42, 47
Dolovich, Sharon, 90
Doomsday Machine, 114–116, 168
double jeopardy, regarding registration and notification requirements of Megan's Law, 1–2
draconian, 13
draconian sanctions, 110
draconian sentences, 104, 106
Dressler, Joshua, 67n18
Dr. Strangelove, 48
drugs, illegal, 43, 109
Du Bois, W. E. B., 95
"due process of law," 20, 33

178 Index

Dunn, Kerry, 133
duress, 45, 49, 67n21, 68n22, 71n30, 119, 120, 122–123; and nonwrongs, 45; economic, 66n18
Durham rule, 64n9
Durkheim, 166
Durkheim, Emile, 6, 91, 92; and "we–they" distinctions, 6
Durkheimian model of punishment, 98
dwarf tossing, 36
dynamometer, 111

East Africa Embassy bombings, 146
East German (former judge A), 12–13, 105–106, 110, 112–113, 116, 119–121, 124
East German People's Army, 103
East Germany, 12, 13, 103, 104
economic duress, 66n18
economic instability, 93
educational opportunity, 43
effect, 2
Eighth Amendment, 1, 8, 20, 25, 27–30, 33, 163
Eisenhower High, Decatur, Illinois, 4
electric fence, 114–116
Elster, Jon, 107
emancipation, 87
embezzlement, 52
emotional disorder, 43
empathic judgment, 141
empathy, 14–15, 30, 31, 128, 130, 131, 140–147, 156n54, 166; "dark side" of, 15, 30
end-of-life decision making, 128
enforcement, 97, 121
England, 32, 96
enlightened policy, 33
enlivening value, 35
enterprise of prevention, 118, 120
entitled, 124
epistemic conditions, 68n23
equality, 19, 21
"equal protection of the laws," 20
estate planning, 128
ethic of restraint and sobriety, 23
eugenics, 25
European, 93

euthanasia, 105
evil, 1, 4, 5, 6, 48, 88
Ewick, Patricia, 6, 15, 152; product of imagination, 15; suppression of imagination, 15
excessively harsh sentences, 12
excessively long sentences, 13
excessive punishment, 113, 114, 124
"exclusion and control" penology, 101n17
excuse, generic, 47
execution, 4, 29, 32, 36; chamber, 31, 133, 165; and collective engagement, 32; "death row syndrome," 29; and incompetency, 36; of Karla Faye Tucker, 4; moratorium on, 160; "protocols," 31; team member, 30, 31, 130, 144
expiation of guilt through punishment, 6
ex post facto prohibition, 107
Exquisite Corpse, The, 134–135
exquisite corpses, 165

fair-play theory of political obligation, 79n74
fair-play theory of punishment, 79n74, 80
Fair Sentencing Act of 2010, 160
false imprisonment, 13, 105
Fascist, 117, 168
Fassin, Didier, 144
fear mongering, 93
Feeley, Malcolm, 84, 88; "The New Penology," 84
first-class citizens, 9, 44
first-class citizenship, 164
Florence, Albert, 25
forgiveness, 1
formal sanctions, 118
Foucault, Michel, 85, 93, 99
Fourteenth Amendment, 33
Fourth Amendment, 20
Frampton, Mary Louise, 161
France, 96
Frankfurt examples, 70n26
Frankfurt School, 92, 98
Frankfurt's hierarchical account, 71n29
Frazier, Cornelius, 42, 63n4
freedom qua, 46, 47

freedom qua capacity, 45–46, 48, 69n25
free will, and punishment, 5
Freud, 24
Fundamental Attribution Error, 118–119
fundamental equality of persons, 7
Furman v. Georgia, 8, 28, 33

gangs, 43
Gardiner, Chauncy, 123
Garvey, Stephen, 8–10, 11, 14, 133, 163–164
Gawande, Atul, 29
generic excuse, 47
gentrification, 92
German, 106, 113
Germany, 12, 109
Gilmore, Ruth Wilson, 11, 89–90, 91, 92, 93, 94; *Golden Gulag*, 89
Giuliani, Rudolph, 91–92, 98
Gospel of Matthew, 1
Graham v. Florida, 163
Greenwich Village, 97
grossly disproportionate punishment, 59–60, 67n18
Guantanamo Bay Naval Base, 24, 158
guilt, 86

Hagel, Chuck, 158
Han, Clara, 150
Haney, Craig, 132–133, 165
hardship, 9
harsh criminal punishment, 115
harsh justice, 92, 99
Hart, H. L. A.: *Prolegomenon to the Principles of Punishment*, 1
Harvard Law Review, 106
Harvard Law School, 19
Harvey, David, 97
Heider, Fritz: *The Psychology of Interpersonal Relations*, 118
Henry, Leslie Meltzer, 35
Hertz, Robert, 167
Herzog, Werner, 30, 144–145; *Into the Abyss*, 44
Hester Prynne, 23
Hiroshima, 148
Hirsch, Susan, 146

"hitching post" punishment, 8, 27, 28, 29, 31–32
Hobbes, Thomas, 79n73
Holocaust, 148
homosexuality, male, 24
Hope, Larry, 27, 29
Howard, Ebenezer, 96
Howells, William Dean, 95
Huigens, Kyron, 20
human dignity, 6, 7, 10, 19–41, 39n21, 147; concern for in punishment, 5; "naturalized" account of, 34, and ontological heft, 34; respect for, 34; and subjectivity, 34
human dignity, four principles of abstraction of: arbitrariness, excessiveness, severity, societal unacceptability, 28
humane criminal code, 120
Human Rights Committee, 36
humiliating punishment, 7–8, 24–27, 30, 38n11
humiliation, 23, 24, 34, 39n21, 88
hunger strike, 158–159, 160, 167
Hyde, Alan, 140
hypnosis, 48–49, 72n38
hypnotic suggestion, 73n38
hypocrisy, 10, 52–53, 54, 76n55

"ideological function" of imprisonment, 11
ideological justification of violence, 83
ideology of punitive degradation, 87
ignorance of law, 112–113
imagination: product of, 15; suppression of, 15, 161. *See also* punitive imagination.
immoral laws, 105
impaired or nonexistent cognitive capacity, 71n31
impaired or nonexistent volitional capacity, 71n31
impeachment of former president Clinton, 4
implicit social contracts, 124
imprisonment, 94; rates, 161; without justice, 82–83, 85
incapacitation, 11, 12, 84, 85, 89–90, 99, 160, 162, 165
incarceration, 4, 11, 22, 24, 27, 29, 82, 86, 91,

180   Index

145, 164; rate, 5, 7, 19. *See also* mass incarceration.
incompetent to be executed, 36
indefinite detention, 158
indignity, 35
individual autonomy, 35
individual dignity, 7, 22, 30, 36, 39n31
individualization, 8, 32–34
individual right, 21
individual-rights-based formulation of dignity, 30
industrial economy, 91
industrial factory, 91
informal sanctions, 118–119; criticism, 118; ostracism, 118
insanity, 43, 46, 47, 64n9, 122, 123
insanity defense, 74n49
insecure imagination, 86, 95, 100
International Covenant on Civil and Political Rights, 36
Irish Republican Army (IRA), 159–160
"irresistible impulse" to shoot, 43

Jackson, Jesse, 4
Jacobs, Jane, 96–97; *The Death and Life of Great American Cities*, 96
Jehovah's Witnesses, 12–13, 103–104, 113, 116, 119–120
Jewish refugees, 148
Jim Crow, 91
jujitsu, 159, 160
jurisprudence of life and death, 14, 127–128, 134
justification of violence, ideological, 83
juvenile offenders, treatment of as adults, 7, 19
juveniles facing life without possibility of parole, 35, 163

Kafka, Franz: "The Hunger Artist," 159
Kahan, Dan, 22, 26, 38n11
Kant, Immanuel, 31
Kaplan, Paul, 133
Katz, Leo, 12–13, 168; "Punishment as an Act of the Imagination," 103–126
Kaufman-Osborn, 163
Kennedy, Anthony, 163

King, Martin Luther, Jr., 82
King, William, 42, 50–54, 58–62, 77n58
"knowing misrepresentations," 134
Kozinski, Jerzy, 123

Law and Literature, 83, 85, 98
laws of nature, 46
Lazarus, Jeremy, 158
Le Corbusier, 96
LeDuff, Charlie: *Detroit: An American Autopsy*, 98
legal and moral sanction, 124
legal and political transitions, 107
legitimate authority, 56
lethal aggression, 133
"leveling down," 20
"leveling up," 20
Levinson Funeral Home, 136
liability, 52, 53, 55, 60
liberty, 19, 21
life imprisonment, 60
life sentence, 145
"a life without hope," 163
life without parole, 7, 19, 20, 90, 128
Little Tavern, 42
Locke, John, 79n73
lonely suffering, 129
longue durée, 151
Lopez, Ian Haney, 161
Los Angeles, 43, 92
Luban, David, 34, 163; and ontological heft, 34
Lynch, Mona, 170n28

Madeira, Jodi, 145; *Killing McVeigh*, 145–146
malum in se, 56–59, 78n71, 80n78
malum prohibitum, 56–58, 78n71
mandatory capital sentencing, 33
mandatory death penalty, 32–33; historical consensus against the imposition of, 33
mandatory minimum sentences, 8, 32
mandatory sentences, 19, 32–33
Manhattan, 93
manipulation, 50
manipulation argument, 72n36
manipulator, 74n47
manslaughter, 46, 128

Marcin, Joshua, 37
Marine Corps, 42
Marshall, Thurgood, 8, 28, 135
Marxian, 91
masculine identity, 24
mass imprisonment without justice, 86
mass incarceration, 10–12, 15, 20, 84–91, 93, 94, 98, 99, 100n6, 131, 148, 160–162, 164
"material form" of imprisonment, 11
McCleskey v. Kemp, 140
measured punishment, 23
medical care, 28, 43
medical intervention, 158
Megan's Law, 2–3; as deterrent, 3; as punishment, 2–3; registration and community notification requirements of, 2; retributive, 3; salutary, 3; three-part test, regarding registration and community notification of sex offenders, 2
Memphis, 129
mens rea (mental state), 13, 54, 64n8, 112, 113, 117–118, 121
mental abnormality, 46
mental disease or defect, 46, 47, 74n49
mental health care, 28
mental illness, 29, 36, 43, 64n9
mental states, 113
merciless vengeance, 93
mercy, 1, 19, 88, 99
Minow, Martha, 127, 134
miscegenation, 105
moat, 114–116
Model Penal Code, 49, 77
moral community, 51
moral education, 84
moral imagination, 168
morality, 4, 44, 47, 50, 55–57, 63
morality of responsibility, 44, 45–54
moral law, 54
moral narratives, 85
moral obligations, 56–57, 61
moral power, 44
moral relationship, 164
moral responsibility, 45–46, 51, 82
moral satisfaction, 32
moral wrongs, 58
moratorium on executions, 160

Morris, Norval, 74n49
Moses, Robert, 96
"moving threshold," 128
Ms. White, 48–49
Mulcahy, Aogan, 159
murder, 43, 46, 54, 57, 128, 132, 135, 137–139, 153n19
Murdock, Benjamin, 10, 42–43, 47, 50–54, 58, 60–62, 63n3, 63n6, 64, 65n13, 65n17, 77n58, 80n79
Muslim detainees, 24

nature of its authority, 61
Naucke, Wolfgang, 106, 109, 119
Nazi, 26, 105–106
Nazism, 23
NCIS: Los Angeles, 94
necessity doctrine, 121, 122, 123
negative desert, 122–123
negative responsibility, 122
negative rights, 61
neglect, 53
negligence, 54
neoliberal, 92, 97–98
neoliberal consensus, 87
neoliberalism, 91
neoliberals, 91, 164
New Deal, 87
New Jersey, 2
New Jim Crow, 85
new penology, 84, 88, 90, 100n3
New Republic, 21; "The Stupidity of Dignity," by Steven Pinker, 21
New York, 88, 92, 97, 102n28
New York City, 91–92
New Yorker, 29
New York Police Department, 98
New York Times, 158
Nietzsche, Friedrich: *Genealogy of Morals*, 84
Nilsen, Eva, 20
Nixon, Richard, 5
nonwrongs, crimes committed under duress, 45
norm against retroactive laws, 107, 124
norm against retroactivity, 109
norms of rehabilitation, 119

notice principle, 115
notice requirement, 116
nuclear power, 105
Nuremberg, 107
Nuremberg race laws, 105
NYPD Blue, 94

Obama, Barack, 158–159, 160
obedience, coercion for, 44, 55, 62
objective purpose, regarding requirements of Megan's Law, 2, 3
obligatory military service, 12
obvious cruelty, 27
occupying power, 10, 165
O'Connor, Sandra Day, 135, 138
offenders, 8, 11, 22, 33, 34, 36, 104; enemies of society, 11; petty, 94
Oklahoma City bombing, 145
Old West, 88
ontological heft, and human dignity, 34
operant conditioning, 119
Orange Is the New Black, 99
Orwell, George, 117, 168
ostracism, 118
overcrowded prisons, 8, 28, 29, 32; and disease, 28; medical care provided in, 28; suffering and death in, 28
ownership, 9, 48, 50

pain, physical or psychological, 8, 22, 27–32, 34; as part of punishment, 1, 2, 7–8, 30–31; and execution, 29, 31; rejecting this type of punishment, 31
Payne, Bernice and Carl, 129, 132
Payne, Pervis Tyrone, 128–129, 131, 139
Payne v. Tennessee, 13–15, 127–136, 139–141, 143–145, 147–151, 165
peace, 88; political, 57; social, 57
peace treaty, 121
penal desert, 111–112
penal ideology, 88
penal institutions, 6
penalized, 44
penal spectators, 130, 165
penal state, 11, 85, 86, 92, 160, 162; construction of, 91
penal system, 15, 94

penal tracks, 119
penal violence, 92
penalties, disproportionate, 121
penalty, 44, 62
penitence, 85
penitentiary system, 83
penology, new, 84, 88, 90, 100n3
permission to punish, 44, 54–55, 62, 80n74
perpetrators, 127, 130, 131, 133, 139, 142, 143, 144, 145, 148, 150, 165
personal injury lawsuits, 128
petty offenders, 94
pickpockets, 113
Pinker, Steven, 7, 21, 35, 37; "The Stupidity of Dignity," 21
pink underwear, 24, 39n21
Plessy v. Ferguson, 25; separate but equal, 25
Poe, Edgar Allan, 95
political authority, 8
political criminals, 159
political jujitsu, 159
political peace, 57
political process, 60
politics of revenge, 6
pornographic spectacle, 92
pornography, official, 27, 34
positive desert, 122–123
positive responsibility, 122
Posner, Eric, 106–110
Posner, Richard, 23, 26, 30, 38n11
posthypnotic suggestion, 48–49
postindustrial order, 91
post-traumatic stress disorder, 148
Powell, Lewis F. Jr., 137
power qua authority, 55
predators, 88
premature abortions, 109
prevention, 115, 118, 124
preventive enterprise, 116, 118, 124
prima facie, 44, 55–56, 57, 61, 122
principal, 122
principle of alternative possibilities (PAP), 69n24
principle of proportionality, 115
prison boom, 87–88, 90
prison conditions, barbarous, 23
prisoner experimentation, 26–27

Index 183

prison and jail populations, 6
prisoners at Guantanamo Bay Naval Base, 158–159
prison population, 4, 5, 160
prisons, 5; and "broken windows" policies, 84, 92; and population management, 84; reactionary crackdown in, 86; riots, 86; as "secure communities," 84; as sites of containment, 11, 83, 89; warehouse, 83, 89, 90, 93, 98–99; as zones of dispossession and dehumanization, 82
prison sentences, 103
prison system, 83, 84, 99; correction, 87; justice and injustice, 85; logics of security, 85; massive expansion of the, 89; and the New Jim Crow, 85; prison-industrial complex, 85
privacy, 20, 21
private wrongs, 51
privilege, status-based, 20
Professor Plum, 48–49
prohibitions, 58
proportionality, 4, 20, 21, 118, 124; principle, 15, 116, 163
pro tanto, 51
Protestant ethic, 146
provocation, 46, 47, 77n58
psychological anguish, 29
psychophysicists, 111
psychophysics, 110
psychosurgery, 48, 50
public debt, 90
public humiliation, 23
public order, 36, 90
public space, 94
public shaming. *See* shaming punishment.
public wrong, 9–10
punishment, 6–18, 16n18, 23, 27, 30, 31, 34, 55–56, 78n72, 79n74, 83–84, 87–90, 110–112, 114–115, 118, 122, 124, 131, 138–139, 160–163, 167; "chain of pain," 166; "civilizing" function of, 31; criminal, 20–23; criteria for an act to be considered punishment, 1; culture of, 161; disproportionate, 13, 59–60, 61, 67n18, 110; Doomsday Machine approach to, 168; essential elements of, 1; essential in protecting society and defending society's values, 6; excessive, 113–114; fair-play theory of, 79n74; and free will, 5; "governance of rules," 4; harsh criminal, 115; and human dignity, 5, 20; as a mechanism for racial exclusion, 164; Megan's Law as, 2, 4; permissibility of, 50; and the proportionality principle, 15–116; rejecting physical pain type of, 31; savage, 23; of the socially disadvantaged, 5; state, 22, 29, 33, 44, 50, 51, 55, 57, 59, 60, 67n18, 80n78, 81n83. *See also* shaming punishment.
punishment practices, 22
punitive degradation, ideology of, 87
punitive imaginaries, 142
punitive imagination, 6, 10, 12, 14, 15, 37, 82, 83, 88, 91–94, 138, 148, 151, 168
"The Punitive Imagination" Symposium, 152
punitive imaginings, 127
punitive measure, 24
punitive practices, 127
punitive response, 164
Puritan village, 23

Quantico, Virginia, 42
quasipunishment, 120
quasipunitive, 120, 121, 124
quasipunitive character, 119
quasipunitive practice, 118
"quick attention," 14
"quick glimpse" of life, 14, 127, 132–133, 147, 165

race, 140, 164
racial disparity, 130
racial hostility, 43
racial insult, 47, 77n58
Rao, Neomi, 21
rapid urbanization, 95
Reagan, Ronald, 87
reasonable provocation, 46
Rechtman, Richard, 144
Rechtsbeugung, literally "bending the law," 13, 105, 108–109
redemption, 86, 87
reform, 86

registration and community notification, of sex offenders, 2–4
regulatory and not punitive, protecting the public and preventing crimes, 3
regulatory technique, registration as a, 3
rehabilitation, 11, 84–85, 87–90, 99, 101n17, 119, 124, 162
rehabilitative, 83
rehabilitative enterprise, 119
rehabilitative ideal, 11
Rehnquist, William, 132, 134, 138
Reiman, Jeffrey, 31
relevant evidence, 137
remedial purpose, 2–3
repentance, 4
reproductive rights, 128
respect for humanity, 34
responsibility, 1, 5, 9, 48, 50–51, 118–119; diminished, 64n8; negative, 122; positive, 122
"restorative justice," 109
retribution, 11, 28, 85, 88–90, 93, 101n17, 116, 118, 124, 142, 162, 166
retributive, 83
retributive justice, 78n72
retributive punishment, 84
retributivism, 31, 87
retroactive justice, 109
retroactive laws, 13, 107, 124
retroactive punishment, 109
retroactivity in criminal cases, 107
retroactivity in noncriminal cases, 107
retroactivity norm, 109
retroactivity, norm against, 109
revenge, 142, 166
rhetoric of law and order, 5
Richardson, Charles, 145
Riis, Jacob, 95–97
Roberts v. North Carolina, 33
Rotella, Carlo: *October Cities*, 98
rotten social background, 9, 43, 47
rules abstractly considered, 121–122

salutary, 3
same-sex marriage, 21
Hasan Moqbel, Samir Naji al, 158

sanctions, formal and informal, 118; criticism, 118; ostracism, 118
sanction, legal and moral, 124
Sarat, Austin, 32, 35, 130, 134, 137–138, 152, 166; "Examining Assumptions: An Introduction to Punishment, Imagination, and Possibility," 1–18; *When the State Kills*, 166
savage punishments, 23
Scalia, Antonin, 132
Schick, Frederick, 117–118; *Understanding Action*, 117
second-class citizen, 9–10, 43–45, 47, 50–55, 58, 60–63, 65n16, 66n18, 67n21, 74n47, 80n77, 163–165
second-class citizenship, 133
securitization of public space, 93
segregation, 29, 32, 95
self-control, 46
self-defense, 43, 60, 122, 123
self-mutilations, 167
self-policing neighborhood, 97
Sellin, Thorsten, 110–111
sentences, prison, 19, 103; death, 14, 128, 129, 137; excessively harsh, 12, 104; excessively long, 13; grossly disproportionate, 61; life, 145; life without parole, 7, 19, 20, 35, 90, 128; mandatory, 19
sentencing process, 32, 34; individualizing sentencing determiniations, 33–35
Sentencing Project, 130
separate but equal, 25
severity score of an offense, 112
sex offenders, 2; re-abuse by, 3; registration of, 2–4
sexuality, detention practices involving, 24
shaming punishments, 7–8, 22–27, 30, 34, 36, 38n111; and degradation penalties, 38
Sharp, Gene, 159
Shaw, George Bernard, 1
Shklar, Judith, 107
Siegel, Reva, 21, 35
Simon, Jonathan, 20, 84, 88, 161; "The New Penology" (1992), 84
Smith, Caleb, 10–11, 14, 24, 131, 162; "Imprisonment without Justice," 82–102

Smith, Philip: *Punishment and Culture*, 166
social background, 9, 43, 47, 74n49; rotten, 9, 43, 47
social cognitive theories, 72n37
social contract, 120–121; implicit, 124
social deprivation, 9, 11, 50, 74n49
social histories, 132–133
social inequality, 14
social injustice, 43
social insecurity, 91
social instability, 11, 90, 93
socially disadvantaged, punishment of, 5
social order, 59
social peace, 57
social space, 10, 90
societal value, 7, 21
society, protecting via punishment, 6
Soja, Edward J.: *Seeking Spatial Justice*, 92
Soledad, 86
solitary confinement, 8, 29–30; Senate hearings on, 29
Souter, David H., 136
South Carolina v. Gathers, 129
southern slave discipline, 87
Spanish Civil War, 117, 168
spatial reorganization, 98
standard doctrine, 53
standardless capital sentencing, 33
standing, 51–55, 62, 75n50, 76n56, n57
Stanford Prison Experiment, 26–27
state-imposed obligation, 61
state of nature, 56, 58–62, 80n81; political, 57, 59; social, 57, 59
state power, 90
state punishment. *See* punishment/state.
state qua authority, 55
state-sanctioned justification, 57
state's authority to punish. *See* authority/state's, to punish.
state sovereignty, 128
status-based privilege, 20
Steiker, Carol, 7, 8, 10, 11, 14, 19, 86, 166; "'To See a World in a Grain of Sand': Dignity and Indignity in American Criminal Justice," 19–81
St. Elizabeth's Hospital, 64n9

Stolter-Baloun, Lisa, 145
strip searches, 24, 25
structural violence, 133
subhuman criminals, 93
subproletariat, 11, 12, 92
suffering, 130, 132, 141, 143; during an execution, 32; spectacle of, 142
summary justice, 23
supermax prisons, 7, 19, 32, 90
suppression of emotions, 31
Supreme Court, 8, 14, 24, 27–29, 33, 35, 36, 132, 134, 140, 163
surveillance, 97
survivors, 144, 145, 148
Svengali, 48–49

Tennessee, 129, 131, 139
Tennessee, Millington, 131
Tennessee Supreme Court, 132
terrorists, 5, 159
testicular cancer, 29
Texas, 4, 30
Thatcher, Margaret, 159
theocon, 21
theories: dissociation, 72n37; social cognitive, 2n37
Third Circuit Court of Appeals, 2; decision regarding challenge to Megan's Law, 2, 4
Third Reich, 106
three-part test, regarding registration and notification requirements of Megan's Law: actual purpose, 2; effect, 2, 3, 4; objective purpose, 2
three strikes, 89
Tocqueville, 5
torture, 29; in California's overcrowded prisons, 28; psychological, 29
tough on crime, 84–85
tough-on-crime politicians, 93, 99
transgression, 85, 94
transitional justice, 106–108
transitions, legal and political, 107
truthfulness, 4
Tucker, Karla Faye, 4; and repentance, 4
"tyranny," 5

United Nations, 158
United Nations Human Rights Committee, 36
University of Alabama Law School, 37, 82, 125, 152
urban geography, 96
urban planning, 96
urbanization, rapid, 95
urban renewal, 96–98
urban welfare, 98

vengeance, 84, 86, 88, 99, 100n8, 142; fantasies of, 88; merciless, 93
Vermeule, Adrian, 106–110
victim, 5, 127, 130–131, 133, 138–139, 142–152, 153n19, 165; capital, 14
victim impact evidence, 129, 132, 135, 137, 138, 140, 153
victim impact statement, 14, 130, 145, 146, 153n19, 165
victims' rights movement, 151
Victorian England, 114
violence, 43, 143; cultural, 127; ideological justification of, 83; penal, 92; of punishment, 84; of southern slave discipline, 87; structural, 133
voluntariness requirement, 121

Wacquant, Loïc, 11, 89–94, 164; *Prisons of Poverty*, 1, 89; *Punishing the Poor*, 89
warehouse prisons, 83, 89, 90, 93, 98, 99
war on crime, 6, 160–161
War on Crime, 88, 90, 92
"war theory" of punishment, 87

Watts, 43
Weber, Eugen, 111
Weber, Max, 111
Weber's law, 111
welfare programs, 91; deconstruction of most, 93
welfare state, 11, 97; dismantling of, 90, 98
welfare, urban, 98
Western Europe, 20
West German, 13, 112–113, 116
West Germany, 12, 103–104
White Horse Tavern, 97
Whitman, James, 20, 23
Whitman, James Q.: *Harsh Justice*, 87
Williams, Patricia, 143
willful misapplication of law, 105
Wolfgang, Marvin, 110–111
Woodson v. North Carolina, 33–34
workers' rights, 91
World War II, 12, 103, 105
worth of victims, 139, 149
wrongdoing, consciousness of, 112–113
wrongful act principle, 115
wrongful death litigation, 128
wrongfully convicted, 82
wrong, public, 9–10

Yeats, W. B.: "The King's Threshold," 167

zero-sum choice, 166
"zero-tolerance" policy, 4, 92
Zimbardo, Philip, 26
zone of indeterminacy, 147
"zone of indistinction," 128